STUDY GUIDE

for use with

PRODUCTION/OPERATIONS MANAGEMENT

Fifth Edition

William J. Stevenson

Prepared by

William J. Stevenson
Paul Van Ness
Both of Rochester Institute of Technology

IRWIN

Chicago • Bogotá • Boston • Buenos Aires • Caracas
London • Madrid • Mexico City • Sydney • Toronto

Printed in the United States of America.

ISBN 0-256-20851-4

1 2 3 4 5 6 7 8 9 0 P 3 2 1 0 9 8 7 6

PREFACE

This study guide is intended to provide you with supplemental material that can be used to enhance your understanding of the material presented in the textbook.

Among the important features of this study guide are:

1. Each chapter begins with a set of key ideas. These help to identify the most important elements of the chapter.

2. Many chapters have a section called "Study Tips" or "Tips for Solving Problems." The first of these, gives suggestions for approaching the material, which is important for very long chapters or for chapters having numerous models and/or formulas. The problem-solving tips are more specific to setting up problems, interpreting what a problem is asking for, and similar items. These are based on questions frequently asked by students such as yourself.

3. Each chapter has a sample test containing true/false and multiple-choice questions and a test key.

4. Most chapters have problems similar to those in the textbook. Solutions are provided for all problems.

CONTENTS

1 - Production and Operations Management

KEY IDEAS

1. Society provides goods and services to satisfy individual or collective needs and wants. Production uses capital and human knowledge to transform materials and services into products; these products can either be tangible (goods) or intangible (services). The essence of production/ operations management is managing the conversion of inputs outputs.

2. By systematizing operations, and by conducting training in the use of equipment, management makes it possible for employees to become skilled in their jobs; the productivity and efficiency of the system, and the quality and reliability of products are enhanced by supplementing training with motivation for doing good work.

3. Production/operations management designs the system and controls it; this include arranging facilities, scheduling tasks, developing procedures for inventory acquisition and turnover, as well as providing corrective actions to insure that changes are made whenever it is necessary to do so.

4. Production and operations systems can be classified in a variety of ways: degree of standardization, from highly standardized, such as an automobile assembly plant, to highly customized, such as a job shop; type, such as physical, storage, transportation exchange, entertainment or communication*, and manufacturing vs service. In general manufacturing produces material goods that require a distribution system to get them into the hands of consumers, while service industries tend to deal directly with consumers.

5. Studying the historical evolution of production/operations management gives us an appreciation of how the current state of operations management developed, and some of the key elements of that development, such as *interchangeable parts* and the *division of labor*. it may also provide insight into future developments in the field.

6. There are quite a few current issues that have an impact on operations management, and hence, issues that operations managers (and other managers) must contend with. These issues include global competition, new emphasis on operations strategy, the advantages of flexibility, emphasis on time reduction, emphasis of quality, technology, involving workers in decision making and problem solving, and environmental issues.

7. The central purpose of this book is to provide an understanding of the theory and practice of operations management and the role of the operations manager, and of some of the quantitative techniques used to support good managerial practices at the operating level.

GLOSSARY

degree of standardization

> **customized output:** products or services designed to meet the specifications of a customer.

> **standardized output:** products or services designed to appeal to a broad set of customers.

job shop: production system designed to handle jobs with a variety of customer specifications. Typically produces a number of different products.

lead time: length of time needed to fill an order or to receive an order from a supplier.

operations function: along with marketing and finance, one of the three primary functions in most business organizations. Operations consists of all activities related to producing goods or providing services.

operations management: responsible for systems that create goods or provide services. Includes both design and operation of production systems.

Pareto Principle: a relatively small percentage of items or factors are very important in achieving an objective or solving a problem.

re-engineering: a radical approach that involves "starting from scratch" by asking basic questions about processes such as how and why they are done the way they are, in order to significantly improve them.

production: the creation of goods or services.

transformation process: conversion of inputs into outputs.

type of operation

> **manufacturing:** production of a tangible output such as a toaster, a stereo.

> **service:** implies an act rather than a tangible output (e.g.. wash a car).

type of output

> **batch or unit:** jobs which tend to vary according to the needs of customers. Relatively small number of units. See *job shop*.

> **continuous processing:** uninterrupted homogeneous processing (e.g., chemicals, oil refining, heating, air conditioning).

> **mass production:** used for highly standardized output; involves repetitive operations.

project: a set of activities directed towards a unique goal within a limited time frame.

valued-added: The amount by which the price or value of an output is increased due to the addition of material, labor, or other resource.

TRUE/FALSE QUESTIONS

1. The three primary functions of a firm are financial management, operations management and accounting.

2. Frederick W. Taylor is generally credited with introducing the moving assembly line.

3. The principal activity in all production operations is to convert inputs into outputs that satisfy consumer wants.

4. Human effort, technology, raw materials, information and time are all examples of the necessary inputs to operations.

5. The elements of the transformation process include the production system, equipment, facilities, and employee motivation and skill.

6. Outputs of operations may be classified as goods, raw materials and profits.

7. It is easier to measure productivity for an operation that provides services than for one that produces goods.

8. Both inputs and outputs are more uniform for an operation that provides services than for one that produces goods.

9. System design includes managing personnel, inventory management, scheduling, project management and quality assurance.

10. The operation of the production system includes capacity, location, layout and equipment-acquisition decisions.

11. According to the Pareto principle, a relatively few factors are very important in achieving an objective or solving a problem.

12. Two recent trends in P/OM are flexibility and specialization.

MULTIPLE-CHOICE QUESTIONS

1. Which one of the following would not generally be considered an aspect of operations management?

    a. Schedule work
    b. Secure financial resources
    c. Maintain quality
    d. Oversee the transformation process
    e. Manage inventories

2. Which one of the following is not a typical question dealt with by an operations manager?

    a. How much capacity will be needed in the months ahead?
    b. What is a satisfactory location for a new facility?
    c. Which products/services should be offered?
    d. How can bottlenecks be reduced?
    e. All are typical of operations decisions.

3. Which one of these people was not involved in the Scientific Management movement?

    a. Henry Ford
    b. F. W. Taylor
    c. John D. Rockefeller
    d. Frank Gilbreth
    e. Lillian Gilbreth

4. Which one of these was not mentioned in the list of recent trends in P/ OM?

    a. Total quality management
    b. Worker involvement
    c. Global competition.
    d. Automation.
    e. Environmental issues.

5. Match this list of contributions with the originator:

    a. moving assembly line   2   1. F. W. Taylor
    b. motion study principles   5   2. Henry Ford
    c. principles of scientific management   1   3. Japanese manufacturers
    d. interchangeable parts   6   4. Adam Smith
    e. emphasis on quality and time reduction 3   5. Frank Gilbreth
    f. division of labor   4   6. Eli Whitney
    g. emphasis on manufacturing strategy   7   7. W. Skinner

2 - Productivity, Competitiveness, and Strategy

KEY IDEAS

1. The operations manager makes both strategic broad-scope decisions, and tactical moderate-scope decisions, as well as running the day-to-day operations of the production system. Strategic planning includes selecting products, choosing locations and technology, and overseeing new construction. Tactical decisions include setting employment and output levels, selecting equipment and controlling the flow of funds.

2. A key responsibility of the production manager is to achieve productive use of an organization's resources. This is often measured as the ratio of outputs to inputs which is called a productivity ratio. The closer the ratio is to 1.0, the higher the productivity; the closer the ratio is to 0.0, the lower the productivity. U.S. productivity is high, but many other nations are close behind, and gaining at a rapid pace. Productivity is important because it relates to an organization's ability to compete, and to the overall wealth and standard of living of a nation. Productivity is affected by work methods, capital, quality, technology, and management. A list of ways that productivity can be improved is given in the textbook.

3. The postwar experience of Japanese industry has provided lessons in management effectiveness, quality low-cost production, and employee motivation; it has also enabled Japan to overcome a prewar reputation for low quality, and to become a leading industrial power, even though the country has limited national resources.

4. Business organizations compete with each other in a variety of ways, such as price, quality, product or service features, flexibility, and delivery time. Operations and marketing functions must decide on an approach to competition, and work together to achieve success, capitalizing on strengths and exploiting competition weaknesses.

5. The most successful business organizations have carefully thought out strategies for accomplishing the goals of the organization. Corporate strategy is the overall strategy of the organization. It is affected by both Internal and external factors. These are listed and described in your textbook. Operations strategy should support the corporate strategy. It has a narrower focus; it pertains to the transformation aspect of the organization's activities. Operations strategy often relates to cost, quality, flexibility, and availability of products or services.

6. An important new approach to production of manufactured goods is lean production. It gets its name from the fact that it requires less inventory, time, and other resources than mass production. The evolution of manufacturing began with craft production, where skilled workers using general purpose tools produced custom-made goods. This was supplanted by mass production in the early 1900s. In contrast to craft production, production workers were generally low-skill, machines were specialized, and jobs became narrow. Specialization and division of labor were key concepts. Costs decreased while quality and productivity increased. Mass production is starting to give way in some industries to lean production.

Lean production has the advantage of greater flexibility than mass production, and can usually achieve higher quality than mass production.

GLOSSARY

craft production: a form of production that produced highly customized goods. Hallmarks were highly skilled craftsmen working with simple tools who completed entire items rather than parts of items.

hierarchy of decisions: strategic decisions (broad scope) establish the framework for tactical decisions (moderate scope) which in turn establish the framework for operating decisions (narrow scope).

Lean production: a form of production that uses less resources than more traditional manufacturing. Flexibility and quality are hallmarks of this approach.

mass production: a form of production designed to produce high volumes of standardized goods. Hallmarks are division of labor and specialized equipment.

mission: the basis for an organization; its reason or purpose.

productivity: a measure of output relative to input; the ratio of output to input.

strategy: a general plan for achieving a goal.

tactic: a method or action intended to accomplish a strategy.

TRUE/FALSE QUESTIONS

1. The mission of a firm should be designed to support the firm's overall strategy.

2. Operations managers measure productivity as the ratio of input to output.

3. Workers in lean production systems have more input in decision making than workers in mass production systems.

4. Workers in lean production systems often work as teams to solve problems.

5. Workers in lean production systems often operate under more pressure than those in mass production systems.

MULTIPLE-CHOICE QUESTIONS

1. Which of the following is not a possible negative impact on productivity?

    a. Low propensity of consumers to save.
    b. Use of robots.
    c. Government regulations.
    d. Increasing demand for services.
    e. Emphasis on long-run performance.

6

2. Which one of the following is not generally cited as a negative impact on productivity?

    a. Government regulations
    b. Liability claims
    c. Increased emphasis on services
    d. Emphasis on short-term performance
    e. All are reasons.

3. Which is the correct hierarchy of operations management decisions (highest first)?

    a. Operating, tactical, strategic
    b. Operating, strategic, tactical
    c. Tactical, strategic, operating
    d. Strategic, operating, tactical
    e. Strategic, tactical, operating

4. Which formula correctly describes productivity?

    a. $\dfrac{\text{Output - Input}}{\text{Output}}$ c. $\dfrac{\text{Output}}{\text{Input}}$

    b. $\dfrac{\text{Input - Output}}{\text{Input}}$ d. $\dfrac{\text{Input}}{\text{Output}}$

5. Operations strategy is affected by both internal and external factors. Which one of the following would come under both headings (internal and external)?

    a. Competition
    b. Technology
    c. Suppliers
    d. Markets
    e. Facilities and equipment

6. Which one of these are key aspects of lean production?

    a. specialization and division of labor
    b. highly skilled workers and general-purpose equipment
    c. high volume and dedicated equipment
    d. low-skilled workers and narrowly defined tasks
    e. flexibility and high quality

7. Which of these is not usually a basis for competition?

    a. Flexibility
    b. Price
    c. Quality
    d. Strategy
    e. Product differentiation

PROBLEMS

1. The Cool-Tech Company produces various types of fans. In May, the company produced 1,728 window fans at a standard price of $30.00. The company has 12 direct labor employees whose compensation (including wages and fringe benefits) amounts to $16.00 per hour. During May, window fans were produced on 9 working days (of 8 hours each), and other products were produced on other days. Determine the labor productivity of the window fans.

2. The Cool-Tech Company (see # 1) also produces desk fans at a standard price of $20.00. During May, 1,872 desk fans were produced on 11 working days (of 8 hours each). On one day, two employees called in sick.
    a. Determine the labor productivity of the desk fans.
    b. Was productivity higher for the window fans or for the desk fans in May?

3. Here is additional information about the Cool-Tech Company (see #I & #2). There were 20 working days in May. The direct material cost of window fans is $6.00; the direct material cost of desk fans is $4.00. The annual overhead expense incurred in operating the factory is $114,000.

    a. Determine the multi-factor productivity of the Cool-Tech Company in May.
    b. What is the interpretation of the multi-factor productivity?

2S - Decision Making

KEY IDEAS

1. Managers are decision makers. By making decisions, they exert an influence over the resources of the organization. Hence, decision making is a fundamental part of management. In terms of problem solving, decision making consists of these steps:

    (1) Identify the problem.
    (2) Specify objectives and decision criteria.
    (3) Develop a list of alternatives.
    (4) Analyze alternatives.
    (5) Select the best alternative.
    (6) Implement the alternative.
    (7) Monitor results

2. A key tool in decision making is the use of models, which are abstractions of reality. Models are valuable to decision makers because they enable decision makers to focus on a relatively few important aspects of a decision, they provide the ability to manipulate variables, and they increase understanding of a problem. [See the list of benefits and the list of limitations of models on pages 17-18 of the textbook.]

3. Operations decisions are characterized by the use of models, quantitative approaches, analysis of trade-offs, sensitivity analysis, and a systems approach. These are important concepts that are explained on pp. 17-21 of your textbook.

4. Decision theory is a general approach to decision making that can be used for decisions that involve a set of possible future conditions that will affect the payoff to the organization, a list of alternatives from which to choose, and an estimated payoff for each alternative under each possible future condition. It can be very helpful to organize this information-nation into a payoff table, listing the alternatives down the left side of the table, the possible future conditions across the top of the table, and the payoffs in the body of the table.

5. If estimated probabilities for events are available, the environment is one of risk. A typical approach in such cases is the following:

    a. Compute the expected payoff for each alternative using the probabilities.
    b. The alternative with the best expected payoff is the optimal decision.
    c. Additional information over and above that specified can sometimes be obtained. The *expected value of perfect information (EVPI)* is the difference between the *expected value of the best payoff each* event and the *expected value of the payoffs for the best* (single) alternative; an alternative definition of EVPI is expected regret.

6. If probabilities for events are unknown, the environment is one of uncertainty, and one or more of four decision criteria can help us decide which alternative is best:

maximin (pessimistic): the alternative with the best value of the worst payoffs.

maximax (optimistic): the alternative with the best payoff.

Laplace (equal weights): since the actual probabilities for events are unknown, for each alternative compute the expected value of the payoff, assuming every event has the same probability weight; the event with the highest expected payoff is the one selected.

minimax regret (cautious). the terms "regret" and "opportunity loss" mean the same thing: given an event E, for every alternative A. compute the difference between each payoff and the best payoff obtainable for any alternative with E, that difference is called regret. Calculate the regrets for every (A, E) pair and organize them into a matrix having the same dimensions as the payoff matrix. Select the alternative with the lowest value of the highest regrets, the minimax regret.

7.   Because the four uncertainty criteria all have different psychological bases, varying from extreme pessimism about the outcome to extreme outcomes, it would be most unusual if all of them agreed on what the right decision Is. As a test for the reasonableness of the results obtained from this analysis, the decision maker should select the criterion that comes closest to representing the decision maker's own psychological makeup, and compare results with one or more of the other four criteria.

8.   In this discussion, payoff is considered to be "positive" profit or revenue. The same decision process can be applied to costs, which are considered to be negative, including events, alternatives and payoffs.

9.   In the special case that there are just two states of nature, say El and E2 sensitivity studies can be performed graphically to find ranges of probability values for optimal decision making, without assuming that the probability distribution is known. The type of graph is shown in Example 8 of Chapter 2S. The horizontal axis is p, the probability of event E2, and (1 - p) is the probability of El; the vertical axes show the payoffs. At the lefthand edge $p = 0.0$, denoting that the probability of E2 is 0.0 and the probability of El is 1.0; at the right-hand edge, the probabilities are reversed, 1.0 for E2 and 0.0 for E1. For each decision alternative draw a straight line from the point representing the of (A, El) at $p = 0.0$ to the point denoting the payoff of (A, E2) at $p = I.O$. Every point on that line payoff is the expected value of alternative A for the respective p. The solid line at the top of the graph shows the highest expected payoff for every value of p, and the decision alternative associated with that payoff.

GLOSSARY

alternative: one of the choices available to the decision maker.

certainty: the event that will occur is known beforehand.

event: see state of nature.

expected value: for an alternative, obtained by multiplying each payoff by the column probability and summing the results; the mean.

expected value of perfect information (EVPI): the expected payoff assuming certainty minus the optimal payoff under risk; also expected value of the regret for the alternative that has the best expected value.

Laplace criterion: assign equal probabilities to all events, and choose the alternative with the highest expected value.

maximax criterion: an optimistic approach to decision making under uncertainty; select the alternative with the best overall payoff.

maximin criterion: a pessimistic view of the possible outcomes of the decision process under uncertainty; select the alternative with the best of the worst payoffs.

minimax regret criterion: a cautious approach to decision making under uncertainty; the absolute value of the difference between the payoff associated with an alternative-event pair (A, E) and the highest payoff for any decision in the E column of the matrix.

model: a simplified version of something; an abstraction of reality.

payoff: for every alternative/state of nature combination, the associated profit, cost, etc.

payoff matrix: a two-way layout, the rows representing the decision-maker's alternatives and the columns nature's events; an entry in a cell of the matrix is the payoff associated with the corresponding alternative-event pair.

probability: see probability distribution.

probability distribution: a set of nonnegative numbers called probabilities, each probability represents the chance that its corresponding event will occur; the sum of the probabilities for all events is 1.00.

regret: the difference between the payoff associated with an alternative-event pair (A,E) and the highest payoff for any alternative in the E column of the matrix.

risk: there is a known probability distribution for the events.

sensitivity: the extent to which the results of modelling are influenced by changes in the probabilities or the probability distribution.

state of nature: an event that could occur, that would not be under the control of the decision maker.

uncertainty: the possible events that could occur are known, but the probability distribution is unknown.

TRUE/FALSE QUESTIONS

F 1. States of nature are alternatives available to a decision maker.

2. Certainty is a situation that exists only if the information is perfect, that is, if the probability of the event that actually occurs is 1.0.

3. The expected value of perfect information (EVPI) is the expected value of the difference between the payoff of a decision under certainty and the optimal decision under risk.

4. EVPI is the expected value of the regret for the optimal decision under risk.

5. Minimax opportunity loss and minimax regret are actually the same thing.

6. With both risk and uncertainty the probability distribution for events is known.

7. A decision tree branches out all of the possible decisions and all of the possible events.

8. The expected value of the payoff for the optimal decision under risk is the best payoff that can be had without acquiring additional information.

9. An example of maximax decision making is when people buy lottery tickets hoping for a very big payoff.

MULTIPLE-CHOICE QUESTIONS

1. Which of the following is not a criterion for decision making under uncertainty?

    a. EVPI
    b. Maximin
    c. Maximax
    d. Laplace method
    e. Minimax regret

2. Which one of the following statements is not correct relative to decision making under risk?

    a. The sum of the state-of-nature probabilities must be 1.000.
    b. every probability must be greater than or equal to zero.
    c. All probabilities are assumed to be equal.
    d. Probabilities are used to compute expected values.
    e. Perfect information assumes that the state of nature that will actually occur is known.

The next three questions are based on the following payoff table of the present values:

Alternative	High	Low
buy	90	-10
rent	70	40
lease	60	55

3. The maximax strategy is:

    a. buy   b. lease   c. rent   d. high   e. low

4. The maximin strategy is:

    a. buy   b. lease   c. rent   d. high   e. low

5. If the probability of the state of nature "high" is 0.7, the decision with the highest expected value is:

    a. buy   b. lease   c. rent   d. high   e. low

6. Which one of the following steps is often the most crucial in the decision-making process?

    a. Identifying the problem.
    b. Specifying objectives
    c. Developing alternatives
    d. Analyzing alternatives
    e. Selecting the best alternative

7. Which one of the following would not generally be given as a reason for poor decisions?

    a. Unforeseeable circumstances
    b. Bounded rationality
    c. Suboptimization
    d. Mistakes in the decision process
    e. All are reasons

PROBLEMS

1. Here is a payoff matrix; parentheses designate a loss, The probabilities of the states of nature, $p(1)$ and $p(2)$, are unknown.

| | States of Nature | |
Alternatives	1	2
A	$500	$300
B	700	100
C	(300)	600

    a. Which alternative should be selected under the maximax criterion?
    b. Which alternative should be selected under the maximin criterion?
    c. Which alternative should be selected under the Laplace criterion?
    d. What is the opportunity loss table?
    e. Which alternative should be selected under the minimax regret criterion?

2. Refer to Problem 1. Construct the sensitivity graph, as shown on p. 80 of your textbook.

a. For what range of values of p(2) is alternative A preferred?
b. For what range of values of p(2) is alternative B preferred?
c. For what range of values of p(2) is alternative C preferred?

3. Fall has come, and the department manager of the Purple Pentagon Discount Store must decide how many snow blowers to order for the winter season. He believes there is an association between the weather and the demand for snow blowers: a winter with heavy snow should produce a high demand, and a winter with light snow should produce a low demand. However, if he guesses wrong and orders a large number of snow blowers when the weather turns out to have light snow, he will suffer a loss. Here is his payoff matrix.

	States of Nature		
Alternatives	*Heavy snow*	*Medium snow*	*Light snow*
Large Order	$5,000	$1,000	$(4,000)
Medium Order	2,000	3,000	(2,000)
Small Order	500	500	1,000

a. Which alternative should be selected under the maximax criterion?
b. Which alternative should be selected under the maximin criterion?
c. Which alternative should be selected under the Laplace criterion?
d. What is the opportunity loss table?
e. Which alternative should be selected under the miriimax regret criterion?

4. Refer to Problem 3. Suppose that the following probabilities are available regarding the snowfall next winter:

p(heavy snow) = . 10
p(medium snow) = .50
p(light snow) = .40

a. Which alternative should be selected under the expected value criterion?
b. Which alternative should be selected under the lowest expected loss criterion?
c. What is the value of the EVPI?
d. What is the interpretation of the EVPI?

5. (One step beyond) Here is a payoff matrix, in which the value of one payoff (X) is unknown.

	States of Nature	
	1	*2*
	p = .20	p = .80
Alternative		
A	$500	$1,200
B	x	400

a. Find the value of x for which the decision maker will be indifferent between alternatives A and B.
b. Suppose x = $4,000. .Will the decision maker prefer alternative A or alternative B?

14

3 - Quality Management

KEY IDEAS

1. An organization's reputation for superior quality can give it a competitive advantage in the marketplace. Superior quality can also reduce the risk of liability claims, reduce costs, and increase productivity.

2. Quality is defined as the ability of a product or service to consistently meet or exceed the expectations of the customer. Operational definitions of quality generally refer to one or more dimensions of quality. These include performance, special features, conformance to expectations, reliability, durability, and service after delivery.

3. The determinants of quality are design, conformance to design, ease of use, and service after delivery.

4. The consequences of poor quality relate to image/reputation, liability, productivity, and costs. Costs can be categorized as failure costs, appraisal costs, and prevention costs.

5. Quality can be improved by R & D efforts (explained in Chapter 5 of the textbook), by efforts of improvement teams, and by suggestions from employees and customers. Management plays a key role in improving and maintaining good quality.

6. Modern quality management stresses prevention of mistakes rather than finding and correcting mistakes after they occur. This has placed increased emphasis on both product design and process design. Quality gurus such as Deming, Juran, Crosby, and Ishikawa have greatly influenced current thinking and practice of quality management.

7. Total Quality Management (TQM) is a philosophy that says that quality is the responsibility of everybody in the organization. The focal point is customer satisfaction. Important features include continuous improvement (described in supplement of this chapter), benchmarking, employee empowerment, the use of teams for problem solving, and knowledge of tools (described in chapters 3S and 9 in the textbook).

8. Quality awards, such as the Malcolm Baldrige Award and the Deming Prize have generated interest in quality improvement, and helped to focus attention on the importance of quality. They have also helped to educate business people on quality management.

9. Organizations need to avoid the trap of over-emphasizing TQM, personnel and paperwork costs can quickly mount. A balanced approach is generally the best approach, giving measured emphasis to quality while continuing to give appropriate attention to other aspects of the organization.

GLOSSARY

appraisal costs: costs related to appraising quality, such as inspection, testing, and so on.

Baldrige Award: created by Congress to stimulate efforts to improve quality, and to recognize quality achievements. Limited to U.S. companies.

benchmarking: using another organization's process or product as a standard to improve a similar aspect of your organization's products or processes.

continuous improvement: a never-ending quest for better and better quality. A feature of TQM programs.

Deming Prize: named in honor of American W. Edwards Deming. A Japanese prize that recognizes successful quality efforts.

dimensions of quality: used for operational definitions of quality. included are performance, special features, reliability, durability, and so on.

failure costs: costs related to the occurrence of defects in a product or service. Internal costs include lost production, injuries, damage to equipment and other product, rework costs, and so on. External costs include loss of good will, warranty work, liability claims, complaints, and so on.

ISO 9000: a series of standards that outline the requirements for quality management systems. Developed by the International Organization for Standardization, which is comprised of 91 countries, including the U.S. Essential for companies that want to deal with the European Economic Community (EC).

liability: the legal responsibility of a producer for defects of a product or service that cause injury, harm, or property damage.prevention costs: costs associated with attempts to prevent mistakes from occurring. These include planning and administrative costs, training costs, monitoring operations, working with vendors, and so on.

quality at the source: making each employee responsible for the quality of his or her own work.

quality of conformance: achieving the intent of design in producing a product or delivering a service.

quality of design: the extent to which a product or service possesses features that can meet or exceed customer expectations.

TRUE/FALSE QUESTIONS

1. In the phrase *quality of conformance*, conformance refers to meeting customer specifications.

2. The Deming prize is limited to U.S. companies.

3. One definition of quality is fitness for use.

4. The TQM approach emphasizes customer satisfaction.

5. Liability claims can result from poor quality.

6. One criticism of the Baldrige Award is that applicants sometimes spend tremendous amounts of time and money vying for it.

7. Quality at the source refers to each worker being responsible for the quality of his/her work.

8. Reworking items that fail to pass inspection is an example of an appraisal cost.

9. A common cause of variation is the same as a random cause.

MULTIPLE-CHOICE QUESTIONS

1. Which one of these reflects an internal failure cost?

   a. inspection
   b. rework
   c. liability claim
   d. customer complaint

2. Although closely associated with quality, this name is not on the list of quality gurus:

   a. W. Edwards Deming
   b. Philip Crosby
   c. Malcolm Baldrige
   d. J. M. Juran
   e. Kaoru Ishikawa

3. Which name is associated with the phrase "fitness for use"?

   a. Deming
   b. Crosby
   c. Baldrige
   d. Juran
   e. Ishikawa

4. Which name is associated with a list of 14 points?

   a. Deming
   b. Crosby
   c. Baldrige
   d. Juran
   e. Ishikawa

5. Which name is associated with a cause-and-effect diagram?

    a. Deming
    b. Crosby
    c. Baldrige
    d. Juran
    e. Ishikawa

6. Which name is associated with a Japanese Prize?

    a. Deming
    b. Crosby
    c. Baldrige
    d. Juran
    e. Ishikawa

7. Which term is least likely to be associated with TQM?

    a. Appraisal costs
    b. Benchmarking
    c. Employee empowerment
    d. Continual improvement
    e. Team approach

8. Which one of these would not be considered a determinant of quality?

    a. Ease of use
    b. Service after delivery
    c. Design
    d. Conformance to design
    e. Focus groups

9. Which of the following would not normally be included in a list of the major ways quality affects an organization?

    a. Liability
    b. Reputation
    c. Costs
    d. Productivity
    e. All are factors

3S - Continuous Improvement

KEY IDEAS

1. Continuous improvement is a philosophy towards the improvement of quality that many organizations have adopted: The quest for higher and higher levels of quality should never end. Continuous improvement provides a structured approach to quality improvement. It is directed primarily at improving the *process*.

2. The conceptual basis for continuous improvement is the plan-do-check-act (PDCA) cycle: *Plan* by studying and documenting the current process. Collect data on the process. Develop a plan. *Do* refers to implementing the plan, and collecting data. *Check* involves evaluating the data collected during the do phase. *Act* means to standardize the new method if it is judged to be successful. Also, consider repeating it in other similar situations, communicate it to others, and implement training for the new method. The PDCA cycle is also known as the Shewhart cycle or the Deming wheel..

3. Among the key tools and techniques that are used for continuous improvement are flow charts, check sheets, Pareto analysis, brainstorming, control charts, interviewing, quality circles, benchmarking, cause-and-effect diagrams, and run charts.

4. A basic concept in both decision making and problem solving is that some elements or factors are more important than others. Typically, a relatively few of these are very important, and many are relatively unimportant. This is known as the Pareto phenomenon. The implication for decision makers and problem solvers is that it is important to identify the few key elements of factors and then give them special attention or emphasis.

GLOSSARY

benchmarking: using another organization's processes as a standard to improve your own process. The benchmark need not be in the same type of business, and need not be a competitor.

brainstorming: an idea generating method where a group of people cooperate in a freethinking session, building on each other's ideas.

conformance: the characteristics of the product satisfy the established standard for the characteristics.

continuous improvement: the attitude adopted by many organizations that strives to continually improve quality. The primary emphasis is on process improvement.

control chart: a technique devised by Walter Shewhart to monitor the quality level of work in process.

control limits: the boundaries of the range of random values of a statistic such as a sample mean.

5W2H approach: A set of basic questions, five that begin with a W (Who? What? Where? When? Why?) and two that begin with an H (How? and How much?). Used as a basis for process improvement.

inspection: examining material in process or finished products to determine conformance to standard.

liability: the legal responsibility of a producer for defects of a product or service that causes injury, harm, or property damage.

Pareto analysis: analysis that organizes categories of items according to degree of importance or frequency of occurrence. The purpose is to direct efforts to those items which have the greatest potential for improvement.

Plan-do-check-act (PDCA) cycle: is the conceptual basis for continuous improvement. It provides a structure for improvement efforts.

TRUE/FALSE QUESTIONS

1. Continuous improvement works best in firms that don't need major breakthroughs.

2. Continuous improvement is designed to generate major breakthroughs in process improvement.

3. The plan-do-check-act cycle is also known as the Shewhart wheel or the Deming wheel.

4. The 5W2H approach is a method used for asking questions about a process.

5. The 5W2H approach provides a visual representation of the key steps in a process.

6. A check sheet is a simple tool used for problem identification.

7. Another name for a cause and effect diagram is a fishbone diagram.

MULTIPLE-CHOICE QUESTIONS

1. Which one of these terms is associated with studying another organization's products or operations?

    a. Brainstorming
    b. Benchmarking
    c. Pareto analysis
    d. Continuous improvement

2. Which one of these is the conceptual basis for continuous improvement?

    a. Benchmarking
    b. Cause-and-effect diagram
    c. Pareto analysis
    d. The plan-do-check-act cycle

3. Which one of these terms refers to documenting a process?

    a. Initialize   b. Pareto analysis   c. Check sheet   d. Standardize

4. The term "80-20 rule" is most closely associated with:

    a. Control charts
    b. Pareto analysis
    c. Check sheets
    d. Brainstorming

PROBLEMS

1. The Modern Styles Furniture Company produces a line of disassembled furniture which comes in a carton. The buyer is required to assemble the pieces into a usable object. One of the products is a two-shelf bookcase. Here is the parts list for the product:

1 back panel	2 middle shelves	1 package of screws
1 top shelf	2 side panels	1 cardboard carton

    This problem is concerned only with the cardboard carton and its contents, The pieces of the bookcase are assumed to be satisfactory, but some may be missing in some cartons. This constitutes a simplification, of course, since it ignores the problem of defective or damaged parts. The company provides an 800 number on the carton to assist customers who experience difficulties. Recently, there has been a rash of calls concerning missing parts. The Company promptly ships the missing part(s) to the aggrieved customer.

    Management is concerned about the poor reputation which the Company's products are developing and about the extra expense of the shipments, which should be unnecessary. In an attempt to pinpoint the problem, some employees have been detailed to check every carton before it is sealed up and to keep a record of their findings on a check sheet. Any parts discovered to be missing are replaced before the carton is shipped. Here is a table of their findings for one week.

Piece	Mon.	Tues.	Wed.	Thurs.	Fri.	Total
Back panel	3	1	2	1	1	
Top shelf	2	2	3	1	2	
1 Middle shelf	6	4	7	4	10	
2 Middle shelves	2	-	3	1	-	
1 side panel	7	10	4	8	6	
2 side panels	-	2	1	3	1	
Screws	3	4	5	5	4	
Carton	-	-	-	-	-	
Total						

21

a. Fill in the totals in the Table.
b. Which piece is most often omitted?
c. Suggest a corrective action for the piece in b.
d. Which piece is the next most often omitted?
e. Suggest a corrective action for the piece in d.
f. Which day is most prone to errors in packing?
g. Suggest a corrective action for the worst day.

2. Using the data in Problem #1, construct a Pareto diagram for the missing pieces.

3. Assume that action has been taken to resolve the problem of the missing pieces in Problem #1, according to the suggestions in the answers. In order to find out whether the corrections were effective, all cartons produced in one week have been checked, producing the data in the table, below.

Piece	Mon.	Tues.	Wed.	Thurs.	Fri.	Total
Back panel	1	2	1	2	1	
Top shelf	3	2	3	1	3	
1 Middle shelf	-	-	-	-	-	
2 Middle shelves	1	2	1	-	1	
1 side panel	-	-	-	-	-	
2 side panels	2	1	1	3	1	
Screws	5	6	3	3	5	
Carton	-	-	-	-	-	
Total						

a. How much progress has been made in solving the missing pieces problem?
b. Which piece is now the most often omitted.
c. Suggest a corrective action for the piece in b.

4 - Product and Service Design

KEY IDEAS

1. Relevant considerations in planning a product or service system include: research, design, production, life cycle, safety in use, reliability, maintainability, regulatory and legal problems.

2. A marketable product is not always profitable. The reasons for this include:

    a. poor design that leads to an unsafe product may violate product codes or cause accidents that will result in future product liability lawsuits.
    b. the development may take so long that the product is being marketed past the time of peak demand.
    c. competition may result in obsolescence.

3. There are five stages to the product-demand life cycle: incubation, growth, maturity, saturation and decline. The production/operations system becomes an active participant early in the cycle, because of the need to plan production facilities.

4. Basic research is research that contributes knowledge but not products directly; applied research contributes knowledge about products; development contributes products; production/operations management delivers the products.

5. Computer-aided design and computer-aided manufacturing (CAD-CAM) enhance the productivity of both design and production personnel, because the computer can assimilate enormous quantities of information, display the consequences of a design or a course of action, and institute programmed controls of the manufacturing process.

6. Standardization of parts, components, and modularization, or standardizing larger components that might be used in several different products, has advantages for many reasons, including: reducing inventories; enhancing employee, customer and vendor familiarity; making it easier to purchase raw materials and component parts; and routinizing production and quality assurance activities. There are also some possible disadvantages in reduced consumer appeal and possible freezing of imperfect designs, with subsequent costly changeovers.

7. An important aspect of the design process is to design for manufacturability. This means avoiding designs that would require costly or time-consuming steps, or steps that would make it difficult to achieve desired quality levels. Instead, designers need to be aware of manufacturing capabilities, and create products that are easy to produce, and lend themselves to achieving desired quality levels.

8. The design of services differs in many respects from the design of products, because of certain basic differences that exist between products and services. For example, services tend to have higher customer contact than manufacturing, and services tend to be intangible. Also, services can't be inventoried. Because of these and other differences, the design of services requires attention to many different details than design of products.

9. Robust design refers to products or services that are relatively insensitive to some change in operating conditions. That is, products (or services) with robust design have a broader range of conditions under which they can function in an acceptable manner than products (or services) that do not have this feature. That can be a real advantage in terms of reliability and customer satisfaction.

10. Reverse engineering refers to the dismantling of another firm's product to learn about any special features that can be adapted to one's own products.

11. Quality function deployment (QFD) is a process for integrating the "voice of the customer" into the design of products and services. This intention is to achieve increased levels of customer satisfaction by incorporating customer requirements at the earliest possible stage in the production cycle.

GLOSSARY

applied research: research that is directed at the growth of scientific knowledge, with a specific commitment toward product development.

attribute: a characteristic that has only two possible states.

basic research: research that is directed at the growth of scientific knowledge, without any specific product orientation.

concurrent engineering: bringing engineering and manufacturing personnel together early in the design phase.

development: research and design activities that bring forth a serviceable and marketable product with a profit potential.

end item: a product sold or delivered to the ultimate user.

growth: the second stage of the product life cycle, representing growth in demand and marketability.

incubation: the first stage of the producer's product life cycle; usually it is an idea that is the result of either basic or applied research.

manufacturability: designing products with manufacturing capabilities in mind, and with an eye towards making products easy to produce, and easy to avoid mistakes.

maturity: the third or middle stage of the product life cycle, when the product reaches the peak of demand.

modularization: a high level of standardization, where the standardized components are assemblies or subassemblies of the end item product.

product liability: the legal responsibility of a manufacturer, in case there is a serious injury to a user because of a defect in the design or manufacture of a product.

product design: all activities connected with bringing forth a new product to market.

quality function deployment (QFD): integrating the "voice of the customer" into product and service design.

reverse engineering: dismantling another firm's product to learn about its special features.

robust design: design that results in products or services that can perform over a broad range of operating conditions.

saturation: the fourth stage of the product life cycle, when the demand for the product is just past its peak and *on the decline.*

Uniform Commercial Code: in essence, the code specifies that every product must be usable for its intended purposes.

TRUE/FALSE QUESTIONS

1. Basic research, applied research and development are all part of the product life cycle.

2. Technological obsolescence can be prevented by designing a better product.

3. Standardization of parts and components frequently leads to higher costs of production.

4. The term *robust design* refers to particularly strong and durable products.

5. The term *concurrent enginering* refers to bringing engineering and manufacturing personnel together early in the design phase.

6. Modular design is a form of standardization.

7. CAD uses computer graphics for product design.

8. A service blueprint is typically used to guide construction of a service facility.

9. Quality function deployment is a method of integrating the "voice of the customer" into the design process.

10. Reverse engineering involves taking apart a product to see how it is designed.

MULTIPLE-CHOICE QUESTIONS

1. The advantages of standardization include:

   I. early freezing of the design.
   II. fewer parts to deal with in inventory.
   III. reduced training cost and time.
   IV. more routine purchasing.

   a. I, II   b. I, IV   c. I, II, III   d. II, III, IV   e. I, II, 111, IV

2. The term that pertains to incorporating customer ideas in product design is:

   a. TQM
   b. CAD
   c. QFD
   d. robust design.
   e. reverse engineering

3. Product design that uses computers is referred to as:

   a. QFD   b. CAM   c. RFD   d. CAD   e. TQM

4. Taking apart a competitor's product to better understand how it operates is:

   a. Service blueprint
   b. Concurrent engineering
   c. Robust design
   d. illegal
   e. None of these

5. Which one of these is a tool used for service blueprinting?

   a. Flowchart.
   b. QFD.
   c. CAD.
   d. CAM.
   e. Reverse engineering.

6. The term "House of Quality" is associated with:

   a. Service blueprinting.
   b. The Taguchi approach.
   c. Quality function deployment.
   d. Robust design.
   e. Concurrent engineering.

4S - Reliability

KEY IDEAS

1. Product descriptions and specifications frequently require that a product have a minimum specified reliability. Reliability has both qualitative or descriptive aspects, the ability of the product to perform its intended function, and quantitative aspects, as a measure of the probability of success.

2. The probability of success is measured in one of two ways:

    a. attributes, success or failure: the probability of a success on a single usage or trial; for example, the opening or closing of a switch.
    b. time-to-failure analysis, the probability that the product will perform its intended function for a specified period of time such as, for example, a warranty period for an automobile.

3. If we assume that components succeed or fail independently, the reliability of a serial system is the product of the reliabilities of the components. There is a dual relationship between serial and parallel, redundant or standby systems; for a parallel system the unreliability, or probability of failure, is the product of the unreliabilities of the components.

4. For time-to-failure components or systems, the failure rate tends to follow the bathtub curve: a high but declining failure rate when the product is new, constant failure rate during the normal service period, followed by increasing failure rate, or wearout. The following diagram is typical:

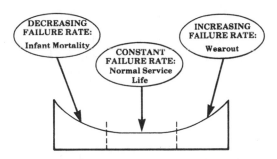

The central period of constant failure rate is characterized by the exponential distributition; it represents the majority of the service lifetime of the product. Manufacturers try to reduce or eliminate the defects that cause early failures through quality assurance activities and employee motivation, in order to increase customer satisfaction and reduce complaints or the possibility of lawsuits. The wearout period is the time that one might expect the customer to strongly consider purchasing a replacement, because of the difficulty in getting satisfactory service. Warranties usually cover early failures and the beginning of non-normal service life, but not wearout.

5. The interpretation of the reliability-MTBF relationship is that during the normal service-life period, if T is a specified lifetime, such as a warranty period, the reliability R is

$$R = e^{-(T/MTBF)}$$

where $e = 2.71828$ is the base of natural (Naperian) logarithms, and T is frequently called the "mission time" of the system.

Elaboration:

In both cases, note that the concern is with failures. Thus, an alternate definition is that the reliability is the probability that a failure will not occur before it is supposed to occur, if ever. Estimating the reliability of a product or system is a statistical problem based upon lifetime and failure data obtained either with laboratory testing or the failure reports of equipment in the field.

The reliability may be estimated for a component, a module, a system or an assembly. The distinctions between the three types is arbitrary. Since the advent of microminiaturization, tiny chips which are a fraction of the size of a fingernail can contain several thousand transistors and diodes, and perform complex electronic logic at amazingly low cost. A convenient distinction is that a component is an element that is tested as a unit. A module is a collection of components; an assembly is a finished product or end item; and a system is a collection of end items intended to perform a specific function.

A system or subsystem for reliability purposes is organized according to a specific logic. If there are n components and all of them must work in order for the system to work properly, it is called a serial system. If all components succeed or fail independently, the reliability of the system is the product of the reliabilities of all n components. If every component is protected by a standby or parallel element that can perform its function, the system is parallel or redundant, and the unreliability or probability of failure is the product of the unreliabilities of the parallel elements.

6. Some companies have found that by reducing the number of components in a product, the reliability of those products has increased. With fewer parts, fewer processes are required (less chance for mistakes), there are fewer interfaces to deal with (so designers can be more focused), and less time is required (less time for mistakes to occur). An alternate approach is to use backup, or redundant, components to increase reliability.

GLOSSARY

availability: The proprotion of time that a piece of equipment is expected to be available to perform its intended function instead of being out of service.

bathtub curve: a description of the changing failure rate of a product over its lifetime decline: the fifth or final stage of the product life cycle, when the demand for the product has just about phased out and it is the time to find new products to produce and market.

exponential functions: mathematical functions that incorporate the constant e, the base of natural logarithms.

infant mortality: the first stage of the product life cycle in use, characterized by high but declining failure rate.

MTBF: the mean time between failures, the inverse of the failure rate.

parallel system: a system for which only one of several alternative components is needed for success.

redundancy: a situation where if a specific component fails, a substitute component is available to take over the specified function.

reliability: the probability of success.

series system: a system for which all components are needed for success.

time-to-failure analysis: for a product or system that is supposed to have a specified lifetime or period of service, time-to-failure analysis measures the length of life, the failure rate or MTBF, and any characteristic changes that may occur over the lifetime of the product in use.

TRUE/FALSE QUESTIONS

1. Reliabilities are typically specified with respect to normal operating conditions.

2. Redundancy is sometimes used in product design to increase reliability.

3. The typical service life of a product usually consists mainly of a period of constant failure rate.

4. The term *availability* refers to having sufficient design personnel to handle product design.

5. If a system is made up of two components that are in series, and both have failure rates of 50%, the probability that the system will fail is 75%.

6. It is theoretically possible that the service life of a component or element can be described by the normal distribution.

MULTIPLE-CHOICE QUESTIONS

1. A system is composed of three components, 1. II, III. All three of these components must function in order for the system to work. Their reliabilities are respectively: I. 0.4; 11, 0.5; III, 0.5. The overall system reliability is:

   a. 0.70
   b. 0.99
   c. 0.10
   d. 0.18
   e. 0.97

2. A system is composed of three components, I, II, III. The reliabilities of the three components are respectively 0.5, 0.4, and 0.9. II is a standby for I that switches on only if I fails, and III is a standby for II. The overall system reliability is:

    a. 0.70
    b. 0.99
    c. 0.10
    d. 0.18
    e. 0.97

3. A life test has shown that coffeemakers fail in use at the rate of 0.04257 per month. The manufacturer warranties that a coffeemaker will last for 12 months of ordinary usage. Assuming that the lifetime failure distribution is exponential, the reliability of a coffeemaker is:

    a. 0.4   b. 0.5   c. 0.6   d. 0.7   e. 0.8

4. In Problem 3, the MTBF would be (fill in answer) _____ months.

5. In Problem 3 assume that the lifetime distribution is normal with a mean equal to the answer you obtained in 4 immediately above, and a standard deviation of 10 months. What is the reliability of the coffeemaker in this case? (fill in)

PROBLEMS

1. A system has four components, A, B, C, D. The probability that each component will work is p(A) =.90, p(B) = .70, p(C) =.95, and p(D) = .60; all components must operate in order for the system to work. Since the probabilities associated with components B and D are low, backup components, B-B and D-D, with the same probabilities are provided:

    a. Draw the box and line diagram for this system.
    b. What is the probability that each component will not work?
    c. What is the probability that the system will work without the backup components?
    d. List the ways in which the system can work with the backup components.
    e. What is the probability that the system will work with the backup components?
    f. How much improvement in reliability do the backup components provide?

2. (One step beyond) A simple system consists of three components, A. B, C, as shown below, with the probability that each component will work. Component A costs $20,000 each, B costs $10,000 each, and C costs $6,000 each.

    >—| p(A) = .99 |—| p(B) = .99 |—| p(C) = .75 |—>

a. What is the probability that the system will work?

b. Management wishes to have at least a .95 probability that the system will work, and proposes to achieve this goal by adding redundant component C's to the system, which are identical to the existing component C. Each new C would switch on if the preceding C's failed. How many C's will be required?

c. Draw the diagram of the new system.

d. How much will it cost to achieve a .95 probability by adding C's?

3. The mean operating life (MTBF) of TV picture tubes is 4,000 hours, and the failure rate of the tubes can be modeled by a negative exponential distribution. Use Table 4S-2 in your textbook, or use the ex or In x keys on your pocket calculator to solve these problems.

a. Determine the probability that a picture tube will fail within 3,200 hours.

b. Determine the probability that a picture tube will last at least 6,400 hours.

c. The manufacturer wishes to provide a warranty on which he will be obligated to make a replacement of only 2% of the picture tubes sold. For how many hours should the picture tubes be warranted?

d. Does the MTBF come in the middle of this distribution?

4. The service life of automobile tires is modeled by a normal curve; the Mean Time Between Failures (MTBF) is 20,000 miles and the standard deviation is 800 miles. Use Table A in Appendix to solve these problems.

a. Determine the probability that a tire will fail before 22,000 miles.

b. Determine the probability that a tire will last at least 19,000 miles.

c. The manufacturer wishes to provide a warranty on which he will be obligated to make a replacement of only 1% of the tires sold. For how many miles should he warrant the tires?

d. Does the MTBF come in the middle of this distribution?

e. What is the difference between modeling the service life with the negative exponential distribution or with the normal curve?

5. The office copier is a very temperamental machine; it seems to break down about once a month (of 20 working days). When it does, it is necessary to have the manufacturer send out a service technician to repair it, which takes two days.
a. What is the MTBF?
b. What is the MTR?
c. What is the availability?
d. What is the interpretation of the availability?

6. (Refer to #5) The office manager has decided to investigate the possibility of replacing the copier with a competitors machine. The competitor has installed his machine in the office for a trial run. After several months, the office manager has concluded that the new machine breaks down about once every five weeks (25 working days). The manufacturer then dispatches a service technician to repair it, which takes three days.
a. What is the MTBF?
b. What is the MTR?
c. What is the availability?
d. Should the manager replace the old copier with the new one?

31

5 - Process Selection and Capacity Planning

KEY IDEAS

1. Process selection involves making choices concerning the way an organization will produce its products or provide services to its customers. It has major implications for capacity planning, layout and work methods.

2. Organizations which make rather than buy products, or provide rather than subcontract for services, naturally become more involved in process selection than those who buy or subcontract. [See the list of factors relating to make vs. buy in the text, page 182.]

3. Organizations can select from three types of processing: continuous, intermittent, and project. Note that many organizations use all three, but for different aspects of their operations. However, many other organizations rely primarily on one type of processing. Essentially, continuous processing is used for high-volume operations that have Standardized output, intermittent processing is used for lower-volume, customized operations, and projects are used for limited-time, unique sets of tasks.

4. Process selection may lead to automation or computer-aided manufacturing. [You should find it helpful to list the different types of computer-aided manufacturing, along with a brief description and advantages and limitations of each type.]

5. A key issue in process selection is the management of technology. See the discussion under the Operations Strategy section. Another key issue in process selection is flexibility.

6. Production-system design and capacity planning are twin concepts: the system is designed for a stated capacity.

7. Strategically, capacity and financial decisions are made first, followed by decisions on location of the facility, design of the product, layout and work systems.

8. Capacity is the maximum rate of output for the system under normal operating conditions.

9. If products are similar enough, capacity is measured in common units or rates of output; when products are dissimilar, for example, as in a job shop, capacity is in units of resources used: machine time, labor hours, etc. Capacity is not measured in dollar units, because there can be substantial changes in prices over the life cycle of the product.

10. The capacity decision is often difficult and/or costly to modify.

11. Effective capacity is less than the design capacity, because the system may have alternative product-mix strategies, because of changes in design of the product and quality specifications, job requirements or work rules. Actual output would usually be less than effective capacity, because of shortages, delays, bottlenecks or changes in demand. Efficiency and utilization are ratios, expressed as percentages, that show the relationships between actual output and measures of capacity:

efficiency is the ratio of actual output to effective capacity; utilization is the ratio of actual output to design capacity.

12. Planning considerations involve long-run trends. seasonal shifts in demand, and joint and competing products and services.

13. Cost-volume (breakeven analysis, supplemented by marginal analysis on the optimum size of a plant, helps in determining the optimum design capacity, for a variety of output rates.

14. The linear breakeven model discussed in this chapter assumes that there is only one product, all production is sold, variable cost per unit of output is constant, and that there is no change in fixed costs or in per unit revenues, regardless of volume. If there are major deviations from these assumptions, a nonlinear model should be used instead of a linear one.

GLOSSARY

breakeven analysis: see cost-volume analysis.

breakeven point: the output level at which total cost = total revenue.

capacity: the upper limit on the planned rate of output.

capacity alternatives: different levels of planned output having different cost structures for a range of outputs.

cost-volume analysis: focuses on relationships between cost, revenue, and volume of output. *cyclical* factors: factors that affect the rate of output, based on the business cycle. design capacity: a specified rate of output that the plant is theoretically capable of producing.

effective capacity: an achievable rate of output that is usually less than the design capacity because of operational difficulties.

efficiency: the ratio of actual output to effective capacity, expressed as a percentage.

external factors: circumstances that affect the plant capacity and the rate of output, which are either externally imposed, such as health and safety regulations, or else negotiated, such as by union work rules.

facilities factors: environmental factors that affect the rate of output, based on the design or the location of the plant.

financial analysis: planning for receipt and payout of funds and maintaining cash flow, taking into account the present value of funds to be received or paid out in the future.

fixed cost: those expenses which do not increase (or decrease) when the volume of output increases (or decreases).

human factors: psychological and physical aspects of the layout of the facility and work spaces that affect employee morale, performance and output.

operational factors: scheduling problems, bottlenecks, equipment failures, or breakdowns in communication between different sections of the plant that affect performance and output.

process factors: technology, specifications or special customer requirements that affect performance and output.

product/service factors: factors that affect the rate of output, based on the degree of specialization in the product or service, or in the design of the production system.

seasonal factors: factors that affect the rate of output, based on seasonal changes in demand or in production activity.

trend factors: factors that affect the rate of output, based on long-run changes in tastes, costs, demand levels, taxes, etc.

utilization: the ratio of actual output to design capacity, expressed as a percentage.

variable cost: the total of per-unit material, labor and operational cost, assumed to be constant per unit of product in a linear breakeven model.

TRUE/FALSE QUESTIONS

1. Short-run variations in demand can influence design capacity.

2. Intermittent systems are designed for high volume output.

3. Flexible manufacturing systems can handle a variety of dissimilar products.

4. Systems that produce highly standardized items are sometimes called continuous systems.

5. A project approach is often the best choice when a complex set of tasks has a limited life span.

6. Design capacity is not the same as effective capacity.

7. Peak loads and seasonal requirements affect design capacity planning, as well as effective capacity and actual output.

8. Linear breakeven analysis does not consider when in time the breakeven point is achieved.

9. A capacity decision is irrevocable.

10. Plant efficiency increases as the ratio of design capacity to actual output increases.

MULTIPLE-CHOICE QUESTIONS

1. Efficiency, in capacity terms, is the ratio of.

   a. actual output to effective capacity.
   b. actual output to design capacity.
   c. effective capacity to actual output.
   d. design capacity to effective capacity.
   e. design capacity to actual capacity

2. Which one of the following statements is incorrect?

   a. Short-term capacity is less concerned with trends or cycles than with deviations from the average.
   b. Long-term capacity needs are obtained by converting trend forecasts into capacity requirements.
   c. Product standards and specifications do not restrict management's options of increasing capacity or using existing capacity.
   d. Human factors that influence capacity are more subtle than quantifiable factors, such as the rate of output.
   e. Employee motivation has an important connection with capacity, as do both absenteeism and labor turnover.

3. Seasonal variations are often easier to deal with in capacity planning than trend, because seasonal variations tend to be:

   a. predictable.
   b. smaller.
   c. larger.
   d. controllable.
   e. none of the above is correct.

4. The assumptions of the linear breakeven cost-volume analysis model include:
   I: the variable cost per unit is the same regardless of volume
   II: fixed costs do not change when the volume changes
   III: revenue per unit is the same regardless of volume

   a. I only.
   b. I and II only.
   c. II only.
   d. II and III only.
   e. I, II, and III.

5. What is the breakeven quantity of weekly production for this particular situation?

   fixed cost: $1,500 per week
   variable cost: $3 per unit
   revenue: $6 per unit

a. 200   b. 500   c. 100   d. 600   e. 300

6. Product variety in a job shop tends to be:

   a. high.   b. moderate.   c. low.   d. very low.

7. The system that has the highest equipment flexibility is:

   a. Job shop.
   b. Batch.
   c. Repetitive/assembly.
   d. Continuous flow

PROBLEMS

1. The Crystal Sparkle Co. produces glass tumblers. The plant Is designed to produce 400 tumblers per hour, and there is one eight-hour shift per working day. However, the plant does not operate for the full eight hours: the employees take two 15-minute breaks in each shift, one in the first four hours and one in the second four hours, the first thirty minutes of the shift are spent raising the kilns to the required temperature for firing glass. The plant usually produces about 10,000 tumblers per five-day workweek. Answer the following questions by adjusting the data to one eight-hour shift.

   a. What is the design capacity in tumblers?
   b. What is the effective capacity in tumblers? As a percent?
   c. What is the actual output in tumblers'?
   d. What is the efficiency?
   e. What is the utilization?

2. The Goode and Cooke Company produces several models of frying pans. There is little difference in the production time required for the various models; the plant is designed to produce 160 frying pans per eight-hour shift, and there are two shifts per working day. However, the plant does not operate for the full eight hours: the employees take two 12-minute breaks in each shift, one in the first four hours and one in the second four hours; two hours per week are devoted to cleaning the factory and performing maintenance on the machines; one four-hour period every four weeks is devoted to the meeting of the quality circle. The plant usually produces about 3,500 frying pans per four-week period. You may ignore holidays in solving this problem. Answer the following questions by adjusting the data to a four-week time period.

   a. What is the design capacity in frying pans?
   b. What is the effective capacity in frying pans? As a percent?
   c. What is the actual output?
   d. What is the efficient.
   e. What is the utilization?
   f. Re-work the problem using a time period of one eight-hour shift.

3. The selling price of the product is $199.95. The variable costs per unit are:

Labor	$60.25
Raw material	25.70
Purchased component	21.50
Variable overhead	17.50

The fixed costs total $300,000 per year. Perform a breakeven analysis of this company.

a. What is the total revenue function?
b. What is the total cost function?
c. What is the profit function?
d. What is the breakeven point in units of the product?
e. What is the revenue at the breakeven point?
f. What is the income at the breakeven point?
g. Estimate the profit when 9,000 units of the product are sold in a year.
h. How many units must be sold for the company to make $900,000?

4. The Lade & Bach Company produces office chairs. The price of the chairs is $99.75 and the variable cost per chair is $49.75. The following fixed costs are incurred:

Depreciation of plant and equipment per year	$20,000
Property taxes per year	12,000
Manager's salary and fringe benefits per month	5,200

Perform a breakeven analysis of this company:

a. What is the total revenue function?
b. What is the total cost function?
c. What is the profit function?
d. What is the breakeven point in number of chairs?
e. What is the revenue at the breakeven point?
f. What Is the income at the breakeven point?
g. Estimate the profit when 1,500 chairs are produced in a year.
h. How many chairs must be sold for the company to make $75,000 in a year?

5. The telephone company has three billing plans.

A: An unlimited number of local telephone calls per month for $20.00
B: Fifty (or fewer) local telephone calls per month for $16.00 plus $0.08 per call above 50 calls.
C: Twenty (or fewer) local telephone calls per month for $12.00 plus $0. 10 per call above 20 calls.

The subscriber is uncertain as to whether the number of local telephone calls will be about 60 per month, or about 90 per month, or about 120 per month, or about 160 per month. Use decision theory to determine which billing plan the subscriber should select:

a. What is the payoff table?
b. Which plan should be selected under the minimax regret criterion?
c. Why is it improper to use the maximax criteria here?

d. Suppose that the subscriber assesses probabilities as follows:

p(60 calls) = .40   p(120 calls) = .20
p(90 calls) = .30   p(160 calls) = .10

Which plan should be selected under the best expected value criterion?

e. Which plan should be selected under the least expected regret criterion?

6. (One step beyond) PC Fun & Games, Inc., produces a game for personal computers on a CD-ROM disk which is entitled: Armageddon, the Final Battle. The company sells the disk to software retailers for $20.00, each, with a 5% discount for orders of 100 copies or more. virtually every retailer takes the discount. The variable costs of producing the disks are low, totaling only $7.00 each for the blank disk onto which the game is copied, the wages of the machine operator, and the packaging.

The game has become a best seller, and the production manager must plan to expand the capacity of the plant to turn out CD-ROM disks. CD-ROM disks are produced on a machine which makes copies of a master disk, one at a time. Each copy takes fifteen minutes, which includes inserting the blank disk, imprinting the game, and removing the finished disk.

At present, the Company has four machines; each machine cost $80,000 and has a service life of five years. The Company operates two eight-hour shifts per day, 50 weeks per year, and the machines require servicing and adjustments for one hour every day.

New machines can be purchased for $85,000. They also have a service life of five years and require one hour of servicing, but they can make copies in ten minutes. Because of the savings in copying time, the variable cost will drop to $6.00 per disk.

a. What is the annual effective capacity of one present machine?
b. What is the annual depreciation expense of one present machine? (Use straight line depreciation expense = cost/service life.)
c. What is the present breakeven point?
d. What is the annual effective capacity of one new machine?
e. What will be the annual effective capacity of the plant if one new machine is purchased?
f. What will be the new average variable cost per unit?
g. What will be the new breakeven point?
h. Suppose a second new machine is purchased. What will be the annual capacity of the plant?
i. What will be the new average variable cost per unit?
j. What will be the new breakeven point?

5S - Linear Programming

KEY IDEAS

1. A linear programming (LP) model is a linearized mathematical representation of a system of relationships about a set of decision variables. The objective is to maximize or else to minimize a linear objective function, subject to a set of linear constraints and bounds for the variables.

2. The job of an analyst is to recognize the problem, formulate the model to solve the problem and supply the necessary input data. Because of the availability of computers and standardized LP codes, solving the model is now a routine task; students, however, acquire a working familiarity with the mechanics of a solution, in order to understand the meaning of the output.

3. An LP problem consists of an objective function, a set of constraints, plus a set of bounds for the decision variables, all linear functions. The objective function is a linear function with an unspecified value, Z. that is to be either maximized, if the problem deals with revenues or profits, or minimized, if it deals with costs. Because Z is not a specified constant, in graphical LP the objective function is represented by a family of parallel straight lines.

   The feasible space is the area of the first quadrant bounded both by the axes and by all of the constraints. A solution is a point in two-dimensional space, whether it satisfies the model or not. A feasible solution is a solution inside the feasible space. The optimal solution is the feasible solution that either maximizes or minimizes the objective function.

   The optimal solution is always a corner point of the feasible space. In order to find the exact values of x and y for a corner point, two constraint-boundary equations are solved simultaneously.

4. Small problems with just two decision variables, are usually solved graphically. The text includes detailed step-by-step procedures for: (1) plotting the constraint boundaries that enclose the space of feasible solutions; (2) drawing the *isoproftt (or isocost)* lines that are parallel to the objective function; and (3) identifying the corner point of the feasible space at the intersection of two constraint boundaries, representing the optimum solution.

   Two-variable maximizations with all less-than-or-equal-to ($\leq$) constraints have feasible spaces that are entirely enclosed inside upper-limit boundaries; if both variables are also nonnegative (>0), the (0,0) origin is feasible. Minimizations with all greater-than-or-equal to ($\leq$) constraints have feasible spaces that are entirely enclosed by the x- and y-axes, unbounded from above and bounded from below by lower-limit boundaries.

5. The simplex method, one of the most useful achievements of modern mathematical science, is a general-purpose linear programming solution method that has been widely computerized. A two-variable problem, or a problem of almost any size, can be solved by simplex.

   The simplex algorithm is a sequence of tableaus, with each tableau or iteration representing the exchange of a zero-valued variable for a nonzero variable. The initial tableau representing the (0,0)

41

origin, has m nonzero slack variables and n zero-valued decision variables. The first pivot results in the exchange of one decision variable for a slack variable. At the start of the second tableau, the decision variable, now > 0. is at the comer point of the feasible space on its own axis, the slack variable is zero-valued, meaning that there is no slack in the constraint because it is at its limit, and the comer point is a better trial solution than the origin of the initial tableau. Subsequent iterations result in further exchanges. A *stopping* rule tells the analyst when the optimum is reached and the iterations can be stopped.

When the system has $\geq$ or = constraints, the feasible space does not include the origin, which is the starting point of simplex pivoting. In that case, the simplex tableaus are augmented by an artificial variable for each $\geq$ or = constraint, in order to ""kick"" the set of solutions away from the origin, into the feasible space. By contrast to slack variables or decision variables, which can be ≥ 0 at the optimum, an artificial variable is always = 0 at the optimum.

The simplex method is an algorithm; this means that if the input conditions satisfy the requirements for an LP model, the output is always the best solution.

6. After the optimum is attained, sensitivity analysis can determine;

    a. The range of feasibility, which is the range of values of the RHS quantities of a constraint for which the shadow prices and the variables in solution remain the same.

    b. The range of optimality, which is the range of values over which the objective function coefficient of a decision variable can change without changing either the list of variables in solution or their optimal quantities, although the value of the objective function will change.

    c. The range of insignificance, which is the range of values over which the objective function coefficient of a variable that is not in solution can change and still not cause the variable to come into solution.

GLOSSARY

algorithm: a procedure that always results in an optimum solution if the input data conform to the requirements for a mathematical model of this class.

artificial variable: a variable added to an LP problem, one for each $\geq$ or equality constraint, in order to facilitate a simplex solution; an artificial variable is required to be zero-valued at the optimum.

C row: in a simplex tableau, the row containing the objective-function coefficients.

C - Z row: in a simplex tableau, the row that supplies the test values in order to determine whether an optimum solution has been attained.

constraint: a linear function of the decision variables that defines boundaries for the feasible space; a constraint could be an inequality of either the less-than-or-equal-to ($\leq$) or the greater-than-or equal-to ($\geq$) type, or else an equality (=).

continuous variable: a variable that is not restricted to integer or discrete values.

corner point: a corner point of the feasible space could occur whenever two linear constraint boundaries intersect; the optimum solution of an LP problem is at a corner point.

decision variable: a variable whose value can be set by a decision maker.

feasible solution: a solution that satisfies all constraints and boundary conditions, with all decision variables and all slack variables nonnegative (≥ 0).

graphical linear programming: an LP problem with two decision variables, x and y, where the solution is obtained on a two-dimensional grid that displays the constraint boundaries, the feasible space and the corner points of the feasible space.

heuristic: a procedure for solving a mathematical model that is not always guaranteed to result in the best possible solution.

integer variable: a variable that is required to assume only integer values, 1, 2, 3, etc. integer programming: LP with some or all of the decision variables integer-valued. isoprofit line: every point on the line will yield the same profit.

iteration: see pivoting.

linear programming (LP): a procedure for finding the values of decision variables, that results in the best solution of an optimization problem with linear constraints and a linear objective function.

linear function: a mathematical function of the form $m = ax + by + cz + ...$, where a, b, c, etc. are constants, x, y, z, etc. are variables; and m could be either a constant or a variable. maximization: a requirement that at the optimum, the objective function shall be at its highest possible value, within the feasible space.

minimization: a requirement that at the optimum, the objective function shall be at its lowest possible value, within the feasible space.

nonnegativity: all decision variables and all slack variables are required to be ≥ 0.

objective function: a linear function of the decision variables, that is either maximized or minimized by the LP solution.

optimal solution: the best feasible solution, one that either maximizes or minimizes the value of the objective function.

pivoting: exchanging a decision variable for a slack variable or another decision variable, or a slack variable for another slack variable or decision variable.

range of feasibility: the range over which the righthand side value of a constraint can change without changing its shadow price.

range of optimality: the range over which the value of an objective function coefficient can change and not change the optimal solution.

43

sensitivity analysis: an extension of simplex used to assess the impact of a change in the value of an objective function coefficient or a change in the right-hand-side value of a constraint.

shadow price: for the final, or optimal, tableau of a solution, the value in the C - Z row for a slack variable; a shadow price is a measure of the relative degree of improvement possible by modifying the corresponding constraint in the right direction.

simplex method: the algorithmic procedure for finding the optimal solution of an LP problem.

simplex tableau: a table corresponding to a comer point of the feasible space, each column representing a decision variable. a slack variable, or an artificial variable, and each row a nonzero variable.

simultaneous solution: finding the coordinates of the point at which two straight lines intersect.

slack variable: a variable whose value is zero if the corresponding constraint is at its boundary, or > 0 if the lefthand side of the constraint does not equal the righthand side.

solution: a set of decision variables, and their respective values.

suboptimization: in LP, suboptimization implies that the proposed solution attained is not actually the overall optimum; it can be a comer point of the feasible space other than the optimum, or else any point in the feasible space, even if it isn't a corner.

TRUE/FALSE QUESTIONS

1. LP operations are performed in an environment of certainty.

2. LP always involves either maximizing or minimizing an objective function.

3. The optimum solution of an LP includes at least one corner point of the feasible set.

4. A circle would be an example of a feasible solution space for an LP problem.

5. Without exception, all of the functions in graphical LP are either straight lines. or families of straight lines.

6. It is possible to have more than one corner point of the feasible set as an optimum solution to an LP problem.

7. All constraints are either ≤ or ≥ inequalities.

8. A simplex solution cannot be attempted when there are just two variables; the solution in that case must be obtained graphically.

9. Artificial variables are used in connection with ≤ constraints and = constraints.

10. A shadow price tells how much a decision variable can be increased or decreased without changing the value of the solution.

11. The range of optimality gives ranges of values for the objective-function coefficients within which the values of the decision variables are optimal.

MULTIPLE-CHOICE QUESTIONS

1. Which objective function is parallel to the line $4x + 2y = 200$?

    a. $2x + 4y$
    b. $2x + y$
    c. $2x + 2y$
    d. $2x - y$
    c. $2x - 4y$

2. Which of the choices below is a simultaneous solution of these two equations: $3x + 4y = 10$ and $5x + 4y = 14$?

    a. $x = 2, y = 0.5$
    b. $x = 49, y = -0.5$
    c. $x = 2, y = 1$
    d. $x = y$
    e. $y = 2x$

3. Choose the best answer: In an LP problem

    a. two-variable problems cannot be handled by simplex.
    b. calculus is used to achieve the optimum solution.
    c. both maximization and minimization can be achieved in the same problem.
    d. an optimum solution has to include a corner point.
    e. all of the above statements are correct.
    f. none of the above statements is correct.

4. Which of the statements below about shadow prices is appropriate?

    a. A shadow price refers only to the optimum solution, not to any of the intermediate tableaus.
    b. A shadow price appears in a slack variable column of a simplex tableau.
    c. Shadow price and market price are the same thing.
    d. a and b above.
    e. a and c above.
    f. b and c above.

5. A constraint that forms the optimal corner point of the feasible solution space is called

    a. redundant.
    b. slack.

    c. surplus.
    d. binding.
    e. optimal.

6. Which of these is not an assumption of linear programming models?

    a. Divisibility
    b. Certainty
    c. Negativity
    d. Linearity.

7. Which one of these would not be considered as a component of an LP model?

    a. Shadow price
    b. Decision variable
    c. Constraint
    d. Parameter
    e. All are components

PROBLEMS

1. Given this LP problem:

Maximize $4x_1 + 3x_2$
s.t.
A $14x_1 + 6x_2 \leq 84$
B $7x_1 + 12x_2 \leq 84$
    $x_1, x_2 \geq 0$

Solve the problem using the graphical method:

a. Plot and label the constraints.
b. Indicate the feasible solution space.
c. Plot the objective function and use it to identify the optimum point of the graph.
d. Use simultaneous equations to determine the optimal values of x_1 and x_2.
e. Compute the optimum value of the objective function.

2. Solve problem #1 using the simplex method.

a. What is the initial tableau?
b. What is the final tableau?
c. What are the optimal values of x_1 and x_2?
d. How much is left over in constraints A and B?

3. Given this LP problem:

Maximize $5x_1 + 8x_2$
s.t.
A $\quad 2x_1 + 2x_2 \leq 100$
B $\quad 10x_1 + 35x_2 \leq 700$
C $\quad\quad\quad x_2 \geq 15$
$\quad\quad x_1, x_2 \geq 0$

Solve this problem using the graphical method.

a. Plot and label the constraints.
b. Indicate the feasible solution space.
c. Plot the objective function and use it to identify the optimum vertex.
d. Use simultaneous equations to determine the optimal values of x, and x_2.
e. Compute the optimal value of the objective function.

4. Solve the previous problem using the simplex method.

a. What is the initial tableau?
b. What is the final tableau?
c. What are the optimal values of x_1 and x_2?
d. What is the slack for each constraint in the optimal solution?

5. The Check-Mate Company produces chess sets and checker sets. It is necessary to plan the production schedule for next week. The sets are made of pine, of which the company has 350 feet in the for-m of cylindrical rods which can be cut into pieces which will be turned into chessmen or checkers. A checker set consists of 15 red disks and 15 white disks, and requires 24 inches of rod. A chess set consists of 16 red pieces and 16 white pieces, and requires 84 inches of rod. The company has a power saw for cutting the rod into circular sections; a checker set requires 30 minutes on the saw and a chess set requires 60 minutes. Next week, the saw is expected to be available 30 hours. The company has a special purpose machine, which resembles a lathe, for turning the pieces; a checker set requires 30 minutes to be turned, and a chess set requires 90 minutes. Next week the machine is expected to be available for 36 hours. Checker sets sell for $7.95 and have a unit variable cost of $3.95. Chess sets sell for $19.95 and have a unit variable cost of $10.95.

a. Is this a problem in maximization or minimization?
b. What are the decision variables?
c. What is the objective function?
d. What are the constraints?
e. Graph the constraints on a piece of graph paper. Indicate the feasible solution space.
f. How many checker sets and chess sets should be produced next week?
g. How much profit will be made by selling the sets?

6. Refer to your solution to Problem 5.

a. How much of the rods will be left over?
b. How much idle time does the saw have?

c. How much idle time does the special purpose machine have?
d. What is the name of the amounts in 6a, 6b. 6c?
e. Suppose the schedule produces an insufficient number of sets to meet the demand. What would be . required in order to produce more sets next week: more rods, more saw time, or more turning time?

7. Refer to Problem 5.

a. Set this problem up in the form of a simplex tableau.
b. Solve the problem with the simplex algorithm and compare your answer with the graphical solution.
c. What is the shadow price for the saw?
d. What is the interpretation of the shadow price for the saw?

8. A dietitian in a hospital is required to devise a recipe for a food which will provide at least the following amounts of vitamins: 500 units of vitamin A. 500 units of vitamin B. and 1,000 units of vitamin C. The dietitian may use two ingredients, P and Q, in the recipe which are described below.

Units per Kilogram:

Ingredient	A	B	C	Cost per Kilogram
P	2,000	3,000	5,000	$5
Q	6,000	3,000	0	$3

a. Is this a problem in maximization or minimization?
b. What are the decision variables? Suggest symbols for them.
c. What is the objective function?
d. What are the constraints?
e. Graph the constraints on a piece of graph paper. Indicate the feasible solution space.
f. How much of each ingredient should be used in the recipe?
g. How large is one serving of this food, in kilograms? In ounces? (I kg. = 2.2 lbs., or 35.2 oz.)
h. What is the cost of one servings

9. Refer to your solution to Problem 8.

a. How much excess vitamin A is provided?
b. How much excess vitamin B is provided?
c. How much excess vitamin C is provided?
d. What is the name of the quantities in 9a, 9b, 9c?
e. If it is necessary to economize on the recipe, which should be reduced: the requirements for vitamin A. or for vitamin B. or for vitamin C?

10. Refer to Problem 8.

a. Set up the simplex tableau for this problem.
b. Solve the problem by using the simplex algorithm. Compare your solution with the answers obtained in the graphical solution.
c. What is the shadow price for vitamin C?
d. What is the interpretation of the shadow price for vitamin C?

11. The Fairley and Winn Company produces hockey sticks, hockey pucks, and baseball bats; it is necessary to plan the production schedule for next week. The hockey sticks, hockey pucks, and baseball bats are made of oak, of which the company has 600 board feet. A hockey stick requires 4 board feet, a puck requires 2 board feet, and a baseball bat requires 3 board feet. The company has a power saw for cutting the oak boards into the appropriate pieces; a hockey stick requires 3.0 minutes, a puck requires 1.5 minutes, and a baseball bat requires 1.5 minutes. The power saw is expected to be available for 3.6 hours next week. After cutting, the pieces of work in process are hand finished in the finishing department, which consists of 4 skilled and experienced craftsmen, each of whom can complete any of the products. A hockey stick requires 60 minutes of finishing, a puck requires 30 minutes, and a baseball bat requires 90 minutes. The finishing department is expected to operate for 40 hours next week. Hockey sticks sell for $29.95 and have a unit variable cost of $17.95; a puck sells for $11.95 and has a unit variable cost of $4.95; a baseball bat sells for $16.95 and has a unit variable cost of $8.95. Determine the linear programming form of this problem, do not attempt to solve it.

    a. Is this a problem in maximization or minimization?
    b. What are the decision variables? Suggest symbols for them.
    c. What is the objective function?
    d. What are the constraints?

12. Solve Problem 11 using whatever software is available to you.
    a. How much of each product should be produced?
    b. How much profit will be generated by selling all of the output?
    c. How much oak will be unused?
    d. How much idle time will there be in the finishing department?
    e. How much idel time will there be in the finishing department?
    f. If it is necessary to produce more baseball bats, would more oak, more saw time, or morefinished time be required?
    g. Suppose an additional need for at least 80 hockey sticks arises. How could this be incorporated in the model?
    h. What is the shadow price of oak?
    i. Interpret the shadow price of oak.

6 - Facilities Layout

KEY IDEAS

1. Production/operations systems are classified into three fundamental types, according to the way the service is performed or the end item is put together: continuous flow, for example, an assembly line; intermittent or batch-flow processing as in computer jobs; and project, as in the building of a house. In some cases, there can be mixtures of the three types, for example, putting up a cement mixer at a construction site involves both intermittent and project processing.

2. There are three fundamental types of plant layout, respectively corresponding to the three different types of production operations situations. A product layout implies that a single product or else a single type of product, for example, automobiles, is manufactured on an assembly line, with the production tasks assigned to workstations along the line. A process layout involves the movement of batches of goods between departments via forklift truck, moving belt, or some other type of conveyance. A fixed-position layout is appropriate for a large end item such as a house or airplane, where all material is assembled to a major structure or product at a specified site.

3. Each type of layout has its own advantages and disadvantages. Production workers must learn to perform their jobs efficiently. However, if the tasks are overly repetitive and there is no opportunity for variety or for participation in the decision-making process, lethargy or antipathy can set in that would reduce the effectiveness of the best layout planning. That is why automation is advantageous; the machine takes over the highly repetitive jobs, while the employees concentrate on troubleshooting, machine maintenance and other operations requiring a combination of human logic and intuition.

4. Product layout such as that associated with Detroit automobile factories is a good idea when it is justified by the volume. The advantages of product layout are that it involves continuous flow of the work in process, minimum work-in-process inventory, maximum specialization, low material handling costs, efficient utilization of labor and equipment, and systematized routing, purchasing, accounting and inventory control. The disadvantages are dull repetitive jobs, inflexibility and susceptibility to frequent shutdowns.

5. A process layout allocates floor space to work centers so as to sustain a logical flow of semifinished goods, and minimize transportation and inventory costs. it is more flexible than product layout in the sense that a variety of products can be made without incurring extensive changeover costs. It also makes better use of the specialized skills of employees, so that incentive pay systems can be effective in enhancing productivity. Process layout is appropriate when each type of product or semifinished goods has low volume, but there are potentially high costs for unused equipment, excess inventory, slow or irregular movement, and a need for extensive production control paperwork.

6. A fixed-position layout is appropriate for large construction projects or for assembly of very large products such as airplanes, which are difficult to move. An example of a fixed position service system is a subway, which is an economical way to move large masses of people.

7. An assembly line is balanced to smooth the flow of semifinished goods, and to achieve the best possible utilization of both the labor force and the plant. The work is subdivided into groups of tasks, and each group is performed at some specific location along the line called a workstation. A workstation might be a single employee, or possibly a small cluster of employees, if the services of more than one person are required for the tasks.

8. The cycle time is the span of time a unit of product is at a workstation. In balancing the line, we determine both the cycle time and the number of workstations, based on the number of units of product to be produced in a working day, the total of the times of the tasks needed to make one unit of product, and the amount of effective clock time available in a day, after allowing for rest periods, breaks and planned shutdowns of the line.

9. There are several different meanings of the term "cycle." The minimum cycle time is the time required for the longest task. The maximum cycle is the sum of the task times for a single unit of product. The actual cycle time is somewhere between these two extremes; it is the amount of time at the workstation with the largest sum of task times.

$$CT = \frac{OT}{D}$$

10. The minimum number of workstations in the product layout is the sum of the task times for a single **unit** of product divided by the cycle time, to the next highest integer. Assigning tasks to workstations is done with heuristics (rules of thumb):

$$N = \frac{D\Sigma t}{OT} = \frac{\Sigma t}{CT}$$

   a. Consider precedence; make sure that all jobs are done in a logical sequence.
   b. Try to keep all stations busy all of the time by filling up the cycle time with tasks. Do not assign a station more tasks than it has time to perform.
   c. The greatest positional weight rule, one of several heuristics for assigning tasks to stations, assigns tasks according to the greatest sum of remaining task times to a free station. Other heuristics are: most following tasks, most preceding tasks, and greatest sum of task times for tasks that precede.

11. Measures of effectiveness guide decision makers to satisfactory, but not necessarily optimum, decisions on process layouts. The simplest approach involves ranking of departments or work centers according to work flow (Distance x Number of loads carried), and assigning work center locations so as to minimize the total intraplant transportation costs.

12. The Muther grid is an alternative approach to process layout planning that allows for subjective opinions that consider multiple criteria on the closeness of work centers to one another. Work centers are rated in pairs on a six-point closeness scale from A (absolutely necessary) to X (undesirable). First the As are paired, and then the Xs are separated; then the Es (very important) are paired, etc., until all centers are accounted for.

GLOSSARY

assembly line: a product layout where a sequence of operations and tasks is performed on the end item at workstations strategically located at points along the length of the line.

balance delay: the percentage of idle time of a line.

cell: a group of machines assembled to perform the operations needed for a set of similar items (part families).

cellular manufacturing: *see* cell.

combination layout: a layout form that combines some of the features of both an assembly line for a product layout and the specialization of a process layout.

computer-aided manufacturing (CAM): manufacturing with some of the work performed by robots or cutting tools that are controlled by computer programs.

continuous processing: refers to an assembly procedure such as a product layout that is dedicated to a single product or type of product.

cycle time: the span of time a unit of material Is at a workstation on an assembly line.

desired output rate: the effective demand for units of a product, translated into a daily rate of output.

fixed-position layout: a production layout such as for the construction of a house or the building of an airplane, with all material brought to the site where construction is being performed.

flow systems: *see* continuous processing.

group technology: grouping items that have similar design or processing characteristics into part families.

heuristic: a rule of thumb for setting priorities among a group of alternatives.

idle time: for a workstation the idle time in a cycle is the difference between the cycle time and the sum of the task times for the tasks performed at that station; for a plant, the idle time in a day is the sum of the workstation idle times multiplied by the number of cycles in a day.

industrial robot: a labor-saving device that performs highly repetitive production tasks such as spot welding or transferring material about over short distances, at very high speeds, under program control.

intermittent processing: refers to layouts for production of end items of one type in batches, with the same plant, equipment and personnel used to produce batches of another type of end item, possibly in a different configuration and sequence of operations.

job shop: *see* process layout.

line balancing: assigning tasks to workstations so as to have approximately the same amount of work performed at every workstation.

maximum cycle time: the sum of the task times required for one unit of product.

measure of effectiveness: in the context of process layouts, a measure of effectiveness of a proposed layout is a measure of the cost of the proposal in distance or time.

minimum number of workstations: the sum of the task times for all of the units of product produced in a day, divided by the operating time.

minimum cycle time: the time required by the longest task.

Muther grid: a chart that displays an index of closeness ratings for every pair of departments or work centers. It is used to assign work centers to positions in a process layout.

numerically controlled (NC) machines: cutting machines that are directed by a tape produced by a digital computer.

operating time: clock time available in a day of production, after subtracting scheduled stops and breaks.

precedence diagram: a diagram that shows the sequence of tasks to be performed on a unit of product in an assembly line.

process layout: a layout such as a job shop, with specialized workstations that perform activities or services on batches of material.

product layout: a layout such as an assembly line dedicated to the production of a single product or service or type of product or service.

project: nonroutine production or developmental planning and construction with relatively long task times for a network of tasks requiring specialized skills and services.

task time: the time required to perform a given task on a unit of product.

tiebreaker: when a decision process assigns identical priorities to two or more alternatives, a tiebreaker is a heuristic for deciding which priority is to be given first.

workstation: a location on an assembly line where a series of tasks is performed on units of a product.

work center: a location in a process layout where a specified group of tasks is performed on a unit or batch of material.

TRUE/FALSE QUESTIONS

1. Product layouts usually require less-skilled workers than process layouts.

2. The term *group technology* relates to the term *part families*.

3. Units Produced per day divided by Cycles per day equals Operating Time per day.

4. Cycle time is the average amount of clock time required to produce a unit of output.

5. A cycle is the same as the total of the task times needed to produce a single unit of output.

6. Subjective rating scales are not useful in process layouts.

7. The "greatest positional weight rule" assigns tasks according to the largest sum of preceding task times.

8. The percentage of idle time for a line is sometimes referred to as its balance delay.

9. One drawback of process layouts is that equipment utilization rates are lower than in a product layout.

10. The minimum cycle time in an assembly line is equal to the time for the longest task.

MULTIPLE-CHOICE QUESTIONS

1. Heuristic rules are usually used when:

    a. an optimum is necessary.
    b. a computer program isn't available,
    c. a program has a small number of possibilities.
    d. no optimizing routine is available.
    e. all other approaches have failed.

2. A production line is to be designed for a job with three tasks. The task times are 0.3 minutes, 1.4 minutes, and 0.7 minutes, respectively. The maximum cycle time, in minutes, is:

    a. 0.3   b. 1.4   c. 2.4   d. 2.8   e. none of the above

3. Which one of the following would not generally be regarded as a reason for redesign of a layout?

    a. Change in the volume of output or product mix
    b. Morale problems
    c. Accidents or safety hazards
    d. Inefficient operations
    e. All are potential reasons

4. A precedence diagram:

    a. shows the sequences in which tasks are performed.
    b. is in the shape of a network.
    c. shows all of the paths from beginning to end of completion of the product.
    d. a and c only.
    e. all of the above.

5. There are 9 assembly tasks for a product. The task times, predecessor relationships and workstation assignments are given in the following table.

Workstation	Task	Time (min.)	Predecessors
1	a	2	-
	b	7	a
	c	5	-
	d	2	-
2	e	15	c, d
	f	7	a, e
3	g	6	-
	h	4	b, g
	i	9	a

The cycle time for this product is:

a. 16 minutes.
b. 19 minutes.
c. 22 minutes.
d. 57 minutes.
e. none of the above choices is correct.

6. Which one of the following is not generally regarded as an advantage of product layouts?

a. Material handling costs per unit are low.
b. Labor costs are low per unit.
c. The system is fairly flexible to changes in volume of output.
d. Accounting, purchasing, and inventory control are fairly routine.
e. There is high utilization of labor and equipment.

PROBLEMS

1. Producing widgets involves fourteen production tasks, lettered a through n, below. For each task, the time required to accomplish it is given, and the immediately preceding task.

Production Task	Time (min.)	Preceding Task
a	.2	-
b	.4	a
c	.5	b
d	.4	c
e	1.0	a
f	.5	e
g	1.1	d, f
h	.7	g
i	.8	g
j	.4	h
k	1.2	i
l	.9	k
m	.6	l
n	.4	j, m
	9.1	

The manager expects to produce 300 widgets per eight-hour shift. The workers are allowed two 10-minute coffee breaks per shift, and 40 minutes is allocated to cleanup and maintenance tasks.

    a. Is it possible to accomplish the objective of 300 widgets per shift with one workstation?
    b. What is the maximum possible output with 14 workstations?
    c. Draw the precedence diagram for this process.
    d. What is the minimum number of workstations which will be required to achieve an output of 300 pieces per shift?

2. Refer to the data in Problem 1.

    a. Assign the tasks to workstations according to the heuristic rule of the largest number of following tasks.
    b. How many workstations are required under the rule of the largest number of following tasks?
    c. What is the percent of idle time (or the balance delay) for this layout?

3. Refer to the data in Problem 1.

    a. Assign the tasks to workstations according to the heuristic rule of the positional weight.
    b. How many workstations are required under the rule of the greatest positional weight?
    c. What is the percent of idle time (or the balance delay) for this layout?

4. The XYZ Co. manufactures a variety of specialized products according to the orders of the customers. The plant consists of 5 departments, numbered 1 through 5 below. While some variation in the work flow is experienced, depending on the composition of the orders received, the following matrix is considered to be representative of the traffic between the departments per five-day workweek, measured in the number of forklift loads or the number of pull truck loads.

From	1	2	3	4	5
1	0	100	50	0	30
2	70	0	60	0	80
3	10	30	0	140	10
4	50	40	0	0	60
5	50	40	80	10	0

The floor plan of the factory is displayed in the diagram below. The plant has an L shape, and the lettered areas represent spaces that are to be occupied by the five departments.

a. In how many ways can these five departments be arranged in the factory?

b. Obtain the distance matrix by measuring from the center of one space to the center of the other space. For example, the distance from area B to area E is $18' + 24' = 42'$. The distances are the same, both ways.

c. Assign departments to the areas. Try to keep departments with heavy traffic close to each other.

d. Obtain the load-distance index for your layout. (The load-distance index is the sum of the products of the traffic between two departments and the distance between the two departments.)

e. Have you obtained the minimum value of the load-distance index?

5. (Advanced) The textbook mentions some software packages which per-form the lengthy computations involved in obtaining the load-distance index and which also test several layouts in search of a low value of the index. If you do not have access to any of these packages, you can obtain the load-distance index on your computer by multiplying the traffic matrix and the distance matrix. Let us symbolize the traffic matrix as $L(i,j)$ and the distance matrix as $D(i,j)$. Then the product matrix is: $P(i,j) = L(i,j)-D(i,j)$.

a. Show how to construct the traffic matrix and the distance matrix so as to perform this multiplication for the layout in 4-c. Hint: consider the traffic matrix to be fixed, and rearrange the distance matrix.

b. Show that the load-distance index is the trace of the product matrix.

6. Here is the Muther diagram for the departments in Problem 4.

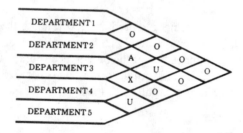

a. Assign the departments to the areas so as to satisfy, as far as possible, the conditions of the Muther diagram.

b. What is the value of the load-distance index of this layout?

7 - Design of Work Systems

KEY IDEAS

1. This chapter covers both job design and work measurement; it brings together both qualitative and the quantitative aspects of designing a job and the working environment so as to achieve employee satisfaction and high productivity, and measuring the result

2. Job design specifies the content of a job and the methods used, job design has significant effect upon the efficiency and productivity of the working force.

3. Job enlargement, which is sometimes called "horizontal loading," means diversifying tasks assigned to a worker. Job enrichment, which is also called "vertical loading," me increasing the skill level within the present job. Both job enlargement and job enrichment help sustain morale and improve efficiency and productivity, if the worker understand the reasons for the changes made in his assignments.

4. Automation is the substitution of mechanical or electronically controlled devices human energy in performing highly repetitive tasks. Although automation has been a important facet of production activity ever since the Industrial Revolution started over 250 years ago, it has become even more important in recent years because of t expanded usage of industrial robots.

5. Specialization is essential, because without it there would not be enough skill to sustain competitive position in the marketplace for goods or services, However, if specialization is too narrow, the employee does not learn very much about the production and operation system. For that reason, managers are frequently rotated in their assignments to provide depth as well as breadth.

6. Motion study provides guidelines for interfacing the worker, his tasks, and the environment. If there are substantial changes in the tasks or environment, new methods analysis may become necessary.

7. Flow process charts, work-machine charts and multiactivity charts are useful for methods analysis and balancing the work flow.

8. Properly scheduled work breaks help improve efficiency and morale.

9. The operations manager must ever be mindful of his or her responsibility to provide a safe working environment. The pressures that make this necessary are personal responsibility, public opinion, potential legal liabilities, possible interference with production due to lost-time accidents, industrial grievances, and OSHA (Occupational Safety and Health Administration) rules.

10. Time studies provide information on how much time a job can take. Since these studies involve repeated observations and measurements, the cost is justified if the task is repeated frequently and if there is substantial evidence that pre-existing time standards are not adequate. One of the problems of time study is worker resistance or non-cooperation, for example, by deliberately slowing down to give the analyst the impression that the job takes more time than it actually does.

11. In work sampling, a worker is observed at random times during working hours. Work sampling provides a measure of employee efficiency by showing what proportion of the time is spent working. The sample size is a function of the proportion of idle time and how much confidence we want to have in the results.

GLOSSARY

allowance: the difference between normal time and standard time, which consists of planned nonworking time.

allowance factor: the ratio of standard time to normal time.

automation: substituting mechanical and electronic devices for human energy in performing routine and highly repetitive jobs at very high speeds.

behavioral school: the school of thought that emphasizes the relationship between productivity and satisfying the wants and needs of the employee.

color coding: adopting a color scheme for the plant that enhances visibility and safety.

efficiency school: the school of thought, founded by F. W. Taylor, that emphasizes the relationship between productivity, pay incentives, and the configuration of the work space.

flow process chart: a symbolic chart that shows the sequence of operations and tasks performed by an employee in a particular job.

gang-process chart: a multiactivity chart showing a cross section of the tasks performed by a team of employees.

group incentive plans: incentive pay plans for all of the employees of a company based on savings in labor and material costs, or profit sharing; among the plans discussed in Chapter 7 are the Scanlon, Kaiser, Lincoln and Kodak plans.

job rotation: varying assignments among a group of employees by shifting tasks and responsibilities.

job design: assigning tasks and planning the working environment and system for an employee or a group of employees, taking into account the costs and benefits of the alternatives available.

job enlargement: giving an employee a greater number of tasks without a corresponding shift to another assignment or a higher level of responsibility.

job enrichment: increasing the level of responsibility of an employee as a motivation towards better performance.

knowledge-based pay: paying workers for the level of knowledge and skill they master; workers are paid for their ability to perform multiple tasks or jobs.

methods analysis: studying the requirements of a job in order to propose new and possibly better ways to perform it.

motion study: a technique for studying the human motions needed to perform an operation or series of tasks, developed originally by Frank and Lillian Gilbreth.

normal time: the actual amount of time required for an employee to complete a cycle of operations. Normal time is less than standard time: the difference between the two is the allowance time.

observed time: the average of the observed times for a task in a single cycle.

occupational Safety and Health Administration (OSHA): the federal agency that has the responsibility for administering laws relating to employee and environmental safety.

output-based systems: systems of incentive compensation to individuals based on output.

performance rating: the ratio of normal time to observed time.

quality of work: a term that characterizes the entire working environment, including facilities, work space and equipment, and the camaraderie among employees and between employees and supervisors.

random number table: a table of random numbers with many uses; in the context of Chapter 7, it is used to establish random times for making observations in work sampling.

specialization: division of labor so that each employee has the best opportunity to become proficient at the operations he will perform.

standard time: the average clock time it would require for a qualified employee to complete a specified task, determined from a time study, including allowances for non-working times.

standard elemental times: standard times for jobs or tasks derived from historical data, rather than from current time-study data.

stopwatch time study: a widely used method of work measurement, developed by F. W. Taylor, for establishing the standard times for relatively small repetitive tasks.

therblig (Gilbreth spelled backward): an elementary unit of human motion in a motion study: common therbligs are: search *select, grasp,* hold, transport loaded, and release load.

time-based compensation systems: systems of compensation based on the amount of clock time an employee works.

work sampling: a statistical technique developed by L. H. C. Tippett for determining what proportion of the time an employee is engaged in a task, by having the analyst walk through the area at random times; if the employee is engaged in a series of highly repetitive tasks, work sampling can be used to set standard task times.

worker-machine chart: a chart that displays the portions of a work cycle in which the worker and the machine are active or idle.

z-statistic: the unit normal deviate of the standard normal distribution that is used to look up probabilities in the normal probability table.

TRUE/FALSE QUESTIONS

1. Work sampling results in less disruption of work than time study does.

2. Time study results in less detail about the time taken for a given task than work sampling does.

3. The sample size needed for a work sampling study increases as the amount of error allowed increases.

4. Work sampling is performed by having the analyst spend a period of time with the employee and take measurements of the amount of time needed to complete tasks.

5. A flow process chart reveals the overall sequence of operations by focusing on the movement of materials on an assembly line.

6. A standard elemental time for a task is the standard time derived from historical data rather than current data.

7. Job enrichment is otherwise known as vertical loading.

8. It is usually difficult or impossible to perform time studies on creative or intellectual jobs such as those of a college professor.

9. The standard time for an activity is usually less than its normal time.

MULTIPLE-CHOICE QUESTIONS

1. The symbols of a flow process chart stand for:

    a. inspection, delay, transportation, storage, operation.
    b. transportation loaded, search, grasp, store, perform operation.
    c. release, transport. store, grasp, search.
    d. circle, arrow, pentagon, square, triangle.
    e. none of the above choices is correct.

2. Analysis of therbligs is most closely related to:

    a. methods analysis.
    b. simo chart.
    c. learning effect.
    d. motion study.
    e. all of the above choices are correct.

3. In a work sampling study, an analyst collecting data would most likely have either with him or attached to his clipboard:

    a. a random number table.
    b. a list of employees cross listed with the tasks they are performing.
    c. a clock.
    d. a and c only.
    e. b and c only.
    f. a, b, and c.

4. Task times derived from a firm's historical data are known as:

    a. predetermined times.
    b. standard elemental times.
    c. judgmental times.
    d. micromotion times.
    e. MTM.

5. Among the following, all are advantages of specialization except:

    a. simplifies training
    b. difficult to motivate quality
    c. high productivity
    d. relatively low wages
    e. all are advantages

6. Which of the following is not an advantage of specialization?

    a. low education/skill requirements
    b. little mental effort needed
    c. low wage costs
    d. work can be monotonous
    e. minimum responsibilities

7. The following are true about stopwatch time except:

    a. Several repetitions are usually timed.
    b. A performance rating is usually necessary.
    c. There is no record of the method used by the worker.
    d. It is well-suited for repetitive jobs.
    e. Jobs that have varying task requirements can pose some difficulty.

8. Which one of the following statements concerning work sampling is not true?

    a. Observations are made at random intervals.
    b. A detailed description of activities is obtained.
    c. Multiple observations are necessary.
    d. It can be used to estimate the percentage of delay.
    e. There is little or no disruption of work.

9. The need for methods analysis might come from any of these sources except:

    a. changes in seasonal demand.
    b. changes in product design.
    c. new products or services.
    d. government regulations.
    e. changes in tools and equipment.

PROBLEMS

1. A time study analyst is planning a work sampling study to estimate the percent of idle time in the packing department. The department consists of a foreman and three workers. The hourly wage of the foreman is $12 and the wage of the workers is $5. A time study technician has made 300 observations of these four employees at random times, producing the data below.

        Idle observations   60
        Working observations   240
           Total observations   300

    a. What is the point estimate of the percent of idle time?
    b. What is the standard error of the percent?
    c. What is the 95% confidence interval for the percent of idle time?
    d. What is the interpretation of the confidence interval?
    e. Estimate the weekly loss due to idle time in the packaging department. The department works a 40-hour week.
    f. Suppose that an estimate of idle time within 2 percentage points, either way, is required. How many more observations should be taken?
    g. What will be the point estimate of the percent of idle time after the additional observations are taken?

2. In the course of manufacturing an amplifier, an off-on switch must be attached to the front panel. A time study analyst wishes to determine how long it takes an experienced employee to perform this operation; he therefore times a worker during several repetitions, producing the data below.

Time (x)	x^2	Time (x)	x^2
9.5	90.25	8.5	72.25
8.2	67.24	10.0	100.00
9.0	81.00	8.5	72.25
8.8	77.44	10.0	100.00
9.3	86.49	8.7	75.69
9.8	96.04	8.0	64.00
8.0	64.00	8.9	79.21
7.9	62.41	8.0	64.00
		141.1	19252.27

a. What is the true (population) mean time for attaching the off-on switch?
b. What is the observed time for attaching the off-on switch?
c. What is the sample standard deviation of the time?
d. What is the standard error of the time?
e. What is the 95% confidence interval for the mean time for attaching the switch?
f. Suppose it was desired to estimate the mean time within 9 seconds either way. How many more measurements would be required?

3. Use the data in Problem 2 to solve this problem.

a. The analyst has determined that the worker has a performance rating of 125 percent while being measured. What is the normal time?
b. Was this worker working rapidly or slowly?
c. The plant manager allows for these delays and interruptions during the working day.

   Coffee breaks (2 per 8 hr. shift) 10 min. each
   Personal time   20 min. per shift
   Maintenance and adjustment
     of equipment   30 min. per shift
   Delays and bottlenecks   20 min. per shift

   What are the allowances as a percent of job time?
d. What is the standard time for attaching the off-on switch?

4. Use your work in Problem 3 to solve this problem. The workers who install the off-on switch are paid $9.00 per hour, with fringe benefits of 35 percent.

a. Estimate the number of off-on switches which one worker should be able to install in one 8-hour shift.
b. Determine the standard labor cost of installing the switch.

5. (One step beyond) The text book mentions, but does not explain, allowances based on working time (i.e., a full day) rather than on job time. This problem demonstrates working time allowances using the data in problems #2 and #3.

a. What are the allowances as a percent of working time?
b. What is the standard time for attaching the switch?

7S - Learning Curves

KEY IDEAS

1. Repetitive operations performed by humans are subject to a learning effect that causes the time per repetition to decrease as the number of repetitions increases.

2. The improvements are due to the combined effect of actual learning by those performing the jobs and the contributions of indirect personnel (e.g., industrial engineers) who change work methods, job design, etc.

3. According to the learning curve theory, the time per repetition decreases at a constant percentage with every doubling of total number of repetitions. For instance, with an 80 percent curve, the time for the 10th unit will be 80 percent of the time needed for the 5th unit; and the time for the 16th unit will be 80 percent of the time needed for the 8th unit.

4. The textbook contains a table that can easily be used to obtain both individual times and cumulative times for selected learning rates.

5. Applications of the learning curve theory include negotiated purchasing, scheduling, pricing new products, budgeting, and inventory planning.

GLOSSARY

learning curve: a mathematical relationship used to describe the learning effect.

learning effect: the continued reduction in the amount of time required to complete a new task, sequence of tasks, or project, as a result of acquiring experience and skill in the job.

log-log scale: a type of graph paper that has logarithmic scales in both the horizontal and vertical directions.

negotiated purchasing: used for special purchasing situations such as when a limited quantity of a customized product is involved.

unit time: the number of direct labor hours required for the n-th unit in production.

TRUE/FALSE QUESTIONS

1. According to the learning curve, every time the cumulative output doubles, the learning rate increases.

2. A learning curve of 80 percent will result in more improvement than a 90 percent curve over a given number of units.

3. Learning curves only apply to humans, not to machinery.

4. Learning curve results are due strictly to worker learning.

5. Every time the cumulative output doubles, the time per unit will decrease by a constant percentage, assuming the learning curve is pertinent.

MULTIPLE-CHOICE QUESTIONS

1. If a learning situation has a learning curve of .80 and a time of 20 hours to build the initial unit, the estimated time for the 4th unit in hours is:

   a. 20   b. 16   c. 12.8   d. 10.24

2. In which of these activities would learning curves be least useful?

   a. budgeting
   b. pricing new products
   c. manpower planning
   d. assembly-line scheduling
   e. negotiated purchasing

3. A manager is trying to estimate the learning rate for a new job. The first unit required 16 hours and the fourth unit required just under 13 hours. The learning rate is:

   a. 70%
   b. 75%
   c. 80%
   d. 85%
   e. 90%

4. A job will have a learning rate of 75 percent. If the 3rd unit requires 10 hours, the 12th unit should require about this many hours:

   a. 5.6   b. 6.5   c. 7.4%   d. 8.3%   e. 9.2

PROBLEMS

1. Solve the following exercises by referring to Table 7S- I in your textbook.

    a. In the production of cargo planes, an 80 percent learning curve is experienced. It takes 2,000 direct labor hours to produce the first plane. Estimate the direct labor hours required to produce the 10th plane.
    b. In the above case, estimate the total direct labor hours required to produce the first 10 planes.
    c. In the construction of tract houses, a 90 percent learning curve is experienced. It takes 3,000 direct labor hours to construct the first house. Estimate the direct labor hours required to construct the 15th house.
    d. In the above case, estimate the total direct labor hours required to construct the first 6 houses.

2. The Emperor Shipyards Co. has a contract to build 20 identical oil tankers. The production manager believes that an 85 percent learning curve is appropriate for direct labor time. The wages of the workers average $9.00 per hour, with fringe benefits of 30 percent. The following accounting data have been accumulated on the first tanker.

    Direct labor   25,000 hr.
    Direct materials $200,000

    a. What is the interpretation of the 85 percent?
    b. Estimate the direct labor time required to build the 5th tanker.
    c. Estimate the total direct cost of the 5th tanker.
    d. Estimate the total direct labor time required to build all 20 tankers.
    e. Estimate the total direct cost of all 20 tankers.
    f. Find the price per tanker which is 150 percent higher than the total direct cost per tanker.

3   The formula for the learning curve is: $T_n = T_1 \times n^b$, where:

    T_n = time f or the nth unit
    T_1 = time for the first unit
    b = ln(learning percent)/ln 2

    Use the e^x key or the ln x key on your calculator, or use Table #4S-1 to solve these problems:

    a. ln 2 = ?
    b. Learning percent = 85%, Ln(learning percent) = ?
    c. b = ?
    d. $T_1 = 5,000$ hrs. $T_4 = ?$

4. Use the formulas in problem #3 to solve these problems:

    a. Learning percent = 82%, Ln(learning percent) = ?
    b. b = ?
    c. $T_1 = 7,000$ hrs. $T_5 = ?$

8 - Location Planning

KEY IDEAS

1. A plant location decision is either a choice to expand existing productive facilities, add new locations, or substitute a new facility for an existing one. Subcontracting may also be used as a substitute for substantial plant expansion.

2. A plant location decision can be made either before the capacity decision is made, concurrently with the capacity decision, or after it.

3. The criteria for choosing sites are not based solely on economics or cost. Many environmental and quality-of-life factors are relevant to the decision.

4. Service operations and public utility systems have different guidelines for choosing locations than do more conventional production operations. Service operations must concentrate upon accessibility to markets. A production facility decision is usually based on least cost, providing there are not some overriding considerations such as accessibility to raw materials or skilled labor, quality of life, etc.

5. There is a location problem at more than one level of decision making. Not only must a decision be made as to where to put the production facility, but also where to put the warehouses and distribution centers, and how to build support networks that take care of the relevant logistical problems.

6. In recent years multinational companies have been putting production facilities in foreign countries to take advantage of lower labor costs. In many cases, these plants produce semifinished goods and components to be integrated into larger products, via the production process. International operations management introduces new problems such as taxes, import duties, additional transportation costs, different sets of laws, foreign social and political structures, and trade practices and restrictions.

7. Localities frequently offer special incentives for industrial development by buying land for industrial districts, constructing special buildings, and offering favorable leases, tax incentives or loans.

8. Location preferences may reflect organizational policy on decentralization versus centralization.

9. Regional factors include location near the sources of raw materials, both for service and to minimize transportation costs.

10. Community location factors are primarily quality of life and quality of the work force available, as well as taxes, availability of public utilities, support for plant development, and whether or not there are costly local regulations. Special incentives offered by communities to attract industry are also relevant.

11. Site location factors include costs, access to all transportation media, zoning restrictions and land.

12. The factor rating scale method evaluates alternative locations by computing weighted averages of **the** factor rating scores of the various alternatives. The recommended location is the one with the highest weighted average.

13. The center of gravity method is useful in establishing an approximate (geographic) location for a distribution center. The method minimizes total shipping cost between the distribution center and multiple shipping points (destinations). if shipping quantities for all destinations are equal, the distribution center will be located at the arithmetic averages of the x and y coordinates of the destinations; if shipping quantities are unequal, the location of the distribution center is found by using a weighted average approach, where the weights are the quantities to be shipped.

GLOSSARY

center of gravity method: used to determine location for centralized distribution.

environmental regulations: regulations imposed by agencies such as the federal Occupational Safety and Health Administration (OSHA) or by local regulatory bodies that restrict the way a plant can be built or operated, based upon the potential effect on the environment.

factor rating: assigning numerical weights to factors in order to facilitate the plant location decision.

location: the site for a plant, raw materials, markets or a labor supply.

locational break-even analysis: break-even analysis adapted to the cost analysis of alternative plant locations.

multinational company: a firm with plants in more than one country.

semi(finished goods): component parts or modules of an end item in the production system, that will require further processing.

tax abatement: reducing the tax base of a potential plant as a special incentive for the plant to locate in a particular region or community.

threshold: a minimum required value for an average factor rating score, if an alternative does not meet the threshold value, it is eliminated from further consideration,

TRUE/FALSE QUESTIONS

1. Factor rating scales is a proven method of choosing the best of a set of decision alternatives.

2. A location decision may be either to expand an existing facility, add a new one, or else replace an existing facility with another one.

3. The sum of factor weights in a rating scale can be greater than 100%.

4. A break-even point in location analysis is a case where two different locations have the same total cost.

5. It is more important for a service facility to be near the potential market than for a production facility.

6. Companies which use multiple plant strategies may have plants devoted to specific products, specific markets, or specific processes.

7. In choosing one of a set of location alternatives based on a factor rating scale, the scale usually does not accurately reflect dollar differences in costs between the various alternatives.

8. The center of gravity method is used to minimize production costs.

MULTIPLE-CHOICE QUESTIONS

1. Pick the statement about location decisions that is not true.

    a. They are often long term.
    b. Mistakes can be difficult to overcome.
    c. Both fixed costs and variable costs are usually affected.
    d. It is important to identify the optimal location.

2. Which of the following would not generally be classified as a regional factor in location decisions?

    a. Location of raw materials
    b. Location of markets
    c. Labor supply
    d. Taxes
    e. All are regional factors.

3. Which one of the following is more a community factor than a site factor?

    a. Rail access
    b. Zoning
    c. Environmental regulations
    d. Room for expansion
    e. Utility hookups

4. Here is a list of steps used in making location decisions. Which step should occur first?

    a. Identify a general region
    b. Identify factors that are important. such as location of markets
    c. Identify some community-site alternatives
    d. Identify criteria that will be used to evaluate alternatives
    e. Evaluate the alternatives

5. Which of the following would not usually be cited as a reason for U.S. companies locating in foreign countries?

    a. Increased quality of output
    b. Cheaper labor
    c. Availability of raw materials
    d. Access to markets
    e. All are reasons

6. Faced with the choice of location for a plant, a firm is considering four different possible alternatives. The decision will be made by using a scoring model. Give the order of preference for the four different locations based on the following data.

		Alternative			
Criterion	Weight	1	2	3	4
raw material availability	0.2	g	p	ok	vg
community support	0.1	ok	ok	ok	ok
transportation costs	0.5	vg	ok	p	ok
labor relations	0.1	g	vg	p	ok
quality of life	0.1	g	vg	p	ok

points: vg (very good) = 5 points; g (good) = 4 points; ok (acceptable) = 3 points; and p (poor) = 1 point

The order of preference for the four alternatives is:

    a. 1, 2, 3, 4.
    b. 4, 3, 2, 1.
    c. 1, 4, 2, 3.
    d. 4, 1, 3, 2.
    e. 2, 1, 4, 3.
    f. none of the above choices is correct.

PROBLEMS

1. Two plant locations are under consideration for a new battery factory. Here are estimates of the fixed and variable costs at each location.

Location	Fixed Cost per Year	Variable Cost per Unit
A	$1,500,000	$1.25
B	1,250,000	1.75

    a. What is the total cost function for each location?
    b. Plot the total cost functions on the same graph.
    c. On the graph, identify the range of output for which each location has the least cost.
    d. Which location should be selected for an output of 400,000 batteries per year.9 800,000 batteries per year?
    e. Find the cutoff point algebraically.

2. Four plant locations arc under consideration for a new microchip plant. Here are estimates of the fixed and variable costs at each location.

Location	Fixed cost per year	Variable cost per unit
A	$3,500,000	$600
B	3,000,000	800
C	4,000,000	500
D	4,500,000	400

   a. What is the total cost function for each location?
   b. Plot the total cost functions for these locations on the same graph.
   c. On the graph, identify the range of output for which each location has the least cost.
   d. Which location should be selected for an output of 4,000 chips per year? 12,000 chips per year?
   e. Find the cutoff points algebraically.

3. Two locations are under consideration for building a condominium. (A condominium is a building in which each apartment is owned by the resident, rather than rented.) One location is in suburb A of a large Eastern city, and the other is in suburb B. The marketing manager has identified the following factors which bear upon the location decision and their relative weights.

Factor	Desirable Status	Weight
1. Proximity to public transportation	Should be close	.20
2. Space for a parking lot	Should be large	.40
3. Property taxes	Should be low	.25
4. Electricity rates	Should be low	.15

Each factor will be rated on a scale of I = unsatisfactory to 10 = outstanding. Rescarch has revealed the following information about each location, and the marketing manager has rated each factor at each

Factor	Location		Rating	
	A	B	A	B
1. Public transportation	1 block	6 blocks	9	2
2. Parking lot	1 acre	3 acres	3	7
3. Property taxes	$600/year	$800/year	6	4
4. Electric rates	$.09/kwh.	$.06/kwh.	5	8

   a. Construct a rating analysis worksheet in the style of Example 2 in your textbook and determine the composite score for each location.
   b. Where should the condominium be built? Why?

4. Business has been good for the Black & White News Company, which receives magazines from the publishers and distributes them to the news racks of drugstores and supermarkets. At present, it has five customers, each of which is serviced once a week; expired magazines are collected and new editions are displayed on the racks. (This problem is obviously artificially small.) Here are the x and y coordinates of the locations of the customers and the number of truck loads of magazines which go to each destination.

The company operates out of a single warehouse, whose coordinates are also included. The company has outgrown the warehouse, and the partners are discussing whether to expand the present facilities or to construct a larger warehouse at a new site.

Customer	x	y	Weekly Loads
A	2	3	1
B	5	2	3
C	3	6	2
D	10	4	6
E	6	5	2
Warehouse	3	4	

a. Plot the locations of the customers on graph paper.
b. What is the mean of x?
c. What is the mean of y?
d. Plot the optimal location of the warehouse on your graph.
e. Based solely on this analysis, should the partners enlarge the present warehouse or construct a new one?

8S - The Transportation Model

KEY IDEAS

1. A transportation problem involves distributing stocks or supplies from multiple sending points (origins) to multiple receiving points (destinations) in such a way that the total transportation cost is minimized.

2. The transportation model is a special-purpose linear programming model that permits manual solution of fairly large problems with relative ease. Problems must be set up in tabular fashion, such as shown in the textbook.

3. The first step in a transportation problem is to make sure that supply and demand are equal. If they are not, add a dummy row or column with a supply (row) or demand (column) equal to the difference between supply and demand. Assign a zero transportation cost to each cell in the dummy row or column.

4. Next, obtain an initial feasible solution. Use the intuitive method.

5. Evaluate the solution to determine if it is optimal. Use either the stepping-stone method or the MODI method.

6. If all cell evaluations are positive or zero, the solution is optimal. A zero cell evaluation signifies the existence of an alternate solution that will result in the same total cost as the current solution. One or more negative cell evaluations indicate a non-optimal solution. Use the stepping-stone method to obtain an improved solution.

7. Repeat steps 5 and 6 until the optimal solution has been obtained.

8. One application of the transportation model is for location decisions. In such cases, two (or more) competing location alternatives are each used in a different version of the transportation table to see which one will provide the lowest total cost solution.

GLOSSARY

See also GLOSSARY for Chapter 5S on "linear programming."

cell: a location at the i-th row and the j -th column of a transportation matrix that identifies a shipment from the i-th source of supply to the j-th destination.

completed cell: an assigned shipment from source, i, to destination, i. under the solution of the transportation model for the current iteration.

degenerate solution: for the transportation model, a degenerate solution is one that is feasible, but does not have the required number of shipments to make possible a test for optimality; in that case, an E (nearly zero) shipment is assigned to one of the empty cells to make possible further progress in verifying the solution.

dummy: see unequal supply and demand.

empty cell: a cell that does not contain a shipment.

epsilon (ε): when the solution is degenerate, an e (nearly zero) shipment is assigned to one of the empty cells; the E is placed so as to facilitate the tests for feasibility and optimality.

feasible solution: for the transportation model, a feasible solution is a solution that exhausts the available supply capacities and at the same time satisfies all of the demand requirements.

intuitive approach: assigning units to cells, lowest cost first, to obtain an initial feasible solution of a transportation model.

iteration: improved feasible solutions of the transportation model are obtained in a series of stages called iterations; the term iteration comes from the fact that the same procedure is followed for each successive stage of improvement.

modified distribution (MODI) method: an efficient method for evaluating a feasible solution of a transportation problem based on index numbers.

optimal solution: an optimal solution of a transportation model is a feasible solution with the smallest total transportation cost.

solution: for the transportation model, a solution is a set of shipments.

stepping-stone: a method for improving a feasible solution by shifting shipment amounts at right angles around a closed path so as to reduce the overall transportation cost.

suboptimal solution: a feasible solution that is not optimal.

transportation matrix: a table consisting of m rows, each row representing a source of supply, and n columns, each column denoting a destination, and each (i, j) cell (i = 1 9 ..., m,j = 19... . n) contains cost data about a shipment from the i-th source of supply to the J-th destination.

transportation model: a linear programming technique for minimizing the overall transportation cost of shipments of a commodity from m sources, such as warehouses, with limited capacities, to n destinations, such as stores, with specified minimum demand requirements.

unequal supply and demand: a situation where the total of the capacities of the m sources of supply and the total of the demand requirements for the n destinations are not equal; in that case it is necessary to assign a dummy row or else a dummy column in order to balance the transportation model; if there is a surplus, the sum of the capacities or availabilities exceeds the sum of the requirements-in that case a dummy column absorbs the unused demand; if there is a shortage, a dummy row absorbs the backorders for unsatisfied demand.

TRUE/FALSE QUESTIONS

1. The transportation model of linear programming assumes homogeneous commodities, deterministic supply, deterministic demand, that every source is capable of shipping to every destination, and that there is a known per-unit shipping cost from every source to every destination.

2. The transportation model is guaranteed to identify the optimum solution for a given transportation problem.

3. The steppingstone method of cell evaluation involves making a series of alternating additions and subtractions of equal amounts to occupied cells, and to the cell being evaluated.

4. When an empty cell is filled artificially in order to complete a degenerate solution of the transportation model, the filled cell is called a dummy.

5. When developing an improved solution, quantities can be shifted hortizontally, vertically, or diagonally.

6. The total transportation cost of a set of shipments for the transportation model is the sum of the products of the per-unit shipping costs multiplied by the shipment amounts.

MULTIPLE-CHOICE QUESTIONS

1. A transportation table consists of five destinations and twelve sources of supply. in order for a solution to be non-degenerate, what is the number of filled cells required?

   a. 59
   b. 44
   c. 43
   d. 16
   e. 15
   f. None of these

2. You are given a transportation matrix with three sources of supply, A, B. and C and three destinations, D, E. and F. and the following set of per-unit transportation costs:

	D	E	F
A	9	8	7
B	6	7	5
C	3	4	8

A non-optimal solution is provided with the following cells filled: A-D, A-E, B-E, C-D and C-F. At the first iteration of the transportation model, which of the four empty cells will get the shipment?

   a. A-F   b. B-D   c. B-F   d. C-E

3. In Question 2 the shipment amounts for the matrix are:

A-D: 5 units
A-E: 6 units
B-E: 4 units
C-D: 7 units
C-F: 3 units

Which of the five filled cells will become empty at the next iteration of the transportation model?

    a. A-D   b. A-E   c. B-E   d. C-D   e. C-F

4. At the next iteration of the transportation model, which of the five filled cells will become empty?

5. What is the total cost of the optimal set of shipments?

    a. $100
    b. $140
    c. $150
    d. $185
    e. none of these

PROBLEMS

1. A firm has four factories, # 1, 2, 3, 4, which ship their output to two warehouses, A and B. The capacities of the factories for one month, the requirements of the warehouses for one month, and the costs of shipping one unit from each factory to each warehouse are given below.

Factory	Capacity (units)	Warehouse	Requirements (units)
1	250	A	600
2	400	B	700
3	450		1300
4	350		
Total	1,450		

	To:	A	B
	1	12	10
From	2	14	11
	3	9	12
	4	8	7

Determine the least-cost shipping schedule for the month by the stepping-stone algorithm.

a. Set up the transportation matrix.
b. Find the initial solution by the intuitive (lowest-cost) method.

   c. What is the cost of the initial solution?
   d. What is the optimum shipping schedule?
   e. What is the cost of the optimum schedule?
   f. What is the interpretation of the 150 items in the dummy column?

2. Solve Problem 1 by the MODI method.

   a. Find the row and column indexes for the occupied cells.
   b. Find the row and column indexes for the unoccupied cells.
   c. What is the optimum shipping schedule?
   d. What is the cost of the optimum schedule?

3. A firm has two factories, # 1 and 2, which ship their output to four warehouses, A, B, C, D. The capacities of the factories for one month, and the requirements of the warehouses for one month, and the costs of shipping one unit from each factory to each warehouse are given below.

Factory (Rows)	Capacity	Warehouse (Columns)	Requirements
1	500 units	A	300 units
2	900 units	B	200
	1,400 units	C	400
		D	200
			1,100

From-to	Shipping Cost	From-to	Shipping Cost
1 - A	$15	2 - A	$9
1 - B	13	2 - B	11
1 - C	13	2 - C	12
1 - D	10	2 - D	16

Determine the least-cost shipping schedule for the month by the stepping-stone method. This problem is degenerate.

   a. Set up the transportation matrix.
   b. Find the initial solution by the intutive (lowest-cost) method.
   c. What is the cost of the initial solution?
   d. What is the optimum shipping schedule?
   e. What is the cost of the optimum schedule?
   f. What is the interpretation of the 300 units in the dummy column?

4. Solve Problem 3 by using the software on your computer.

   a. What is the linear programming version of the problem?
   b. Find the values of the variables on the printout.
   c. Find the value of the objective function on the printout.

9 - Quality Assurance

KEY IDEAS

1. There are two principal types of ways of measuring quality: attributes (counting the number of occurrences in one or two categories) and variables (measuring a characteristic or the deviation from a standard).

2. There are two principal types of Quality Assurance: sampling inspection of incoming outgoing materials (acceptance sampling) and control charts for ongoing processes (process control). Each type may be applied to attributes or variables.

3. Control charts differentiate between the process being in control (within an accept range of random variation) and out of control (outside the acceptable range). Process control involves making frequent small sample inspections to detect whether the process in control or out of control. Out of control means either above the upper control limit below the lower control limit.

   The limits for control charts are established first by obtaining 20 to 25 small samples of same size at different times from the process. This forms the basis for judging future samples.

4. The four types of control charts described in this chapter are: x-bar chart for means, range chart, *p-charts* for attributes with proportion defectives, and c-charts with number of defects.

   The x-bar charts are based on the mean and a known standard deviation. The UCL and LCL are frequently based on ± 2-sigma or 95.5% limits or ± 3-sigma or 99% limits of the normal distribution.

   Use range to simplify calculations by using the range instead of the standard deviation. Tables of control chart factors A_2, D_3, D_4 are used in conjunction with range data to obtain control limits for x-bar charts.

   A c-chart for attributes gives the number of defects in a standard small sample for very large lots. It is based on the theory that the distribution of the number of defects, c, Poisson, so that c is the mean number of defectives in the sample, the standard deviation the number of defects is MMM-.

5. To be effective, controls may need to be revised from time to time to reflect such factors a changes in the process due to changing standards, technological changes, etc.

6. Run tests such as the number of runs with respect to the median, and the number of runs up and down, can be useful in checking for nonrandomness. Run tests should be used in conjunction with control charts. Both approaches test for randomness. A process that is in control will exhibit randomness in a sequence of observations; the appearance of nonrandomness suggests that the process is not random (i.e., not in control).

7. A process capability index provides an indication of the ability of the process to meet specificiations. It is computed as the ration of a specified dimension to the process width on that dimension. A value of 1.00 means the two are equal; the greater the value of the index, the mosre likely it is that the process output will fall within the allowable variation (specification).

TIPS FOR PROBLEM SOLVING

A frequent issue in problems in this chapter involves determining the value of z that will be used to calculate upper and lower control limits for mean, p, and c charts.

Here are some typical ways the information is given, and how to obtain the value of z:

1. "Use 2-sigma limits." The "2" refers to z; hence use $z = 2$.

2. "Determine control limits such that 95% of the sample values will fall within the limits when the process is in control." To obtain z, divide the percentage by 2 (e.g., .95/2 = .4750) and then locate this value in Appendix Table A. That enables you to determine the value of z (for .4750, the value is 1.96).

3. Some problems refer to an alpha risk, or the risk of making a Type I error (e.g., 5%). Note that these two terms both essentially refer to the area in the tails of a normal distribution. In these cases, subtract the percentage from 100%, divide by 2, and find the value of z in Appendix Table A (e.g., 1.00 - .05 = .95; .95/2 = .4750; $z = 1.96$).

Note that for control chart problems, Appendix Table A is the preferred table rather than Table B.

Finally, if a problem does not reference a probability of a z-value for control limits, simply use a reasonable value such as $z = 2$.

GLOSSARY

attribute: a characteristic that has just two choices, e.g., defective or acceptable.

c-chart: for a continuous process, a type of control chart based on the number of defects per unit.

conformance: the characteristics of the product satisfy the established standard for the characteristics.

control chart: a technique devised by Walter Shewhart to monitor the quality level of work in process.

control limit: see upper control limit and lower control limit.

inspection: examining material in process or finished products to determine conformance to standard.

liability: the legal responsibility of a producer for defects of a product or service that causes injury, harm, or property damage.

lower control limit (LCL): in a Shewhart-type control chart, the lower limit of the random scatter of a sample statistic, to define whether a process is in control or out of control.

p-chart: for attribute process control, a type of control chart based on the proportion of defective items in a sample.

process capability: the variation allowed by the design specification relative to the inherent variability of process output.

process control: automated computer-controlled operations in a production process; for example, a chemical plant refinery.

quality: a measure of the conformance of a product to an established standard; quality may be defined either qualitatively or quantitatively.

range (R): the range of values of the observations in a sample.

range chart: a control chart for variation in the ranges of output samples.

tolerances: specifications pertaining to a dimension or characteristic of a product.

Type I error: incorrectly concluding a process is out of control.

Type II error: incorrectly concluding a process is in control.

upper control limit (UCL): in a Shewhart-type control chart, the upper limit of the random scatter of a sample statistic, to define whether a process is in control or out of control.

variable: common usage is any measurable characteristic, for quality assurance, it usually means a measurable characteristic on a continuous scale, such as height. weight, pressure, speed, etc.

x-bar chart: a type of control chart for variables, based on the mean and standard deviation of a sample.

TRUE/FALSE QUESTIONS

1. Two key issues is inspection are how much to inspect and how often.

2. The cost of inspection may outweigh the benefits of 100 percent inspection.

3. Range and p-charts both deal with sampling for attributes.

4. An attribute is counted rather than measured.

5. An attribute control chart can have a computed negative LCL.

6. As the sample size gets larger, the control limits move closer to the process mean.

7. x-bar charts are based on the normal distribution.

8. x-bar and range charts are used with measurement data.

9. The theoretical basis for a control chart is a sampling distribution.

10. Acceptance sampling is performed primarily on products during production.

MULTIPLE-CHOICE QUESTIONS

1. Which one of the following is not usually an advantage of centralized inspection?

   a. Special testing equipment
   b. Quick decisions
   c. More favorable testing environment
   d. All are advantages
   e. None are advantages

2. Which term is most closely associated with the term "quality of conformance?"

   a. 100% inspection.
   b. On-site inspection.
   c. Quality at the source.
   d. Control chart.

3. In order to monitor the number of defects in the output of a process for making rope, one would use this type of control chart:

   a. x-bar   b. p   c. c   d. R

4. In order to monitor the number of defectives in the output of a process for making iron castings, one would use this type of control chart:

   a. x-bar   b. p   c. c   d. R

5. Tolerances are:

   a. statistical limits.
   b. limits on inherent process variability.
   c. limits of natural variability.
   d. limits established by customers.
   e. b and c.

6. The number of runs up and down in the data set 8 9 12 10 11 12 is:

   a. 2
   b. 3
   c. 4
   d. 5
   e. none of these.

86

7. The number of runs with respect to the median in the data set 8 9 12 10 11 12 is:

   a. 2   b. 3   c. 4   d. 5   e. none of these. *B B A B A A*

8. An x-bar chart is best suited for this type of data:

   a. Count.
   b. Attribute.
   c. Measurement.
   d. None of these.

9. Tolerances refer to:

   a. Control limits.
   b. Specifications.
   c. Process capability.
   d. Process variability.

10. Process capability calculations take into account the process width and:

    a. Process standard deviation.
    b. Process dispersion.
    c. Specifications.
    d. Control limits.

PROBLEMS

Note: Control chart factors can be found in Table 9-2 of your textbook and in Table D of this study guide.

1. The Perfect Circle Company manufactures bushings. Once each hour a sample of 125 finished bushings is drawn from the output; each bushing is examined by a technician. Those which fail are classified as defective; the rest are satisfactory. Here are data on ten consecutive samples taken in one week:

Sample no.	1	2	3	4	5	6	7	8	9	10
Defective	15	13	16	11	13	14	20	25	30	45

   a. What type of control chart should be used here? Why.?
   b. What is the center line of the chart?
   c. What is the lower control limit (LCL)? The upper control l
   d. What statistic should be plotted on the control chart for
   e. Draw the control chart on a piece of graph paper.
   f. Is this system under control?
   g. What should the quality control engineer do?

2. Use the data in Problem 1 in this problem. Assume that an assignable cause has been found for **Sample #10** and has been corrected.

a. What is the value of the center line of the revised control chart?
b. What is the lower control limit of the revised chart?
c. What is the upper control limit of the revised chart?
d. Compare the revised control chart to the original control chart.

3. The Take-Charge Company produces batteries. From time to time a random sample of six batteries is selected from the output and the voltage of each battery is measured, to be sure that the system is under control. Here are statistics on 16 such samples.

Sample	Mean	Range	Sample	Mean	Range
1	4.99	0.41	9	5.01	0.49
2	4.87	0.57	10	5.19	0.56
3	4.85	0.59	11	5.40	0.44
4	5.26	0.74	12	5.15	0.63
5	5.09	0.74	13	5.00	0.35
6	5.02	0.21	14	4.89	0.45
7	5.13	0.56	15	4.99	0.554
8	5.09	0.92	16	5.05	0.33

a. What type of control chart should be used here? Why?
b. What is the center line of the chart?
c. What is the lower control limit? The upper control limit?
d. What statistic should be plotted on the control chart for each sample?
e. Draw the control chart on a piece of graph paper.
f. Is this system under control?
g. What should the quality control engineer do?

4. Use the data in Problem 3 to draw an R chart.

a. What is the lower control limit? The upper control limit?
b. What statistic should be plotted on the control chart for each sample?
c. Draw the control chart on a piece of graph paper.
d. Is this system under control?
e. What should the quality control engineer do?

5. Assume that an assignable cause has been found and corrected for sample # 11 in Problem 3.

a. What is the value of the center line of the revised control chart?
b. What is the lower control limit of the revised chart? The upper control Limit?
c. Compare the revised control chart to the original control chart.

6. Tinker Belle Peanut Butter is sold in .50 kilogram jars. The plant produces thousands of jars of peanut butter per working day; the process is rather simple and quite standardized, and is thought to be highly stable, with a standard deviation of .016k. Occasionally, a random sample of five jars of peanut butter is selected from the output and weighed, to be sure that the system is under control. Here are data on ten such samples. Measurements are in kilograms.

Sample	1	2	3	4	5	6	7	8	9	10
	.50	.50	.50	.51	.51	.51	.50	.50	.51	.50
	.47	.48	.49	.51	.50	.50	.51	.52	.48	.51
	.50	.48	.51	.52	.49	.52	.49	.47	.50	.49
	.49	.48	.47	.51	.52	.51	.50	.49	.49	.50
	.51	.47	.49	.51	.50	.51	.48	.49	.50	.47
	2.47	2.41	2.46	2.56	2.52	2.55	2.48	2.47	2.48	2.47

a. What type of control chart should be used here? Why?
b. What is the center line of the chart?
c. What is the lower control limit? The upper control limit?
d. What statistic should be plotted on the control chart for each sample?
e. Draw the control chart on a piece of graph paper.
f. Is this system under control?
g. What should the quality control engineer do?

7. (One step beyond. Use Table D in this study guide.) Use the data in Problem 6 to construct an R chart.

a. What is the lower control limit? The upper control limit?
b. What statistic should be plotted on the control chart for each sample?
c. Draw the control chart on a sheet of graph paper.
d. Is this system under control?
e. What should the quality control engineer do?

8. The Poseidon Fabric Co. produces large beach towels (among other things): they are supposed to be brightly colored and have a fringe on each end. From time to time, a towel is selected from the finished goods and subjected to an intense inspection in search of any and all defects. A defect is a stain, a badly dyed spot, a hole, a missing fringe, etc., each occurrence counts as a distinct defect. Here are data on 12 sample towels.

Towel	1	2	3	4	5	6	7	8	9	10	11	12
Number of defects	2	1	3	0	1	4	0	1	3	2	3	1

a. What type of control chart should be used here? Why?
b. What is the center line of the chart?
c. What is the lower control limit? The upper control limit?
d. What statistic should be plotted on the control chart for each sample?
e. Draw the control chart on a piece of graph paper.
f. Is this system under control?
g. What should the quality control engineer do?

9. Here is an x-bar chart with 20 sample means plotted on it. Use this chart to perform a test for runs above and below the center line. See next page.

a. What is the expected number of runs?
b. What is the standard deviation of the number of runs?
c. What is the actual number of runs?

d.   What is the z-statistic?
e.   What are the critical values of z for 95 percent?
f.   Is this process under control? Explain.

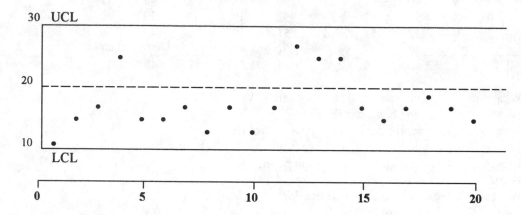

9S - Acceptance Sampling

KEY IDEAS

1. The optimal level of inspection balances the cost of inspection and the cost of allowing undetected defectives to pass through the system.

2. Each situation calls for a different type of inspection process; the stages of production where inspection may take place include: raw materials and purchased parts, finished product end items, before costly operation, before taking an irreversible step, or before painting or plating or some other covering that hides potential defects. Also some inspections take place at the production site and others at the customer's designated location, or in a laboratory.

3. Acceptance sampling pertains to incoming batches of raw materials (or purchased parts) and to outgoing batches of finished goods. Current emphasis in quality assurance is away from acceptance sampling and towards 1) improving the process so that there is less need for inspection, and 2) improving supplier quality so that there is less need for inspection of incoming goods.

4. Acceptance sampling can be applied to either attributes or variables. Attributes are those characteristics of a product or service that are counted (e.g., pass-fail, defective-nondefective), and variables are characteristics that are measured (e.g., width, thickness, weight),

5. The technical starting point for an acceptance sampling plan is the operating characteristic (OC) curve, which gives probability of acceptance, P_{ac} vs. quality level (i.e., the proportion of defects p). The higher p is or the greater the deviation from standard, the lower P. is. A widely used type of OC curve has two clearly identifiable points, the AQL, acceptable quality level, a designated "good" quality, and the LTPD, lot tolerance percent defective, a designated "bad" quality.

   For the AQL, $P_{ac} = 1 - \alpha$, where α is the probability of rejection of a lot with quality AQL. For the LTPD, $P_{ac} = \beta$, where β is the probability of accepting a lot with quality LTPD.

6. The AOQ is the average outgoing quality, frequently shown as a curve with AOQ as a function of p. When rejected lots are inspected 100 percent to remove all defective items and the defectives are replaced with good items, the AOQ is better than with intermediate quality lots because of the extra inspection.

   For lots where the number sampled, n, is small relative to the lot size, N, the AOQ is approximately $P_{ac} \times p$. The highest AOQ (poorest outgoing quality) for a sampling plan is known as the AOQL, average outgoing quality limit.

GLOSSARY

acceptable quality level (AQL): for a given sampling plan, a specified quality level for which there is a low probability of rejecting a good lot.

acceptance number: in attributes sampling, for a given sample size, the maximum number of allowable defectives for acceptance.

acceptance sampling: sampling of lots of incoming material to determine conformance to standard.

attribute: a characteristic that has just two choices, e.g., defective or acceptable.

average outgoing quality (AOQ): given the sampling plan, for a specified incoming lot quality level, a function showing the average quality level of the outgoing lot, as a result of it, replacing defective units of material by good ones.

conformance: the characteristics of the product satisfy the established standard for the characteristics.

consumer's risk: the probability that a lot that has a quality worse than the lot tolerance percent defective will be accepted, or passed.

inspection: examining material in process or finished products to determine conformance to standard.

lot tolerance percent defective (LTPD): for a given sampling plan, a specified quality level for which there is a low probability of accepting a bad lot.

operating characteristic (OC): a mathematical function that yields, for a given sampling plan, the probability of accepting the lot, as a function of the percent defective.

producers risk: the probability that a lot that has an acceptable quality level will be rejected.

quality: a measure of the conformance of a product to an established standard; quality may be defined either quantitatively or quantitatively.

sampling plan: a procedure that identifies a lot . as being of either acceptable or rejectable quality; for example, with attributes, a typical acceptance sampling plan would specify for a given lot size, the sample size and the maximum number of allowable defects for acceptance.

Type I error: rejecting a good lot.

Type II error: accepting a bad lot as good.

TRUE/FALSE QUESTIONS

1. Acceptance sampling can be applied to attributes or to variables.

2. The ability of a sampling plan to discriminate between good and bad lots is described by its operating characteristic curve.

3. Acceptance sampling is performed primarily on products during production.

4. An "accept" decision for a lot of material implies that the lot does not contain any defectives.

5. The AQL is the probability of rejecting a lot of material that is of acceptable quality.

6. The acceptance number in a sampling inspection plan is the lot tolerance percent defective.

7. The AOQL is the worst case of outgoing quality.

MULTIPLE-CHOICE QUESTIONS

1. Acceptance sampling is used for all but which one of these?

    a. Incoming raw material.
    b. Intermediate production.
    c. Final goods.
    d. Incoming purchased parts.

2. In which instance would acceptance sampling not be appropriate?

    a. Destructive testing is required.
    b. The cost consequences of passing defectives is low.
    c. A large number of items must be processed in a short period.
    d. Fatigue and boredom lead to inspection errors.
    e. All are appropriate applications.

3. The letters AQL stand for:

    a. average quality limit.
    b. average quality level.
    c. acceptable quality limit.
    d. acceptable quality level.
    e. average quality of lots.

4. Which is a list of the elements of an acceptance sampling plan?

    a. The lot size, the sample size, and the lot tolerance percent defective.
    b. The lot size, the sample size, and the acceptance number.
    c. The sample size, the acceptance number, and the lot tolerance percent defective.
    d. The sample size, the acceptance number, and the average outgoing quality limit.
    e. The acceptance number, the lot tolerance percent defective, and the AOQL.

PROBLEMS

1. A 10 ampere fuse is a weak link in an electrical circuit; if the fuse is defective. it could fail to blow, even though the current exceeded 10 amps, thereby risking damage to equipment and personal injury. An electrical manufacturer uses enormous quantities of 10 ampere fuses in its products, which are purchased in lots of 100,000 from an outside supplier. The contract provides that each lot will be examined by the buyer according to this acceptance sampling plan: a random sample of 20 fuses will be drawn from the lot and tested by being subjected to a current of 10 amperes; if 0 or 1 of them fail to blow, the lot will be accepted; if 2 or more of them fail to blow, the lot will be returned.

   a. Which probability distribution should be used here? Why?
   b. Calculate some points on the operating characteristic curve for this sampling plan.
   c. Draw the OC curve on a piece of graph paper. Use Table D in your textbook.
   d. The acceptable quality level (AQL) is 5 percent defective fuses. What type of sampling error might be made at the AQL?
   e. What is the probability of suffering a sampling error at the AQL? What is the name of this probability?
   f. The lot tolerance percent defective (LTPD) is 15 percent defective fuses. What type of sampling error might be made at the LTPD?
   g. What is the probability of suffering a sampling error at the LTPD? What is the name of

2. The Major Convenience Appliance Company produces small appliances, such as drip coffee makers, for home and office use. It purchases the indicator lights, which indicate whether the appliance is off or on, from an outside supplier. Indicator lights are bought in lots of 10,000, the contract specifies that each lot will be examined by the buyer according to this acceptance sampling plan: a random sample of 150 indicator lights will be drawn from the lot and tested, if five (or fewer) defective lights are found, the batch will be accepted; if more than five defective lights are found, the batch will be returned.

   a. Which probability distribution should be used here? Why?
   b. Calculate some points on the operating characteristic curve for this sampling plan.
   c. Draw the OC curve on a piece of graph paper.
   d. The acceptable quality level (AQL) is 2 percent defective lights. What type of sampling error might be made at AQL?
   c. What is the probability of suffering a sampling error at the AQL? What is the name of this probability?
   f. The lot tolerance percent defective (LTPD) Is 6 percent defective lights. What type of sampling error might be made at the LTPD?
   g. What is the probability of suffering a sampling error at the LTPD? What is the name of this probability?

3. Calculate some points on the AOQ curve for the acceptance sampling plan in Problem 2.

   a. Draw the AOQ curve on a piece of graph paper.
   b. What is the approximate value of the average outgoing quality limit (AOQL)?
   c. What is the significance of the AOQL?

10 - Forecasting

KEY IDEAS

1. Successful operations planning requires good forecasts.

2. Forecasting is imprecise, but the errors in prior forecasts are measurable.

3. There are both qualitative and quantitative forecast systems.

    a. The qualitative systems include expert or executive opinions, sales force composites, opinion surveys and the Delphi technique. The Delphi method includes a sequence of questionnaires administered to a select group of qualified experts; the design of each questionnaire is based upon the results of the previous questionnaire.
    b. Quantitative forecasting methods include exponential smoothing, moving averages, and associative (regression-based) systems. A forecast system may be a combination of several of these.
    c. The "naive" model is a simple special case: the value for the next period is predicted to be the same as it was in the previous period. An alternative version of a naive model is that the difference between the value for this period and the value for the next period will be the same as the difference between the last period and this one.

4. The accuracy of a forecast system depends upon:

    a. accuracy of the historical time series data
    b. similarity of patterns between the past and the future
    c. grouping or aggregation of the data series
    d. time lapse between the historical periods and the period for which the prediction is being made
    e. choice of a model.

5. Exponential smoothing is an of adaptive forecasting technique with some advantages over other types of moving averages and other statistically based measures. These advantages include:

    a. the calculations are simple.
    b. the weighting pattern can be changed simply by changing the smoothing constant.

    Both exponential smoothing and simple moving averages smooth the data and lag changes in a time series.

6. If there is trend in the historical data, single exponentially smoothed forecasts tend to lag behind the actuals. Therefore, it is necessary to incorporate trend adjustments, with double smoothing.

7. Associative techniques involve the use of predictor (independent) variables in equation form to estimate values of the variable of interest (dependent variable). Least squares analysis is used to obtain the coefficients of the regression equation. [Note the comments on the use of linear regression analysis in your textbook.]

8. Moving averages and trend lines can be used to compute monthly, weekly or daily indexes that show how one part of a "season" compares to the average value of a time series. These indexes are used in conjunction with trend calculations to generate spot predictions that take account of the cycle of demand or economic activity within a period of a year, as well as of the long-run changes over a period of several years.

9. This chapter shows how to continuously monitor and control the accuracy of ES forecasts. The mean absolute deviation (MAD) is a measure of how far the actual values were from the predictions for previous periods, on the average. 'Me tracking signal (TS) is a measure of the biasedness of the differences between the actuals and the predictions.

TIPS FOR SOLVING PROBLEMS

Many of the end-of-chapter problems are fairly specific in terms of what you are required to do. However, two frequently encountered questions are (1) Which technique should I use? and (2) How can I tell if the forecast is working properly?

In terms of which technique to use, begin by plotting the data. Does the plot reveal a trend? If so, either a trend line or trend-adjusted exponential smoothing should be used. A linear trend line requires less effort than trend-adjusted smoothing requires. If no trend is present, select one of the averaging techniques, such as moving average or exponential smoothing. Whether trend or averaging is used, you may also want to consider whether seasonal variations are a factor. Again, examine the plot to determine if major ups and downs occur periodically. Note that when annual data are plotted, seasonality cannot be discerned because these values have been aggregated into annual amounts, thereby concealing any possible seasonal variation.

In terms of the forecast working properly, the preferred approach is to use a control chart to analyze forecast errors. A forecast can be said to be working properly if (a) all errors are within the control limits, and (b) a plot of errors does not reveal any patterns such as trends, cycling, etc.

GLOSSARY

action limits: for a tracking signal, the "tracks" or outer limits of the value of the TS; a tendency to go outside the action limits is an indication that some feature of the forecasting model, such as the value of one of the smoothing constants, might be changed so as to keep the TS inside the limits.

alpha (α): *see* single exponential smoothing.

associative forecasting: forecasting such as regression that estimates the effects of a causal variable or variables upon a dependent variable.

autoregressive series: a set of time series data that shows a great deal of dependence of the results for one period on the results of previous periods.

bias: The tendency of forecast errors to be successively possitive or negative.

Box-Jenkins technique: a sophisticated forecasting technique used to analyze times series data.

causal variable: a variable whose changes in value cause fluctuations in other variables; for example, the duty on imported steel affects the price of steel in the USA.

centered moving average: a moving average that is positioned at the middle of the group of numbers it represents.

composite: a forecast taken by averaging the results of opinion surveys of employees or specialists in the field, such as, for example, salesmen.

control chart: a technique that shows the extent to which the differences between forecasted and actual values stay within predefined statistically computed ranges; control charts are used extensively in quality control and are discussed at greater length in Chapter 9.

correlation: the degree to which the values of two variables have a tendency to change in the same (or opposite) directions.

decomposition: isolating seasonal cyclical, trend and random effects in a time-series data.

Delphi technique: forecasting that forms a consensus of qualified experts, in a series of stages; the results of the questionnaire at one stage are used to redesign the questionnaire at the next stage, and, if necessary, to redefine the problem for which the predictions are being made.

double exponential smoothing: removing the lag inherent in single exponential smoothing, by a model that combines single exponential smoothing of the raw data with secondary exponential smoothing of the predictions.

judgmental forecast: a forecast based entirely upon the experience and personal opinions of a qualified expert.

lag: a specified difference between actual and forecasted values, expressed in time units (e.g., years), rather than in customary physical or monetary units.

linear regression: see regression.

mean absolute deviation (MAD): the average of the absolute differences between the actuals and the predictions.

mean square error (MSE): the variance computed by averaging the squared differences between the predicted and the actual values.

moving average: a sequence of averages, derived from a set of time-series data, for a period of time, such as a season, week, month or day; each average covers n such periods and is computed by deleting the first period from the previous MA, and adding in the most recent period.

naive model: a prediction that the value in the next period will be the same as what it is in the current period, or *else* that the difference between the current period and the next one will be the same as the difference between the current period and the most recent one.

regression: a technique for generating forecasts by computing a linear (straight-line) equation that shows the influence of time or some other causal variable upon the dependent variable whose values are being forecasted.

seasonal relative: an index that expresses the degree to which the value of a series in a particular season tends to vary from the "average" if there were no seasonal variations.

simple (unweighted) average: an average that assigns equal weight to every member of a data series included in the average.

single exponential smoothing: smoothing by computing the weighted average of the current value and the most recent prediction; the current value has a weight of (x, $0 < $(x < 1$, and the most recent prediction has a weight of I - α.

smoothing constant: see single exponential smoothing.

technological forecasting: forecasting that takes account of future anticipated technological changes.

time series: a time-ordered sequence of observations, made at regular intervals.

tracking signal (TS): a measure of the biasedness of the difference between the forecasted and the actual values; a good forecast will always have a TS within a range centering on zero, for example ± 4, and there would be about the same number of values above zero as below zero.

trend: a long-term tendency of a time series to increase or decrease.

trend-adjusted smoothing: see double exponential smoothing.

TRUE/FALSE QUESTIONS

1. Accurate forecasting can be done with inaccurate historical data, providing the forecasting model is a good one.

2. Aggregated (grouped) data frequently generate better forecasts than non-aggregated data.

3. Simple exponential smoothing is a type of forecasting for which the forecasted values tend to lag behind the actuals.

4. Generally, it does not matter how far in time the forecast series is removed from the actual data series, provided good data are available.

5. If a particular season of the year shows greater than average sales, the seasonal relative for that season is greater than 1.00.

6. The Delphi technique is a forecasting model that incorporates the use of multiple regression.

7. A double exponentially smoothed model is more responsive to trend in the data series than a single smoothed model.

8. The MAD is the average of the squared differences between the actual and the forecasted values.

9. The tracking signal is supposed to run between the action limits,

10. The tracking signal is directly proportional to the MAD.

11. The MSE is the average of the squared differences between the actual and the forecasted values.

12. Forecast errors should be within a range centering on zero, Such as ±3cr, and for a forecast to be a good one, about half of the errors should be randomly scattered above zero and half below zero.

13. Double exponential smoothing includes trend calculations.

14. The variance is not a measure of error.

15. Seasonality refers to data patterns that recur every year (week, month, etc.) at about the same time.

16. Associative forecasting techniques are used to obtain seasonal indexes.

MULTIPLE-CHOICE QUESTIONS

1. Which of the following forecasting techniques generates trend forecasts?

    a. Delphi method
    b. Sales force composites
    c. Moving averages
    d. Single exponential smoothing
    e. None of the above

2. For this set of errors: - 1, + 4, 0, + 2, + 3, MAD is:

   a. 1.0
   b. 1.6
   c. 2.0
   d. 2.5

3. Which probability distribution is used most extensively in dealing with forecasting errors?

   a. Normal
   b. Poisson
   c. Exponential
   d. Beta
   e. Pareto

4. Select the statement about moving averages and exponential smoothing that is not true.

   a. Both tend to lag changes in a series.
   b. Both smooth data.
   c. Both involve fairly simple calculations.
   d. Both can be used obtain seasonal index numbers.

5. Demand data with relatively little variation about the mean value will tend to have a:

   a. low cumulative forecast error and a high MAD.
   b. high cumulative forecast error and a low MAD.
   c. low cumulative forecast error and a low MAD.
   d. high cumulative forecast error and a high MAD.

6. The cumulative forecast error is important for determining the:

   a. Mean squared error.
   b. Bias in forecast error.
   c. Mean absolute deviation.
   d. Control limits.

7. Of these values, the value of alpha that would track the data most closely is:

   a. 0
   b. .01
   c. .10
   d. .20
   e. .30

PROBLEMS

1. The data below consist of the closing price of the common stock of the American Telephone and Telegraph Corporation on some recent Fridays. Common stock prices are quoted in eighths of a dollar ($1/8 = \$.125$).

Time(t)	Price	Time(t)	Price
1	$21.125	5	$23.250
2	22.250	6	23.875
3	23.500	7	23.875
4	23.250	8	24.500

    a. Using a five-period moving average, forecast the price of the stock for period 9.
    b. In period 9. the actual price was $24.125. What is the error of the forecast?
    c. Using a five-period moving average, forecast the price of the stock for period 10.

2. A product is manufactured in distinct batches of various sizes. The cost accountant wished to obtain an equation to use for estimating the cost of a batch. He obtained data on a number of batches, consisting of the size of the batch, measured in number of pieces, and the total cost of the batch, consisting of the setup cost and the variable costs of labor, material, etc. The total cost is stated in thousands of dollars. Here is the data.

Size of Batch	Cost of Batch
20	$1.4
30	3.4
40	4.1
50	3.8
70	6.7
80	6.6
100	7.8
120	10.4
150	11.7
650	$55.9

    a. Which is the dependent variable? The independent variable?
    b. Draw the scatterplot of this data. Does a straight line look like a reasonable fit?
    c. Obtain the x^2, xy, and y^2 columns.
    d. What is the value of the slope?
    e. What is the interpretation of the slope?
    f. What is the value of the y intercept?
    g. What is the interpretation of the y intercept?
    h. Estimate the cost of a batch of 125 pieces.
    i. What is the value of the coefficient of correlation? Does it appear to indicate a high degree of association between the size of the batch and the cost?

3. The president of the Rich and Greene College of Business Administration wishes to forecast the enrollment for next fall. The enrollment is measured in Full Time Equivalents (FTE) which

represent the number of full-time students which is equivalent to the existing mixture of full-time and part-time students. Data representing the fall enrollment for the past ten years is given below:

Time(t)	Enrollment
1	907
2	981
3	1014
4	1015
5	1050
6	1071
7	1123
8	1118
9	1175
10	1216

a. Draw a scatterplot. Does the data appear to contain a linear trend?
b. Obtain the t, y, and ty columns.
c. What is the value of the slope?
d. What is the interpretation of the slope?
e. What is the value of the y intercept?
f. What is the interpretation of the y intercept?
g. Forecast the enrollment for next fall.

4. The table below contains data on the monthly amount, in millions of dollars, which was spent by "leading national advertisers" for advertising apparel and accessories in magazines, in four recent years.

	Year			
Month	1	2	3	4
January	$6.7	$7.9	$ 8.8	$ 7.4
February	6.2	8.4	10.3	17.4
March	12.1	15.1	20.4	26.1
April	14.4	15.9	17.3	26.6
May	11.1	11.8	15.7	17.0
June	7.4	5.5	9.0	10.4
July	6.4	7.6	8.9	7.9
August	12.9	13.0	20.0	24.7
September	21.1	23.2	32.6	35.6
October	15.4	17.2	24.2	24.8
November	16.5	16.7	22.0	22.2
December	11.6	11.9	16.9	19.8

Source: Survey of Current Business, U.S. Department of Commerce, Washington, D.C., various dates.

Use this data to obtain a set of 12 monthly seasonal indexes.

a. Obtain the set of 37 12-month moving averages. The first value will fall between June and July of Year 1, and the last value will fall between June and July of Year 4.
b. Obtain the set of 36 centered 12-month moving averages. The first value will fall in July of Year 1, and the last value in June of Year 4.

    c.   Obtain the 36 ratios of the observed values to the centered moving averages. Group them by months.

    d.   Find the mean of the ratios for each month.

    e.   Adjust the means to add to 12. These are the monthly seasonal indexes.

    f.   Describe the seasonal pattern in magazine advertising for apparel and accessories which is revealed by the monthly seasonal indexes.

5. This problem utilizes the data in Problem #4 to make forecasts using the naive methods in your textbook.

    a.   Use the actual value in the previous period to forecast the amount which will be spent on advertising apparel and accessories in January of year 5.

    b.   Use the actual value in the same month of the previous year to forecast the amount which will be spent on advertising apparel and accessories for January of year 5.

6. Use the data for year 1 in Problem #4 for this problem. Calculate the single-factor exponential smoothing forecasts for advertising for the last 11 months of Year 1. Use the first actual value as the starting forecast, and alpha = 0.20.

    a.   Construct the worksheet for single-factor smoothing and obtain the forecasts for the months of February through December.

    b.   Draw the graph of the actual values and the forecasted values.

7. Use your work in Problem #6 in this problem, which involves the mean squared error (MSE), the mean absolute deviation (MAD), and the tracking signal. Use the tracking signal to estimate when a change occurs in the rate of spending on advertising apparel and accessories.

    a.   Obtain the actual column, the forecasted column, and the error column for single-factor smoothing of the data for year 1 in Problem #4. (The actual column will have 12 entries, and the forecasted column will have 11 entries.)

    b.   Obtain squared error column.

    c.   Obtain the MSE for year 1.

    d.   Obtain the absolute error column.

    e.   Obtain the MAD for year 1.

    f.   Beginning with the absolute error of 1.25 for May of year 1, obtain updated estimates of MAD for the months of June through December. Use alpha = 0.20.

    g.   Obtain the tracking signal column.

    h.   Plot the tracking signals on a control chart with limits of ±4.

    i.   What conclusion can be drawn from the tracking signal?

8. Use the data for Year I in Problem 4 for this problem. Calculate the trend-adjusted exponential smoothing forecasts for advertising for the last 8 months of Year 1. Use $alpha_1 = alpha_2 = 0.20$, and use the first four actual values to obtain the starting values.

    a.   What is the starting estimate of the trend, T_4?

    b.   What is the initial forecast, TAF_5?

    c.   Construct the worksheet for trend-adjusted smoothing and obtain the forecasts for the months of May through December.

    d.   Draw the graph of the actual values and the forecasted values.

11 - Inventory Management

KEY IDEAS

1. The chapter describes several different ways of classifying inventory:

   a. raw materials, finished goods, parts, etc.
   b. independent and dependent demand
   c. dollar volumes and sizes: A, B, C. etc.

2. Inventories are held for a variety of reasons, such as customer demand for end items, smoothing production, decoupling Internal operations, a hedge against stockouts and price increases, and economical purchasing.

3. The requirements for effective inventory management are:

   a. an accounting system to keep track of on-hand and on-order merchandise
   b. reliable forecasting of demand
   c. estimates of lead times between placing an order and receiving goods, and lead-time variability
   d. estimates of inventory holding costs, ordering costs and shortage (backorder) costs
   e. a classification system

4. There are numerous examples of electronic automation in retail inventory management, such as UPC scanners, J. C. Penney scanners, and airline reservation systems.

5. The question of how much to order is often answered using some form of an EOQ model. The fundamental variants of the deterministic economic order quantity model include:

   a. EOQ for purchased end items or semifinished goods acquired from outside vendors
   b. economic run length for Internal production orders in batch processing and noninstantaneous replacement
   c. quantity discounts

   In variants *a* and *b* the order quantity is set at a level such that total holding *costs* = total *ordering costs;* unit acquisition (purchase) cost is considered indirectly, but only insofar as it is used to calculate holding cost. In variant *c* order a quantity that minimizes the sum of three costs: acquisition, holding, and ordering costs. In order to implement a quantity discount model, it is only necessary to calculate total cost at an EOQ if it falls between two price breaks, or at a price break. A price break is a quantity at which there is a change in price.

6. An EOQ model tells you how much to order, but it does not say when to order. With uncertainties in delivery schedules and usage rates, there is no guarantee that there will always be material in stock to service production operations. This is where reorder point (ROP) models come into the picture.

   There are four variants of ROP:

(1) constant demand rate and lead time
(2) variable demand, constant lead time
(3) constant demand, variable lead time
(4) variable demand and lead time

The approach to (1) is simple, place the order when the stock gets to a level such that what is in stock now will all be used up when the new shipment arrives. Variants *(2), (3),* and *(4)*, however, add realism by allowing the decision maker to set a safety stock as a buffer against uncertainty. The size of this safety stock depends upon whether the uncertainty is in the demand rate, the lead time, or both, and how much risk of a stockout the decision maker finds acceptable.

In (2), (3), and (4) the fundamental relationship is:

ROP = Expected demand during lead time + Safety stock.

The size of the safety stock is determined by the "service level," the probability of no stockout, that is

Service level = 1.00 - Stockout risk.

There are two fundamental assumptions:

(1) daily demands in lead time are independent
(2) the daily demand rates are normally distributed

In (3), "constant demand, variable lead time," the uncertainty is with the length of the period rather than the demand rate. The lead time (number of days) is assumed to be normally distributed.

7. Chapter 11 includes a discussion of relationships between shortages and service levels for reorder models with fixed lead time (LT) and variable demand. This approach introduces the order quantity (Q) as an element that influences safety stock decisions, and shows the interrelationship between Q, service level (SL), safety stock (SS), annual demand (D), and the standard deviation of demand in LT σ_{dLT}. The greater Q is, all other things being the same, the smaller the safety stock necessary to achieve a specified level of service over the long run.

Table 11-3 gives the unit normal loss function, E(7,), associated with both the corresponding z-value and the lead-time service level (LTSL). For a normally distributed lead-time demand, E(z) is a scale factor that is multiplied by σ_{dLT} to calculate the expected shortage in lead time, E(n). The expected annual shortage, E(N), is the product of E(n) and the number of cycles in a year, D/Q. Since

$$E(N) = (1 - SL_{annual})D,$$
$$SL_{annual} = 1 - E(N)/D$$
$$= 1 - E(n)/Q$$
$$= 1 - \sigma_{dLT} E(z)/Q.$$

8. When ordering is constrained to fixed times, the fixed-order-interval model applies. With the fixed-order-interval model, the safety stock is greater than with the other models, because the ordering is done at fixed time intervals regardless of the stock level.

9. The single-period model is appropriate for cases in which one order is to be placed that is intended to satisfy demand for an entire period. The period can be a day, week, or other interval.

10. Often, the items involved are perishable (e.g., fresh seafood), or otherwise have a limited shelf life (e.g., daily newspapers). Other examples include spare parts for equipment and inventories of rental equipment.

11. Regardless of the application, the single-period model involves computation of a theoretical service level, which is the ratio of unit shortage cost to the sum of unit shortage and excess costs:

$$SL = \frac{C_s}{C_s + C_e}$$

TIPS FOR SOLVING PROBLEMS

This chapter has numerous models, and it can be very difficult in some instances to know which model to use. Part of the difficulty relates to the fact that each model contains several elements, and any one of the elements might be the unknown that solves the problem.

There are two things you can do to enhance your ability to solve these problems. One is to familiarize yourself with the circumstances under which each model is appropriate, and the other is to learn the components of each model and to be able to recognize them in a problem setting. Together, these two skills will greatly contribute to your being able to correctly select the appropriate model.

One way to develop these skills is to refer to Table 11-4 in your textbook. Most of the models are listed, along with the basic formulas and definitions of symbols. Note that the symbols are the components of the models. Thus, you have a list of most of the components. When trying to solve a problem, you might want to begin by listing the symbols and values of as many components as you can from the information given in the problem. By comparing your hst to the formulas in Table 12-4, you should be able to determine which value or values are missing or unknown, and hence, what you need to solve for. Also, make it a point to know which part of an ROP formula relates to risk, to service level, to safety stock, and so on.

The quantity-discount model is not listed separately in the table. However, if a problem has a list of prices and ranges, you can be confident that it is a quantity discount problem. Note that the components of quantity discount problems are essentially the same as those in the basic EOQ model. Also missing are variations of the single-period model (e.g., Poisson, normal, etc.). However, one is never required to make an assumption about type of distribution in such problems-that information will be given.

Example 1

Suppose a pharmacy that dispenses a generic drug, and that daily demand for the drug is 50 mg. and lead time is 4 days, then the average demand in LT is:

$$d \times LT = 50 \times 4 = 200 \text{ mg.}$$

the standard deviation of demand in lead time is:

$$\sigma_{dLT} = \sqrt{4} \times 5 = 10 \text{ mg;}$$

If the lead-time service level (LTSL) 99%, $z = 2.33$, the safety stock (SS) = 23.3 mg. and the reorder point is ROP = 223.3 mg.

1. Suppose Q = 500 mg; what is the annual service level?
2. What value of Q would yield $SL_{nni,1} = 99\%$? What are the corresponding values of the safety stock (SS), the reorder point (ROP) and the order interval?
3. Assuming that Q = 500 mg, what LTSL would correspond to $SL_{nn,1} = 99\%$? What are the corresponding values of SS and ROP?

Solution to Example 1

1. In Table 11-3. for LTSL = 0.99, $E(z) = 0.003$; therefore

$$SL_{annual} = 1 - \frac{10 \times 0.003}{500} = 0.99994.$$

2. In this case the unknown is Q, a formula is derived by algebra:

$$Q = \frac{E(z)\ \sigma_{dLT}}{1 - SL_{annual}} = \frac{0.003 \times 10}{0.01} = 3\ mg.$$

Since $z = 2.33$, both SS and ROP are identical to the original solution, 23.3 mg and 223.3 mg, respectively, Q. however, is very small, just three milligrams, or 3/50 of a day's demand. This means that the order interval is 3/50 of a day and that it would be necessary to place orders 17 times a day.

3. With $Q = 500$ and an annual service level of 99%, in order to solve the LTSL, it is first necessary to find $E(z)$.

$$E(z) = (1 - SL_{annual})/ \sigma_{dLT} = 500 \times 0.001/10 = 0.5$$

the corresponding value of z is approximately -0.2 and the LTSL is 42%. The safety stock (SS) is

$$z\sigma_{dLT} = -0.2 \times 10 = -2\ mg,$$

and the ROP is

$$d + SS = 200 - 2 = 198\ mg.$$

The order interval is 10 days.

In Example 11.1. the standard deviations of daily demand and lead-time demand are small, the *LT* is small and the LTSL is 99 percent. This results in both a large safety stock and frequent orders; therefore, the holding costs are relatively high. Part 3 of Example 10. 1 shows that in the long run needs can be satisfied with only a 1 percent probability of running out of stock, with an LTSL less than 50 percent.

Example 2

Given this information, answer the questions that follow: $EOQ = 447$ cans; $\sigma_{dLT} = 6$ cans; LTSL is 99%; $z = 2.33$; and the demand in LT is 160 cans.

1. What is the annual service level?
2. What is the LTSL that corresponds to an annual service level of 99%? What are the corresponding safety stock and reorder point?
3. In this example, with a lead-time service level of 99%, the safety stock is 14 cans and the holding cost is $0.02 per can per month, or $0.24 per can per year. What would be the annual saving in holding cost in changing from a policy of LTSL = 99% to $SL_{annual} = 99\%$?

Solution to Example 2

1. From Table 11-3, $E(z) = 0.003$. Therefore

$$SL_{annual} = 1 - \frac{6 \times 0.003}{447} = 0.99996.$$

2.

$$E(z) = \frac{446 \times 0.001}{6} = 0.745.$$

From Table 11-3, z is approximately -0.57 and the lead-time service level (LTSL) is approximately 28%. Therefore, the safety stock is

$$SS = 6 \times -0.57,$$

or approximately -3 cans, and the reorder point is

$$ROP = 160 - 3 = 157 \text{ cans}.$$

3. The net reduction in the safety stock is 14 - (-3) = 17 cans. The saving in annual holding cost is 17 x $0.24 = $4.08.

Example 3

In a modernized electronics assembly plant a robotic cart used in production operations moves on a fixed track from one workstation to another, in a preprogrammed way, transferring certain supplies and tools. The circular outer rims of the wheels of the cart have gear teeth that mesh with the gear teeth of the track in a 1: I gear ratio. Because there are very frequent stops and starts, the gear teeth wear out rapidly and it is necessary to have a stock of them on hand in order to facilitate replacement. The supplier of the gear teeth operates a Japanese-style 'Just-in-time*' inventory system, and keeps a very low stock of teeth, servicing orders largely out of new production rather than stock.

Management policy of the electronics firm is to operate a reorder system with an annual service level of 95 percent. The lead time between placing an order for new gear teeth and receiving the order is 2 days; the daily average wearout is 100 gear teeth with a standard deviation of 50-, and the gear teeth are ordered in standard lot sizes of 500 units.

What are the safety stock, reorder point and the corresponding lead-time service level?

Solution to Example 3

The standard deviation of lead-time demand is

$\sigma_{dLT} = \sqrt{2} \times 50 = 70.71$ gear teeth.

The expected unit normal loss is

$$E(z) = \frac{(1 - SL_{annual}) \, Q}{\sigma_{dLT}} = \frac{0.05 \times 500}{70.71} = 0.3535.$$

Referring to Table 11-3, the corresponding z-value is 0.09 and the LTSL is 54%. The safety stock is

$SS = 0.09 \times 70.71 = 6.76$ gear teeth;

the reorder point is

$ROP = 200 + 7 = 207.$

GLOSSARY

carrying cost: see holding cost.

classification system: the A-B-C system classifies inventory items as follows:

A: small percentage of items, but account for greatest proportion of annual dollar usage or other measure of importance.
B: middle-size percentage of items, accounting for middle percentage of value or importance.
C: large percentage of items, accounting for small proportion of annual dollar usage or importance.

continuous system: keeping the count of available stock in an electronic or mechanical device that records additions or removals as they occur.

cost curves: a graphic means for portraying the relationships between the costs that are balanced In lot-size decisions.

cycle counting: physically counting items in inventory.

decoupling (internal operations): strategic placement of inventories so that one section of the plant is not adversely affected by bottlenecks in other sections.

demand: the rate at which stock is used.

demand rate variability: is commonly expressed as a standard deviation.

dependent demand: demand estimates for components and raw materials are determined by demand estimates for finished items.

economic lot size: the lot size that balances holding costs against ordering or setup costs, so as to minimize the net cost of stocking inventory.

economic run size: an economic order quantity, when stock replenishment occurs through production rather than by purchase.

electronic scanner: a device that reads and interprets codes of stock tickets or product code.

end item: an item that is physically transferred out of the plant to the customer or next use as a completed unit.

excess cost: the unrecovered cost per unit of items that are left in inventory at the end of the period.

fixed-order-interval model: a model for inventory control that assumes orders will be place at fixed intervals of time.

hedge: holding inventory as a protection against future possible shortages or price increase.

holding cost: the monetary cost, per unit, of holding a unit of stock for a stated period of time.

Independent demand: demand estimates for an item of inventory that are not governed controlled by demand estimates for any other item.

inventory accounting system: a file that records all transactions relevant to inventory management, and from which reports are periodically processed and prepared.

lead time: the length of time between the placing of an order and receiving it.

lead-time variability: in those cases where the lead time is not known with certainty, lead time variability is measured by the standard deviation of the number of days in lead time.

lot sizing: deciding how many units to order.

optimal stocking level: the quantity for which the service level achieved equals or exceeds the ratio of shortage cost to the sum of shortage and excess cost (see formula in Key Ideas).

part: a component that is ultimately incorporated into an end item.

periodic inventory system: counting available stock at stated periods of t

pricebreak: where quantity discounting is practiced, a price break is a quantity at which a lower price is offered.

purchased parts: assembled or partially assembled components of a product, that have had extensive prior processing and are purchased from subcontractors or suppliers.

quantity discount: a reduction in price per unit, as an incentive for making purchases in larger quantities.

raw materials: components of a product that are used in the production process in bulk.

reorder point: a level of stock at which a replenishment is ordered.

safety stock: a stock level over and above average usage in lead time, maintained as a hedge against unusually high demand.

salvage value: the recoverable cost of an item that remains in inventory at the end of the period. This may be negative; there may be an additional cost to dispose of an item.

service level: defined as the probability of being able to satisfy any order during the normal order cycle from stock on hand.

setup cost: the monetary cost of each production or purchase order placed, not including the purchase price or the costs of direct charges for production.

shortage cost: the loss per unit incurred when demand exceeds supply of an item during a period.

single-period model: inventory model used when items in inventory cannot be carried over from one period to the next. Examples include items with limited shelf lives, and spare parts for machines.

standard normal distribution: the distribution of the standard normal statistic z, with a mean of zero and a variance of one.

stockout: running out of stock, before the next replenishment is received.

supplies: expendable purchased or manufactured elements that are not explicitly incorporated into end items, but are a necessary part of the operation of the plant.

two-bin system: a form of inventory management that is especially useful for C-type items: the first bin is used until it is depleted, then the second bin; when the second bin is opened, an order is placed for replenishment.

UPC system: using electronic scanners to read the *Universal Product Code* of every item purchased, in order to facilitate pricing, order preparation and continuous inventory management.

work-in-process inventory: partially completed, assembled or processed material that is not classified as an end item, purchased part, or raw material.

z-statistic: the random variable of the standard normal distribution.

TRUE/FALSE QUESTIONS

1. A pricebreak is an order quantity at which the purchaser is offered a lower price per unit by purchasing that quantity or more.

2. If the supplier does not offer quantity discounts, the unit cost will not directly affect the decision as to how many units to order, but may do so indirectly if the holding cost is measured as a percentage of the acquisition cost.

3. All reorder-point models assume constant lead time.

4. The two-bin system is a form of a reorder-point model

5. If the production rate in an economic-run-length model is very much larger than the consumption rate, the results are practically the same for economic run length and EOQ.

6. With the quantity-discount model, an order level might not be at an EOQ.

7. In a reorder-point model, the order amount is the EOQ.

8. The expected demand during lead time is greater than the difference between the reorder point and the safety stock.

9. In the single-period model, the service level is equal to the ratio of* "excess cost" divided by excess cost plus shortage cost."

10. In the single-period model, the greater the shortage cost relative to the excess cost, the larger the proportion of times that an order will be satisfied out of inventory.

11. In a discrete model, the actual number of units short must be an integer, while the expected number of units short does not have to be an integer.

12. If excess cost is greater than shortage cost, the optional stocking level will be less than expected demand.

MULTIPLE-CHOICE QUESTIONS

1. In a reorder model the daily demand rate is normally distributed with a mean of 50 units and a standard deviation of 5 units. The lead time is 9 days, Q = 500 units, and the leadtime service level (LTSL) is 90%. What are approximate values for SS and ROP?

     a. 19, 69
     b. 4, 69
     c. 6, 469
     d. 19, 469

2. If both the lead time and daily demand are constant, the ROP is equal to:

   a. Safety stock
   b. Expected demand minus safety stock.
   c. Expected demand plus safety stock.
   d. Daily demand times lead time.
   e. None of these.

3. Which one of the following statements is incorrect?

   a. The EOQ model and a reorder-point model are typically used together.
   b. A service level of 50 percent for lead time implies a 50 percent probability of running out of stock during lead time.
   c. If the mean and standard deviation are known and the distribution of demand is normal, the standard normal distribution with mean of zero and standard deviation of one is used to calculate service level.
   d. The reorder point in safety stock calculations is the EOQ minus safety stock."
   e. None of the above statements is incorrect.

4. Which inventory model does not provide an order quantity?

   a. EOQ.
   b. ROP
   c. Single-period.
   d. Fixed-interval
   e. Quantity discount

5. Which one of the following is not a reason for holding inventories?

   a. To decouple stages of production
   b. As a hedge against inflation
   c. To be able to buy in economical lot sizes
   d. To meet projected demand
   e. All are reasons

6. Which one of the following is not a requirement for effective inventory management?

   a. A system to keep track of inventory on hand
   b. A classification system for inventory items
   c. Reasonable estimates of holding and shortage costs
   d. Using an EOQ model for determining order quantity
   e. All are requirements

7. Which one of the following would not appear on a list of relevant costs of inventory?

   a. Shortage   b. Carrying   c. Order   d. Holding   e. Overtime

8. Which one of the following would not be included in a list of assumptions of the basic EOQ model?

    a. Lead time does not vary.
    b. There are no quantity discounts.
    c. Demand is spread uniformly throughout the year.
    d. Annual demand is a known quantity.
    e. All are assumptions.

9. Which one of the following is a true statement concerning the relationship between holding and ordering costs in the basic EOQ model?

    a. The two arc always equal at the EOQ.
    b. Holding cost is sometimes equal to ordering cost, and sometimes greater at the EOQ.
    c. Holding cost is sometimes equal to ordering cost, and sometimes less at the EOQ.
    d. Holding cost is always greater than ordering cost at the EOQ.
    e. There is no relationship between the two.

10. In the quantity-discount model, if the total cost curves all reach their minimum levels at the same order quantity, this implies that:

    a. holding costs are constant per unit.
    b. holding costs are a percentage of unit price.
    c. ordering costs are constant.
    d. ordering and setup costs are equal.
    e. none of these.

The following three questions refer to this information:

A bakery makes a limited number of croissants each day for sale in its coffee shop. The croissants cost $.35 each to produce and sell for $1.50 each. Leftover croissants are sold in the bakery the following day for $1.00 each, and all of those are sold.

11 The excess cost is:

    a. $.35
    b. $1.50
    c. $1.00
    d. $1.15
    e. $0

12. The salvage value is:

    a. $.35
    b. $1.50
    c. $1.00
    d. $1.15
    e. $0

13. The shortage cost is:

    a. $.35   b. $1.50   c. $1.00   d. 15   e. $0

14. Demand for a perishable item can be described by a uniform distribution that ranges from 18 units per period to 30 units per period. If shortage and excess costs are equal, the optimal stocking level would be:

    a. 18   b. 30   c. 24   d. impossible to say

PROBLEMS

1. An automobile manufacturer uses about 60,000 pairs of bumpers (front bumper and rear bumper) per year, which it orders from a supplier. The bumpers are used at a reasonably steady rate during the 240 working days per year. It costs $3.00 to keep one pair of bumpers in inventory for one month, and it costs $25.00 to place an order. A pair of bumpers costs $150.00.

    a. Which inventory model should be used here: the instantaneous model, the noninstantaneous model, or the single-period model? How do you know?
    b. Write the annual carrying cost function.
    c. Write the annual ordering cost function.
    d. Write the annual total cost function.
    e. What is the EOQ?
    f. What is the significance of the EOQ?
    g. What is the total annual expense of ordering the EOQ every time?
    h. How many orders will be placed per year?
    i. What is the total annual expense of ordering 600 pairs of bumpers every time? How much is saved per year by ordering the EOQ?

2. The Acme Bumper Co. manufactures bumpers for automobiles for one of the big three auto companies. About 60,000 pairs of bumpers (front bumper and rear bumper) are ordered by the auto company per year, at a price of $150.00 per pair. Pairs of bumpers are produced at a rate of about 400 per working day, and the company operates 240 days per year. The company manufactures other products, and it must set up the manufacturing system for a production order for pairs of bumpers, which costs $250.00. It costs $2.50 to store one pair of bumpers for one month.

    a. Which inventory model is appropriate here: the instantaneous model, the noninstantaneous model, or the single-period model? How do you know?
    b. Write the annual carrying cost function.
    c. Write the annual setup cost function.
    d. Write the annual total cost function.
    e. What is the EOQ?
    f. What is the significance of the EOQ?
    g. What is the total annual expense of producing the EOQ every time?
    h. How many production runs will be required per year?
    i. What is the total annual expense of manufacturing 3,000 pairs of bumpers per production run? How much is saved per year by producing the EOQ every time?

3. Use the data from Problem 1 to solve this problem, in addition to the data below. The supplier offers a system of quantity discounts, as follows:

Order Quantity	Cost per Pair	Discount
1 to 299 pairs	$150.00	0%
300 to 499 pairs	$150.00	4%
500 or more pairs	$150.00	10%

   a. Which inventory model is appropriate here: the instantaneous model, the quantity discount model, or the single-period model? How do you know9
   b. Write the annual total cost function for orders for less than 300 pairs.
   c. Write the annual total cost function for orders for 300 to 499 pairs.
   d. Write the total cost function for orders for at least 500 pairs.
   e. Draw the graph of the three total cost functions on a piece of rectangular coordinate paper.
   f. What is the EOQ?
   g. What is the total annual expense, including the purchasing cost of ordering the EOQ every time?

4. The purchasing agent has ascertained that the usage of floppy disks in the company is approximately normally distributed, with a mean of 30 per working day and a variance of 16. The company operates 240 days per year. Floppy disks are obtained from a supplier who is very reliable, when an order is placed (on day 0), it is always received on the ffth working day. The company cannot afford to run out of floppy disks, and the purchasing agent has established a 99.5 percent service level.

   a. Which reorder-point model is appropriate here, fixed lead time and variable demand, variable lead time and fixed demand, or variable demand and variable lead time?
   b. What is the mean usage during lead time?
   c. What is the standard deviation of the usage during lead time?
   d. What is the reorder point? Draw a diagram like the one in Figure 11-11 in your textbook.
   e. What is the significance of the reorder point?
   f. What is the safety stock?

5. The purchasing agent has ascertained that the employees use about 50 pencils per day, with very little variation. Pencils are ordered from a supplier whose shipments are irregular. They are normally distributed with a mean of 10 working days and a variance of 4. He has established a 95 percent service level for pencils.

   a. Which reorder-point model is appropriate here: variable demand and fixed lead tirne, fixed demand and variable lead time, or variable demand and variable lead time?
   b. What is the mean usage during lead time?
   c. What is the standard deviation of usage during lead time?
   d. What is the reorder point? Draw a diagram in the style of Figure 11-13 in your textbook.
   e. What is the significance of the reorder point?
   f. What is the safety stock?

6. The purchasing agent has ascertained that the usage of letterhead paper has an approximately normal distribution with a mean of 200 sheets per working day and a standard deviation of 13 sheets. Letterhead paper is ordered from a printer whose deliveries are variable, with a mean of 25 working days

and a variance of 4 working days. The purchasing agent has established a 99 percent service level for letterhead paper.

a. Which reorder-point model is appropriate here: variable demand and fixed lead time, fixed demand and variable lead time, or variable demand and variable lead time?
b. What is the mean usage during lead time?
c. What is the standard deviation of usage during lead time?
d. What is the reorder point? Draw a diagram in the style of Figure 11-13 in your textbook.
e. What is the significance of the reorder point?
f. What is the safety stock?

7. (One step beyond) The Whirlwind Appliance Store sells freezers for home use. These are large, upright units which resemble a refrigerator. They differ in operation in that the entire interior is kept at a freezing temperature. The store orders the freezers from the factory, which is very reliable and will deliver the order within one week (7 calendar days) almost invariably. Here are the volumes of sales for the past 50 weeks: 2, 1, 4, 5, 2, 0, 3, 6, 7, 3, 4, 2, 2, 4, 3, 5, 5, 1, 3, 6, 4, 5, 1, 0, 1, 4, 3, 5, 7, 6, 3, 5, 4, 1, 5, 5, 4, 5, 6, 4, 3, 2, 5, 4, 1, 5, 2, 5, 4. Future sales are expected to be similar. The store manager wishes to establish a 95 percent service level.

a. What is the frequency distribution for this data? Does it appear to be approximately normal?
b. What are the mean sales of freezers per week?
c. What is the empirical probability distribution?
d. What is the cumulative probability distribution?
e. What is the reorder point? (Hint: use the cumulative probability distribution.)
f. What is the safety stock?

8. An appliance store knows that the distribution of monthly sales of 50" TV sets is approximately normal with a mean of 6 sets and a standard deviation of 1.5 sets. The sets cost $2,750 each, and are priced at $4,000. The sets are ordered from the manufacturer on the 10th of the month (or the preceding business day), and there is a lead time of seven business days. There are 20 business days in a typical month. The manager wishes to maintain a 90 percent service level. The store is open six days a week and Sunday afternoons. On March 31, the store had five 50" TV sets on hand. Here is data regarding sales for the next three months:

Month	Sales
April	4 sets
May	8 sets
June	7 sets

a. Which inventory model is appropriate here: the fixed quantity and variable order interval model, the variable quantity and fixed order interval model, or the single period model?
b. How many sets should be ordered on April 10?
c. What will be the ending inventory on April 30?
d. How many sets should be ordered on May 10?
e. What will be the ending inventory on May 31?
f. How many sets should be ordered on June 10?

9. Use Table 11-3 in your testbook to answer these questions.

   a. What is the expected number of units short per cycle in Example 4?
   b. What is the implication of the expected number of units short in Problem 4?
   c. What is the expected number of units short in Problem 5?
   d. What is the significance of the expected number of units short in Problem 5?

10. Here is a list of 15 items, containing the annual volume of sales and the unit price, An A-B-C inventory system is to be established on the basis of the annual dollar value of each item. Classification A will contain about 60% of the dollar value; B will contain about 30%; and C will contain about 10%. Determine the items which belong in each category.

Item	Annual Volume	Unit Price	Annual Dollar Value
a	800	26	
b	300	20	
c	9,000	7	
d	7,000	5	
e	200	65	
f	100	83	
g	1,000	42	
h	1,800	6	
i.	450	18	
J	7,500	10	
k	350	9	
l	700	28	
m	500	95	
n	750	30	
o	900	72	

   a. Determine the annual dollar value for each item and the total annual dollar value.
   b. Which items should be assigned to the A category? To the B category? To the C category?

11. A delicatessen sells potato salad from trays in the cooler cabinet; the salesperson packs the salad into cardboard containers according to the customers' orders. The supervisor prepares one batch of salad in the morning and disposes of any leftover salad at closing time. Potato salad sellls for $1.49 per pound, and costs $0.80 to prepare. Sales of potato salad are believed to be normally distributed with a mean of 60 pounds per day and a variance of 256.

   a. Which inventory model is appropriate here: The single-period model, the instantaneous model, or the quantity-discount model? How do you know?
   b. What is the shortage cost, C.?
   c. What is the excess cost, C.?
   d. What is the service level?
   e. How large a batch should the supervisor mix up in the morning.

12. Kerey White operates a booth which sells specialty merchandise at the State Fair. This year she is planning to sell t-shirts which are inscribed:

STATE FAIR

The price of the t-shirts will be $25.00. Ms. White buys plain white t-shirts from a factory at a cost of $864 per gross (144 shirts), with a 3% discount for payment within 10 days, which she always takes. Ms. White inscribes the design on the t-shirts, herself, and estimates that her labor is worth $4.00 per shirt. Unsold T-shirts are useless, but can be sold to a scrap dealer for $0.16 per pound; there are eight t-shirts in a pound. The number of t-shirts which will be sold at the State Fair is, of course, unknown. But, based on previous experience, Ms. White estimates that the mean sales are 3 gross, and that the probability of selling more than 3 gross decreases as the quantity increases.

a. Which inventory model should be used here-the instantaneous model, the quantity discount model, the single period model?

b. Which probability distribution should be used here?

c. What is the shortage cost, C_s?

d. What is the excess cost, C_e?

e. What is the service level?

f. How many t-shirts should Ms. White prepare (in gross)?

g. Estimate Ms. White's profits for your answer in f.

12 - Aggregate Planning

KEY IDEAS

1. Aggregate planning is intermediate range planning of general levels of employment and output to balance supply and demand.

2. The term "aggregate" implies that planning is done for groups of products, or product types (i.e., product "families") rather than for specific or individual products.

3. Planners take into account projected demand, capacity, and costs of various options in devising an aggregate plan.

4. Among the variables available to planners are adjustments in output rate, employment level, overtime/undertime, and subcontracting.

5. The goal of aggregate planning is to achieve output objectives at the lowest possible cost.

6. Due to the nature of aggregate planning, it is seldom possible to structure a plan that is guaranteed optimal. Instead, planners usually resort to trial-and-error methods to achieve an acceptable plan.

7. Among the strategies aggregate planners might try are to:

   a. maintain a level work force and meet demand variations in some other manner.
   b. maintain a steady rate of output, and use some combination of inventories and subcontracting to meet demand variations.
   c. match demand period by period with some combination of work force variations, subcontracting, and inventories.
   d. use a combination of decision variables.

   Note: It is unlikely that planners would attempt tomatch demand period by period by vary employment levels alone because that would tend to be costly, disruptive, and result in low employee morale.

8. Choosing a strategy usually depends on the cost entailed and company policy.

9. In order to effectively plan, in addition to knowledge of company policy, estimates of the following items must be available to planners:

   a. Demand for each period
   b. Capacity for each period
   c. Costs (regular time, overtime, subcontracting, backorders, etc.)

10. In order to translate an aggregate plan into meaningful terms for production, it must be disaggregated (i.e., broken down into specific product requirements) to determine labor, material, and inventory requirements.

11. A master schedule indicates the desired quantity and timing of deliveries. A master production schedule takes into account planned production, as well as on-hand inventory.

12. There are three basic inputs to the master schedule: Beginning inventory, forecasts for each period in the schedule, and customer orders. Outputs of the scheduling process include projected inventory, production requirements, and the amount of uncommitted inventory, which is referred to as available-to-promise (ATP) inventory.

GLOSSARY

aggregation: forming groups of similar commodities, represented by a single common unit of measurement, without identifying specific product names.

available-to-promise (ATP) inventory: uncommitted inventory.

chase strategy: adjusting capacity to match demand period by period.

cumulative graph: a graph that displays accumulated output and sales over a period of time such as a year, showing where the periods of shortage and surplus occur.

disaggregation: breaking down an aggregate plan into specific products.

intermediate planning: production planning covering a period of from two to twelve months.

long-range planning: planning for production, covering a period of time of more than twelve months.

master schedule: shows the desired quantity and timing of end items over the schedule horizon.

master production schedule: shows the quantity and timing of planned production, taking into account desired delivery quantities as well as inventory on-hand.

overtime: working time for an employee beyond the normal 40-hour week.

pure strategy: a strategy with a single focal point (e.g., maintain a level work force).

regular time: working time during the normal 40-hour workweek.

short-range planning: planning for production, covering a period of time less than two months.

spreadsheet: a budgeting and scheduling matrix, with the rows representing categories of production or activity and the columns representing time periods.

subcontracting: permitting a portion of the production activity to be carried on by an outside vendor, under a contractual agreement as to price and production levels.

TRUE/FALSE QUESTIONS

1. Aggregate planning is long-range planning (2 years or more) for large products.

2. Aggregate planning is concerned with both the quantity and timing of anticipated demand.

3. Overtime is not considered as a variable in aggregate planning.

4. Keeping a constant level of production in every time division of a planning period (month, week, etc.) is usually the best way to perform aggregate planning.

5. The cost of either a backlog, or a large inventory, or of subcontracting production, is usually very nearly proportional to the number of units involved.

6. The transportation method of linear programming is used differently in developing an aggregate plan as described in Chapter 12, than in solving the conventional transportation model, as described in Chapter 8S.

7. Disaggregating an aggregate plan involves creating a master schedule for production of the end items included in the aggregate plan.

8. A "chase" strategy involves matching demand and capacity in each period.

9. Available-to-promise inventory is uncommitted inventory.

10. A master schedule and a master production schedule are similar, but not exactly the same.

MULTIPLE-CHOICE QUESTIONS

1. All of the following are reasonable strategies aggregate planners might try except:

    a. maintain a level work force and meet demand variations in some other manner.
    b. maintain a steady rate of output, and use some combination of inventories and subcontracting to meet demand variations.
    c. match demand period by period with some combination of work force variations, subcontracting, and inventories.
    d. vary the workforce period by period to match demand.

2. In order to effectively plan, estimates of each of the following items must be available to planners except:

    a. Inventory lot sizes.
    b. Demand for each period
    c. Capacity for each period
    d. Costs (regular time, overtime, subcontracting, backorders, etc.)

3. Which of the following is not a technique used for aggregate planning?

    a. Linear programming
    b. Simulation
    c. Trial-and-error charting
    d. Double smoothing

4. Which term is most closely associated with disaggregation?

    a. Backorders
    b. Overtime
    c. Subcontracting
    d. Master schedule
    e. Trial and error

5. Which one of the following is not a basic option for altering capacity?

    a. Hire and fire workers
    b. Use overtime
    c. Use subcontracting
    d. Use backorders
    e. All are options for altering capacity

6. All of the following are basic options for altering demand except:

    a. pricing.
    b. promotion.
    c. backorders.
    d. inventories.
    e. all are "demand" options.

7. Which statement is false?

    a. Aggregate planners are concerned with the quantity and timing of expected demand.
    b. The basic problem of aggregate planning is balancing supply and demand.
    c. Aggregate planners rely heavily on the master schedule to guide their efforts.
    d. All of these statements are true.

8. Which one of these is not a master scheduling input?

    a. Forecasts
    b. Planned inventory
    c. Customer orders
    d. Beginning inventory

9. Which one of these is not an output of a master production schedule?

    a. Production requirements
    b. Projected inventory
    c. Customer orders
    d. Available-to-promise inventory

PROBLEMS

1. The Snow Mountain Ski Company produces pairs of skis. Its business is highly seasonal, and for the next fiscal year it has the following forecasts of the demand for pairs of its skis for each month. The fiscal year runs from July 1 to June 30.

Month	Forecast	Month	Forecast
July	125	January	500
August	150	February	450
September	300	March	200
October	350	April	150
November	400	May	50
December	600	June	25
			3,300

The company has a beginning inventory on July 1 of 50 pairs of skis. The company has a capacity of 16 pairs of skis per eight-hour shift, and it works one shift per day, for 48 fiveday weeks per year.

Here are financial data on producing, storing, and selling skis.

Variable cost during the day shift (8 AM to 5 PM): $60.00 per pair
Variable cost during the night shift (5 PM to 2 AM): $70.00 per pair
Cost of storing skis for one month: $2.00 per pair in the average inventory
Cost of acquiring skis from a supplier: $64.00 per pair
The selling price of skis: $150.00 per pair

Skis may not be backordered, since they must be available during the skiing season. In case of shortages, the company does have options, however. It may schedule half of a night shift (four hours, with a capacity of 8 pairs of skis); or it may schedule a full night shift (8 hours with a capacity of 16 pairs of skis); or it may purchase from an outside supplier. In the event of surplus production, the company may reduce the day shift to half-time (4 hours per day, with a capacity of 8 pairs of skis). It will not close the plant entirely.

a. Construct an aggregate planning schedule for the fiscal year in the style of Example 1 of Chapter 12 of your textbook. Assume that the company schedules one 8-hour shift per working day with no outside purchases. Unsold pairs of skis will be kept in inventory.
b. How many sales will be lost under the plan in a above?
c. How much gross margin will be made per month under the plan in a? For the entire year9 (Gross margin = Revenue - Cost of goods sold - Storage costs.)
d. It is proposed to schedule half of the night shift beginning in the month in which a shortage appears in the schedule in a (for four weeks) and continuing until the month in which the shortage disappears (for two weeks). Prepare the aggregate planning schedule in the style of Example 1 in your textbook.
e. How many sales will be lost under the plan in part d?
f. How much gross margin will be made under the plan in d per month? For the entire year? Compare this amount to the gross margin in part c.
g. What is one obvious improvement that could be made in the plan in part d.
h. What other options might be explored?

2. Use the data in Problem 1 to .draw a cumulative graph of demand and the inventory, by months, in the style of Figure 12-3 in your textbook, for the plan in la.

3. Use the data in Problem 1 to answer this question. ForTnulate the production problem in the style of the transportation model, as shown in Table 11-4 of your textbook. Construct the table for the months of October, November, December, and January. In each period the alternatives are to produce skis during the day shift, or during the night shift, or both. Backorders are not allowed. You may ignore the beginning and ending inventory. Do not solve.

4. Here is information on the Caribou Beer Company regarding sales of its six-packs for the period of May and June. It is now April 30, and the inventory contains 60 six-packs. The forecasts for each week of the period are given below, along with the firm orders.

Week	ending	Forecast	Orders
May	6	500	400
	13	500	450
	20	500	450
	27	500	1,000
June	3	550	500
	10	550	500
	17	600	600
	24	600	650

Six-packs are produced in lots of 1,200, once a week, if needed.

a. Construct the Master Production Schedule for May and June.
b. When should the Production Manager plan on producing more six-packs?

13 - Material Requirements Planning

KEY IDEAS

1. Manufacturing is performed to meet anticipated needs for future delivery of end items to customers, according to a master schedule that summarizes both the firm orders and the forecasted needs, and translates these into requirements at specified time "buckets" (frequently defined as calendar weeks), for a specified planning period.

2. An end item is a hierarchy of components, assemblies, subassemblies, finished goods and semifinished goods, some of them purchased from outside vendors and some assembled inside the plant. The relationships between elements at different levels are exhibited in a bill of materials (BOM) or its graphical equivalent, a product-structure tree.

3. Low-level coding of a product-structure tree puts a given type of assembly at the same level in the tree, no matter what levels the "parents" may be at, a parent is the next higher level of assembly.

4. MRP releases either Internal production orders or external purchase orders for components, assemblies, subassemblies, etc., time phased so as to permit arrival of goods at the next higher level of assembly when they are needed.

5. The three principal computerized files in an MRP system are a master schedule, a bill of materials and an inventory record. The inventory record contains, for each element: (a) the lead time, safety stock and lot size, and for every time bucket in the planning period, (b) the gross requirements, available quantities, net requirements, scheduled receipts from past orders and planned releases of orders for future production.

6. For elements that go into multiple parents, MRP "pegs" (traces) requirements to specific parents. Low-level coding of the product-structure tree facilitates these assignments.

7. An MRP schedule must be periodically reviewed and updated. The two principal types of review are regeneration and net change. Regeneration periodically revises the plan, recording all changes, and net change makes the changes as they are needed.

8. MRP generates useful information and reports for a variety of management purposes, but there is some potentially useful information it cannot produce. For example, it cannot show which departments are to be assigned a specific production workload. In order to insure that the plan is consistent with departmental and plant workload capacities, it should be tested for realism by being simulated several times with different proposed master schedules, to see which schedule yields the best results.

9. Part-period balancing is a technique for setting order sizes for a component or an end item in a situation of dynamic dependent demands, such as is usually associated with MRP, based on some of the significant theoretical considerations that underlie independent inventory systems. Recall that in Chapter 11, it is shown that the minimum stocking cost for an item is attained when the EOQ or economic lot size is set at a level such that the total of the holding costs is equal to the total of order or setup

costs. Part-period balancing attempts to satisfy this same objective by setting the order interval and the size of an order such that the total order cost is equal to the total holding costs.

10. Capacity Requirements Planning is used in conjunction with MRP. It helps to insure that the MRP production plans are realistic, and that they are consistent with management objectives of smooth flow of materials, continuity of the labor force and balanced workloads between departments. The resulting revisions of the MRP schedules may affect either the master schedule, the rough-cut capacity plan, or the overall production plan, or a combination of several of these plans.

11. MRP II systems actively integrate marketing and finance into rough-cut capacity planning, capacity requirements planning and setting up MRP master schedules.

GLOSSARY

assembly-time chart: displays for an end item, the time phasing of how components are integrated into levels of assembly, including both the lead time and the next level of assembly for every component.

available: inventory on hand, plus scheduled receipts that are available for use within the current time bucket.

bill of materials (BOM): the structural relationship between all the components of an assembly or end item, showing the quantities of components that are needed to assemble one unit of the end item.

capacity requirements planning: adjusting and modifying MRP plans to sustain a free flow of materials and effective utilization of the labor force and plant.

component: any ingredient of a product; this could include, for example, a raw material, subassembly, assembly or end item.

dependent demand: demand for an item derived from the demand for some item or items at a higher level of assembly.

exploding a BOM: printing a BOM, showing all components and their levels.

frozen master schedule: a firm master schedule not subject to modification.

gross material requirements: required minimum size of a lot to be dispatched to the next higher level of assembly.

inventory records file: a record maintained for every component, assembly, subassembly, raw material or end item, of planned and actual order releases and material receipts, and of the customary lead times.

level: in a product-structure tree, a code that assigns a stage number of an assembly, showing how many stages there are between the component and the end item: 0 for end item, 1 or first level, 2 for second level, etc.

level-by-level processing: a search for all the components of a given type at the same level of assembly.

load report: a bar chart that shows planned and actual production releases over a given span of time.

lot-for-lot ordering: MRP with planned-order releases and planned-order receipts matching net requirements exactly.

lot sizing: determining an order size.

low-level coding: a bill of materials or product-structure tree drawn so that all units of a given type of component are at the same level of assembly.

lumpy demand: sporadic, uneven demand resulting in nonuniform batch sizes and usage rates.

MRPII (Manufacturing Resource Planning): an integrated management information system that has all organizational units operating together as a team to develop the production plan, and set schedules that are consistent with the plant capacities.

master schedule: a schedule that specifies the quantity and timing of end items that are to be produced.

net-change system: MRP that is updated continuously, every transaction is posted by the computer, and the changes in available quantities and requirements are made in real time.

net material requirements: the difference between gross material requirements and amount onhand.

part-period balancing: a technique for lot sizing that incorporates economic lot sizes for all components into production planning, based on setting lot sizes such that total holding cost is approximately the same as total setup cost.

pegging: tracing a given set of gross requirements, identifying all of the parents that generated those requirements.

planned-order receipt: a lot of material to be received, based on a prior planned-order release.

planned-order release: a production order for a lot of material, placed a lead time ahead of the planned-order receipt of that lot.

primary reports: reports prepared based on standard MRP parameters, such as planned-order schedules, order releases and changes to planned orders.

product-structure tree: a graphical representation of a bill of materials showing at each level of assembly the number of components of each type that are the ingredients for the assembly at the next level.

regenerative system: MRP that is updated at regular intervals of time.

safety stock: stock maintained over and above that needed to satisfy net requirements. safety time: additional time allowance to compensate for variable lead time.

scheduled receipts: lots scheduled for arrival that are available for use within the current time period; scheduled receipts differ, for example, from planned-order receipts in that scheduled receipts represent executed (instead of "planned") order releases.

secondary reports: reports such as performance control, planning and exception reports, that can be prepared from MRP data.

simulation: computerized studies of the mathematical models of the plant operation, systematically varying the parameters so as to determine the effects of changes in these parameters upon costs, schedules or profits.

stacked lead time: the cumulative lead time required to complete the assembly of all components and subassemblies that go into an end item.

time bucket: a unit of time (e.g.. a week), for purposes of measuring the duration of an MRP operation, such as receiving or releasing an order, or the lead time.

time fences: A series of time intervals in which restrictions are placed on changes to the master schedule. The nearest time fence is the most restrictive.

time phasing: scheduling of the completion of a batch of material, to arrive at the next higher level of assembly, just ahead of the time this material is incorporated into the assembly.

TRUE/FALSE QUESTIONS

1. A departmental load report is one of the primary reports of an MRP system.

2. A bucket in MRP refers to a time period, such as a week, two-week period, etc.

3. Net requirements = Gross requirements - Scheduled receipts - Projected onhand.

4. Low-level coding puts the components and raw materials at the bottom of a product structure tree.

5. Level-by-level processing scans the inventory-status record file in order to determine in which time bucket the scheduled requirements are to be placed.

6. Because of the pyramid relationship for all components in an MRP system, it is appropriate to provide safety stocks at all levels, since this would help to reduce the setup costs.

7. Regeneration as a means of updating an MRP is a better way to update an unstable MRP than net change.

8. There is no relationship between MRP and plant capacity utilization.

9. Safety stock is generally avoided in MRP because it can result in unnecessary inventory buildup.

10. The three principal computerized files maintained for an MRP system include the bill of materials, the product-structure tree and an inventory record.

11. An inventory record file is maintained in MRP for every raw material, component, assembly, subassembly or end item.

12. MRP has been replaced by MRPII. .

13. Lead time is the time between placing an order and receiving the material, it makes no difference whether the order is one to purchase the material or a production order.

14. An MRP worksheet is essentially a "worksheet" showing all the various requirements on hand, planned releases and planned receipts for every item and for every time bucket covered by the current master schedule.

15. In part-period balancing, the size of an order and the length of the order interval are set so that the total of the order costs is approximately equal to the total of the holding costs.

MULTIPLE-CHOICE QUESTIONS

1. The principal files that are incorporated into a computerized MRP system are:

    a. inventory record, master schedule, BOM, MRP computer program.
    b. inventory record, master file, part-period balancing program.
    c. end items, components, and load reports.
    d. capacity requirements planning file, master schedule, inventory record.
    e. MRP computer program, master schedule, capacity requirements planning file.

2. Which of the following statements concerning the level of assembly is correct?

    a. Gross requirements are derived from the planned-order releases at the next higher level.
    b. Gross requirements are derived from the planned-order releases at the next lower level.
    c. Gross requirements are derived from the planned-order receipts at the next higher level.
    d. Gross requirements are derived from the planned-order receipts at the next lower level.
    e. None of the above is correct.

3. Which one of these would not be a possible lot size?

    a. EOQ.
    b. Gross requirements.
    c. Net requirements.
    d. An amount less than net requirements.
    e. All are possible lot sizes.

4. Linking a part with a specific parent is referred to as:

   a. lot sizing.
   b. pegging.
   c. kanban.
   d. capacity planning.
   e. leveling.

5. A list of all parts and materials needed to assemble one unit of a product is called:

   a. a master schedule.
   b. a kanban.
   c. an inventory record file.
   d. MRP.
   e. a bill of materials.

6. Which phrase or term is most clearly associated with the acronym BOM?

   a. Master schedule
   b. Net requirements
   c. Scheduled receipts
   d. Product-structure tree
   e. Inventory record file

7. Which of the following correctly describes the computation of net requirements?

   a. Gross requirements - Scheduled receipts
   b. Gross requirements - On hand + Scheduled receipts
   c. Gross requirements - Scheduled receipts - On hand
   d. Gross requirements - Scheduled receipts + Planned order receipts

PROBLEMS

1. Here are the parts list and the lead time for product TT.

Component/Subassembly	Number Required	Lead time
Product TT		
Subassembly A	2	1 week
Component B	1	2 weeks
Subassembly A		
Component B	3	2 weeks
Component C	1	1 week
Component D	2	1 week

The master schedule for product T is:

Week Number	1	2	3	4	5	6
Quantity	0	0	0	25	50	75

   a. Construct the product-structure tree for product T.
   b. Determine the quantity of each subassembly and component that will be required.
   c. Construct the time-phased plan for each subassembly and component in the style of Figure 13-9 in your textbook; four of them will be required.

2. Use the data in Problem 1 to solve this problem. During the fourth week, an equipment breakdown delayed the production of component D for one week. Thus, the 300 units which were to go into production in the fourth week and be received in the fifth week must be postponed to the fifth and sixth weeks.

   a. Construct a new master schedule for the fourth and subsequent weeks.
   b. Construct new time-phased plans for each subassembly and component for the fourth and subsequent weeks.

3. Here is the usage schedule for component K.

Period	1	2	3	4	5	6
Quantity	60	50	80	70	30	50

It costs $500 to set up the equipment to produce K. and it costs $2 to store one unit of K for one period.

   a. What is the cumulative demand schedule?
   b. What is the economic part-period (EPP)?
   c. What is the lot size (based on the EPP)?

Master Schedule	Week	1	2	3	4	5	6	7	8
	Quantity								

	1	2	3	4	5	6	7	8
Gross requirements								
Scheduled receipts								
Projected on hand								
Net requirements								
Planned-order receipts								
Planned-order releases								

	1	2	3	4	5	6	7	8
Gross requirements								
Scheduled receipts								
Projected on hand								
Net requirements								
Planned-order receipts								
Planned-order releases								

	1	2	3	4	5	6	7	8
Gross requirements								
Scheduled receipts								
Projected on hand								
Net requirements								
Planned-order receipts								
Planned-order releases								

	1	2	3	4	5	6	7	8
Gross requirements								
Scheduled receipts								
Projected on hand								
Net requirements								
Planned-order receipts								
Planned-order releases								

14 - Just-in-Time Systems

KEY IDEAS

1. Just-in-time is an approach to repetitive manufacturing that emphasizes continual effort to remove inefficiency and waste from the production process. It is the aspect of lean production that is concerned with the flow of material through the system.

2. JIT systems achieve important benefits through the use of small lot sizes, high quality, and a team approach.

3. The key elements of a JIT system are listed and explained in the textbook.

4. An important feature of JIT systems is the use of a pull system rather than a push system to move work through a system. Under a push system, work is moved along as it is completed; under a pull system, downstream operations signal preceding operations when they want/need work. Hence, each operation dictates need to the preceding operation; work proceeds in response to demand of following operations.

5. JIT is different than the traditional approach to manufacturing. Important aspects of this are outlined in Table 14-1 in the textbook.

6. Despite the benefits of JIT, conversion to JIT requires considerable planning. See the discussion of this and possible obstacles in the textbook.

7. JIT can also be applied to services, although the majority of applications have been in manufacturing.

STUDY TIPS

There are many elements in a JIT system. A good way to study this chapter is to make a list of the elements, and then write a few sentences about each, explaining what it is (if it is not obvious from your list) and why it is important for a JIT system to have it.

GLOSSARY

andon: a system of lights used to warn of problems or potential problems in a JIT system.

brainstorming: collective, free-thinking approach to problem solving.

delayed differentiation: used when two or more (typically) assembled products are basically the same except for a relatively few components that can be added near the end of production; the basic module is produced without adding the final components. This permits great flexibility and quick response to demand for specific end items.

just-in-time system: an approach to repetitive manufacturing that emphasizes small lot sizes. minimizing waste, high quality, quick setups, and worker involvement in problem solving.

kanban: a signal that authorizes movement or work on parts or material, often in the form of a kanban card.

multifunctional workers: workers who are trained to handle a variety of production, setup and minor repair tasks.

preventive maintenance: emphasizes keeping equipment in good working order and replacing parts which have a tendency to fail before they actually fail.

pull system: work moves through a system whereby work is moved only when it is requested by the next workstation in line.

push system: each station pushes the work along as it completes its set of tasks.

TRUE/FALSE QUESTIONS

1. JIT is basically a pull system.

2. JIT production systems emphasize a fixed, steady rate of production.

3. JIT lot sizes are small compared to those in more traditional systems.

4. Converting suppliers to JIT is one of the first steps in converting to a JIT system.

5. The kanban approach is simpler than MRP II.

6. A goal of JIT is increased flexibility in the ability to change the production mix.

7. Andon refers to a system of warning lights.

MULTIPLE-CHOICE QUESTIONS

1. Which one of these is not generally associated with JIT?

    a. Low inventories
    b. Preventive maintenance
    c. A push system
    d. Problem solving
    e. A fixed, steady rate of production

2. Which one of these is not usually associated with JIT?

   a. Preventive maintenance
   b. Lot-for-lot orders
   c. Multifunctional workers
   d. Process layout
   e. Quick setups

3. Which one of these is not generally thought of in conjunction with JIT

   a. Reduced space requirements
   b. Waiting lines
   c. Management by consensus
   d. Short lead times
   e. High quality

4. Which of these groups would be least likely to resist conversion to a JIT system?

   a. Workers
   b. Management
   c. Customers
   d. Vendors

5. Which one is unrelated to problem solving in a JIT system?

   a. A temporary increase in inventory
   b. Andon
   c. Brainstorming
   d. Worker involvement
   e. All are related

PROBLEMS

1. In the course of manufacturing sunglasses, workstation K must attach the lenses to the frame; lenses come from workstation J. These are the nonprescription type of sunglasses which may be bought off of the rack at the drugstore and this problem is concerned only with the lenses, not the frames. Management has scheduled the production of 160 sunglasses per 8-hour shift. Workstation J requires 3.0 minutes to produce a pair of lenses (left and right); once in a while a pair of lenses is defective, and management allows .20 for inefficiencies. The finished lenses are placed in containers of a dozen each. When workstation K opens a container of lenses, it sends the kanban back to station J which takes 15 minutes, it takes 15 minutes for a container to be transported from station J to station K.

   a. What is the value of D?
   b. What is the value of T?
   c. What is the value of X?
   d. What is the value of C?
   e. How many kanban cards (or containers) should be used in this system?

2. (One step beyond) One step in the manufacture of tennis rackets consists of weaving the cross strings into the head of the racket. This task requires a high level of skill and experience, and is slow. In workstation G, six skilled weavers work on tennis rackets; on the average, it takes 45 minutes for one weaver to weave a tennis racket. The head of the racket is produced by a supplier who has been certified; the supplier is located in Portland. OR, while the manufacturer is located in Los Angeles, CA, a distance of about 1,000 miles. Tennis racket heads are shipped by truck from Portland to Los Angeles; each truckload contains six dozen heads and the trip takes two days, i.e., the truck leaves Portland on the morning of the first day (say Monday) and arrives in Los Angeles on the evening of the second day (Tuesday); the racket heads are available for weaving on the morning of the third day (Wednesday). When any weaver opens the shipment, the kanban is sent to the computer room, where an operator faxes the order instantaneously to the supplier's computer; the order will be on the road the next business day. The six weavers work an eight-hour shift with two 15-minute coffee breaks. Production is continuous; with the current popularity of tennis, the firm can sell all of the rackets it can produce, and is in the happy position of having back orders. The weaving jobs are well done, and management allows .05 for inefficiencies and errors.

    a.   What Is the value of D?
    b.   What is the value of V
    c.   What is the value of X?
    d.   What is the value of C?
    e.   How many kanbans should be in use?
    f.   Suppose that highway construction forces the trucks to take a detour which delays the arrival in Los Angeles one day. What effect will this have on the number of kanban cards?
    g.   After consultation with the supplier, It is decided to experiment with larger shipments of tennis racket heads. A larger truck is rented which can carry eight dozen heads. What effect will this have on the number of kanban cards?
    h.   Suppose one of the weavers retires. An apprentice must be hired and trained. During the training period, the average time required to weave a head is estimated at 60 minutes. What effect will this have on the number of kanban cards?
    i.   During the trial period, management anticipates that the rate of defective weaving jobs will increase, and the allowance is raised to .20. What effect will this have on the number of kanban cards?

14S - Materials Management and Purchasing

KEY IDEAS

1. Materials are the physical items (raw materials, purchased parts, fuel, tools, etc.) that are used during the production process. Materials management is concerned with the purchase, movement, and storage of materials, and with the distribution of finished goods.

2. Purchasing is a subset of materials management; it is responsible for obtaining the material inputs for the operating system. Purchasing objectives are to determine (from operations) the quality, quantity and timing requirements; to obtain the best possible price; to maintain good relations with vendors, to maintain sources of supply; and to be knowledgeable on prices, new products and new services.

3. The purchasing function should periodically perform value analysis on parts and materials to reduce costs and/or improve the performance of purchased items. (See Table 14S-1 in your textbook for an overview of the value analysis process.)

4. From time to time, the question of whether to make or to buy an item comes up. There is a list of nine factors in the textbook that are usually taken into account.

5. Evaluating sources of supply (vendor analysis) involves looking at price, quality, services provided, location, inventory policies of suppliers, and the degree to which a supplier is willing to be flexible.

6. In recent years, there has been a shift in the way buyers view suppliers; more and more, vendors are being viewed as partners rather than as adversaries. (See Table 14S-2 in your textbook for a summary of this.)

7. Bar codes enable companies to monitor goods during production and distribution.

8. JIT II is a philosophy that empowers suppliers to assume responsibilities typically done by a company's own buyers. This may involve planning, order transactions (i.e., ordering), and dealing with problems that relate to the supplier's products.

GLOSSARY

bar code: patterns of lines, spaces, numbers, and symbols attached to labels that can be electronically scanned. They facilitate monitoring items during production and distribution.

distribution: involves the shipping of output from a company through a distribution system to warehouses, retail customers or final customers.

logistics: the movement of materials within a production facility and the handling of incoming and outgoing shipments of goods and materials.

materials: physical items used during the production process. Includes not only parts and raw materials, but also tools, fuels, forms, and anything else that supports the production process.

materials management: concerned with purchasing, storage, and movement of materials during the production process and with distribution of finished goods.

purchasing cycle: the main steps are (1) a requisition is received for a purchase, (2) purchasing selects a supplier, (3) an order is placed, (4) the order is monitored, and (5) the order is received.

value analysis: involves examination of the function of purchased parts and materials in an effort to reduce cost and/or improve performance of those items.

vendor analysis: evaluating sources of supply in terms of price, quality, services offered, location, inventory policy, and flexibility.

TRUE/FALSE QUESTIONS

1. Materials management focuses exclusively on raw materials and purchased parts.

2. Purchasing is responsible for obtaining material inputs for the operating system.

3. The one objective of purchasing is to obtain the best possible price.

4. Value analysis involves choosing a source of supply.

5. Negotiation is a win-lose confrontation.

6. Centralized purchasing means that purchasing is handled by one special department.

7. Nearness of supplier can be an important factor in choosing a supplier.

8. Distribution is often managed by the marketing function in an organization.

9. In JIT II systems, suppliers may order for their customers.

MULTIPLE-CHOICE QUESTIONS

1. Which one of these is not usually a consideration in make or buy analysis?

   a. capacity
   b. cost
   c. quality
   d. lead time
   e. all are considerations.

2. Which is not a factor in vendor analysis?

    a. location
    b. quality
    c. price
    d. inventory policy of supplier
    e. all are factors

3. Which statement most closely describes negotiated purchasing?

    a. It is often a win-lose confrontation.
    b. The main goal is to obtain the lowest possible price.
    c. Each negotiation is an isolated transaction.
    d. It is used for special purchasing situations.

4. Which is true about purchasing relative to materials management?

    a. Materials management is another name for purchasing.
    b. Materials management is a subset of purchasing.
    c. Purchasing is a subset of materials management.
    d. Purchasing is being taken over by materials management.

5. Which one is not usually a benefit of decentralized purchasing?

    a. attention to local needs
    b. quantity discounts
    c. quicker response
    d. ncarness to supplier

15 - Scheduling

KEY IDEAS

1. Production control scheduling involves the timing of specific operations for both workers and machines.

2. The chief objective of scheduling is to utilize manpower and machines to produce goods and services when they are required and to balance the workload so as to reduce costs, idle time, and excess inventories.

3. The hierarchy of decisions in production/operations is: capacity planning for long-term decisions on plant size; aggregate or intermediate planning for general use of facilities, personnel, subcontracting and purchased material; and detailed scheduling of manpower and machines.

4. Material requirements planning (MRP) and capacity requirements planning (CRP) are useful for batch processing with dependent sequential demands. They do not necessarily tell which personnel or machines will work on specific jobs.

5. Each step of production results in a narrower and better defined set of constraints. Scheduling decisions must take all of these constraints into account.

6. Flow systems such as processes and high-volume assembly lines are dedicated to single products or services, with possible variations in sizes, models or mixtures. Scheduling flow systems frequently involves line balancing; but disruptions to the system such as fluctuations in demand or machine breakdowns must be allowed for.

7. Intermediate volume systems have interrupted production schedules. The EOQ models yield lot sizes that minimize setup and inventory costs for a single product with independent demand, but don't always do the job for multiple products.

8. The assignment model of linear programming does one-to-one matching of operators to machines by an easy-to-use algorithm that assigns employee-machine pairs according to the principle of "least relative cost."

9. Job shops typically use Gantt charts. Two specific types are load charts and schedule charts. The load chart shows loading and idle times for a group of machines or departments. Schedule charts show the current status of every job, along with planned and actual starting and ending dates.

10. Job shop scheduling is more complicated than flow systems. Priority rules are used for sequencing in job shops. Different priority rules, first come first served (FCFS), shortest processing time (SPT), due date (DD), slack per operation (S/0), and RUSH, may come up with different sequences. The effectiveness of a rule is measured by average completion time, average lateness, or average number of jobs in the system at any given time.

11. Priority scheduling rules can be local or global. Local rules take into account information pertaining to a single workstation; global rules take into consideration information pertaining to multiple workstations.

12. Johnson's rule minimizes throughput (makespan) time for a group of jobs to be processed in the same order at two work centers by a variation of the SPT rule.

13. Examples of scheduling in service systems are appointments such as in doctors' offices, simple reservations as in restaurants, and computerized scheduling from multiple sources as in airline reservations.

GLOSSARY

assignment method: in situations where there is a one-to-one matching of resources (e.g., workers) available to equipment or facilities (e.g., machines). the assignment method is an efficient alternative for small problems to the simplex method of linear programming for obtaining the optimum (least cost or greatest revenue) one-to-one assignment of resources to equipment or facilities. See also relative cost.

DD (due date): a sequencing rule that gives the highest priority to the job with the earliest due date.

FCFS (first come first served): the sequencing rule that gives the highest priority to the job or customer that arrives at the facility first. FCFS is frequently thought of as being the "fairest" method of assignment for retail or service establishments such as super-markets and automobile service stations, but it cannot be used when there are emergencies, such as in hospitals, and it is frequently less efficient than alternative scheduling systems for job shop production.

Gantt chart: a type of chart designed by Henry L. Gantt, one of the pioneers of scientific management, that shows the progress of a set of jobs over a period of time, and visually displays the difference between planned and actual performance.

high-volume systems: organizations or production systems with standardized equipment and activities that provide highly similar products or services.

intermediate-volume systems: production systems with volume lower than that of a high volume system, but with production quantities greater than those of a job shop.

job shop: an organization with intermittent production activities, and with jobs flowing through the system in batches.

Johnson's rule: an efficient heuristic method for scheduling n jobs through two work centers, where every job goes through both work centers in the same order.

load chart: a form of Gantt chart that shows both the loading and idle times of a set of machines or departments.

loading: assigning jobs to work centers.

makespan: the total time needed to complete a group of jobs.

matching: see assignment method.

relative cost: an aspect of the technique of the assignment method to attain an optimum oneto-one matching of n resources to n facilities. Let us consider an n-by-n matrix with the n rows representing the resources and the n columns the facilities. Out of the n x n potential assignments, representing all the cells of the matrix, the assignment method finds the n assignments, with every resource assigned to a different facility, with the smallest total cost.

reservation system: computerized scheduling systems with multiple numbers of terminals connected on-line to a central computer that maintains master schedule information, and assigns places and times to the customers or users in real time; the best known example of a reservation system is that used by airlines to assign seats on airplanes to customers on specific dates.

schedule chart: a form of Gantt chart used to monitor the progress of jobs through the system.

sequencing: determining job processing order.

SPO (slack per operation): a sequencing and priority rule that gives the highest priority to the job with the smallest ratio of total slack time to the number of operations.

SPT (shortest processing time): a priority rule that gives the highest priority to the job with the least total processing time.

slack: for a job that could be completed before the scheduled due date if it were started immediately and worked on continuously, the slack is the difference in time between the completion date and the scheduled due date.

TRUE/FALSE QUESTIONS

1. Scheduling is primarily concerned with the timing of operations.

2. Job shop schedule by priority rules is inherently deterministic in nature; the scheduler must plan as if both the order of processing and the amount of time each job would take in each work center were known exactly.

3. Line balancing is a characteristic feature of operations for job shops.

4. Scheduling of work for job shops is usually more complicated than it is for flow systems.

5. The assignment method will solve a wide variety of problems that have to do with flow systems.

6. The assignment problem involves matching of tasks and resources.

7. Load charts, schedule charts and charts showing the arrangement of n jobs through two work centers by Johnson's rule are all forms of Gantt charts.

8. The hierarchy of decisions in production operations is, in order:

    (1) long-term capacity planning
    (2) aggregate planning
    (3) material requirements planning
    (4) capacity requirements planning
    (5) scheduling

9. If the first come first served rule were used more in industry, it would probably result in more efficient scheduling of jobs.

10. Johnson'srule, the assignment method, and loading and priority rules are all appropriate methods of scheduling for job shops.

11. Priority rules are simple heuristics for determining job processing sequence.

12. Measures of effectiveness for a processing rule include average completion time, average job lateness and average runout time.

13. Different processing rules can often result in different schedules, and all of these can be called optimal in one sense or another.

14. The DD (earliest due date) rule will generally result in better sequences of jobs or assignments than the FCFS rule.

MULTIPLE-CHOICE QUESTIONS

1. Which one of the following is not an appropriate job-shop scheduling rule?

    a. Due date
    b. Assignment method
    c. First come first served
    d. Shortest processing time
    e. Johnson's rule

2. Which one of the following statements is correct?

    a. Flow systems are generally associated with high volumes of production, and every workstation along an assembly line is assigned a specialized task.
    b. Flow systems are associated with job shops.
    c. Machines in a job shop are rarely idle.
    d. Intermittent systems are fundamentally just-in-time, similar to modem Japanese methods of production.
    e. Fixed-position systems are assembly lines in fixed locations, that produce a high volume of merchandise.

3. The term "loading' in the context of scheduling refers to:

    a. the assignment of jobs to processing centers.
    b. using Gantt charts for scheduling.
    c. balancing a production or assembly line.
    d. transporting finished goods to appropriate distribution equipment such as trucks or rail cars.
    e. expanding (horizontally or vertically) workloads.

4. Which one of the following is an optimizing technique?

    a. Shortest processing time
    b. Assignment method
    c. First come first served
    d. Loading
    e. None of these

5. All of the following are possible reasons for using the first come first served rule in service systems except:

    a. It is easy to apply.
    b. It guarantees the shortest throughput time.
    c. It is viewed as "fair" by waiting customers.
    d. No computations are required.
    e. All are possible reasons.

6. A major disadvantage of the SPT rule is:

    a. it tends to make long jobs wait.
    b. it results in high in-process inventories.
    c. long jobs tend to delay other jobs.
    d. it does not take processing time into account.
    e. none of these.

7. A major disadvantage of the DD rule is:

    a. it tends to make long jobs wait.
    b. it results in high in-process inventories.
    c. long jobs tend to delay other jobs.
    d. it does not take processing time into account.
    e. none of these.

8. Choose the best ending to this statement: Scheduling service systems presents certain problems not generally encountered in manufacturing systems due to:

    a. the inability to store services.
    b. the random nature of customer requests for service.
    c. both a and b.
    d. the systems tend to operate over a longer day than manufacturing systems.
    e. both b and d.

PROBLEMS

1. Mr. Art Point manufactures drawing pencils in his shop: his product line consists of 2B, 3B, 4B, 5B, and 6B drawing pencils. At the first of the month, he has some inventory of each type of pencil, as shown in the table below. He also has an estimate of the volume of sales of each type of pencil. By running a linear programming problem, he has determined the quantity of each type of pencil to be produced this month.

Type of Pencil	Inventory	Estimated Sales per day	Scheduled Production
2B	2,000	500	12,000
3B	3,000	600	9,000
4B	0	1,200	27,000
5B	3,000	1,000	18,000
6B	6,000	500	5,000

   a. What is the runout time for each type of pencil?
   b. In what order should the pencils be produced during the month?
   c. What assumption about the sales of drawing pencils is made here?

2. A construction company has a contract to construct an access ramp from a street to an expressway. The principal activities in the project are shown below, along with the scheduled starting date and the estimated number of working days which each step will require.

	Activity	Starting Date	Working days
(1)	Draw blueprints	May 6	10
(2)	Build temporary bypass road	May 13	5
(3)	Build the grade for the access ramp	May 20	15
(4)	Lay the foundation for the pavement	June 3	12
(5)	Lay the concrete pavement	June 17	5
(6)	Paint lines on pavement, etc.	June 24	5
(7)	Remove temporary bypass road	July 1	5

The company works the customary five-day week and observes holidays on Memorial Day (May 27) and on the 4th and 5th of July. Here is a calendar for May, June, and July:

```
        May                      June                     July
 S  M  T  W  T  F  S      S  M  T  W  T  F  S      S  M  T  W  T  F  S
          1  2  3  4                        1                  1  2  3  4  5  6
 5  6  7  8  9 10 11      2  3  4  5  6  7  8      7  8  9 10 11 12 13
12 13 14 15 16 17 18      9 10 11 12 13 14 15     14 15 16 17 18 19 20
19 20 21 22 23 24 25     16 17 18 19 20 21 22     21 22 23 24 25 26 27
26 27 28 29 30 31        23 24 25 26 27 28 29     28 29 30 31
                         30
```

a. Construct a Gantt Progress Chart as of May 6, showing the schedule of the activities List the activities on the vertical axis and count only working days on the horizontal axis (May 6 = 1).

b. Assume it is June 10. Here Is the history of the project to-date:

Drawing the blueprints started on May 6 and took nine working days.
Constructing the temporary bypass road took six working days, because of heavy rains.
The rains caused a two-day delay in commencing to build the grade, which actually started on May 22, and is incomplete as of June 10.
Laying the foundation for the pavement commenced on June 3. and is incomplete as of June 10.

Prepare the updated Gantt Progress Chart which shows the status of the access ramp on June 10.

3. The Interstate Biology Machines Company leases equipment to hospitals and laboratory for use in medical tests and research on humans and animals. The company has several bureaus in Cities A, B, C and D, which are staffed by technicians who may be sent to t customers' establishments in the event of difficulty with the equipment. One day, requests for service have been received from customers in Cities, 1, 2, 3, 4 and 5. The distance each service bureau to each customer, one way, is given in the table below in kilometers.

			Customer		
Bureau	1	2	3	4	5
A	200	50	500	100	60
B	100	200	80	40	600
C	90	200	400	60	200
D	700	100	200	400	90

It is necessary to assign the technicians to the customers so as to minimize the amount of technicians' travel.

a. What is the initial tableau for solving this problem with the assignment method?
b. What is the final tableau?
c. Which technician should be assigned to which customers?
d. What is the total round-trip distance which the technicians must travel?
e. Who does without in this schedule?

4. (One step beyond.) Refer to Problem #3.

a. The Service Bureau in City C is not equipped to handle the problem of Customer #1. Incorporate this constraint into the problem.
b. Customer #3 has an emergency; if the equipment is not serviced immediately, the patient may die. Incorporate this constraint into the problem.
c. What is the initial tableau?
d. What is the final tableau?
e. Which technician should be assigned to which customer?
f. What is the total round trip distance which the technicians must travel?
g. Who does without in this schedule?

5. A number of jobs are waiting to be processed at a work center. The jobs are listed below in the order in which they arrived. For each job, the due date is showing and an estimate of the processing time in workdays. Only one job can be processed at a time, and it is necessary to determine the sequence. Assume it is October 1.

Job Number	Due Date	Processing Time (days)
1	Dec. 10	6
2	Nov. 13	10
3	Oct. 15	8
4	Nov. 18	12
5	Dec. 6	9
6	Oct. 30	7

a. What is the sequence using the first come first served (FCFS) priority rule?
b. What is the sequence using the shortest processing time (SPT) rule?
c. What is the sequence using the due date (DD) priority rule?
d. What is the difference between these rules and the runout time rule (Problem 1)?

6. A number of jobs are waiting to be processed through two work centers. Each job must be processed through Center A and Center B, in that order. For each job, the processing time in each work center is given below, in minutes.

Job	Time in Center A	Time in Center B
A	10	12
B	8	15
C	15	9
D	20	11
E	18	10
F	17	13
G	11	14

a. Use Johnson's rule to determine the sequence in which the jobs should be processed.
b. Construct a chart showing the sequence of the jobs in each work center, the times the jobs spend waiting, and the times that the work centers are idle.
c. What is the throughput (makespan) time?
d. How much time do the jobs spend waiting to be processed?
e. How much idle time do the work centers have?

15S - Maintenance

KEY IDEAS

1. Maintaining the production capability of an organization is an important function in any production system. Maintenance includes all activities related to keeping equipment and facilities in proper working order, and making repairs when breakdowns occur.

2. The goal of maintenance is to keep the system in good working order at minimal cost. Decision makers have two basic options for this: breakdown maintenance (deal with breakdowns when they occur) and preventive maintenance (reduce breakdowns through periodic adjustment, inspection, and replacement of worn parts before failure).

3. Preventive maintenance is generally scheduled using some combination of the result of planned inspections that reveal a need for maintenance, according to calendar, and after a set number of operating hours.

4. Predictive maintenance is an attempt to determine when to perform preventive maintenance activities.

5. The major approaches to handling breakdowns include:

   a. the use of standby or backup equipment.
   b. stock of spare parts.
   c. operators who can handle minor repairs.
   d. repair people who can diagnose and correct problems with equipment.

GLOSSARY

breakdown maintenance: deal with breakdowns or other equipment problems when they occur.

maintenance: includes all activities related to keeping facilities and equipment in good working order and making repairs when breakdowns occur.

predictive maintenance: an attempt to determine when to perform preventive maintenance activities to avoid breakdowns.

preventive maintenance: intended to reduce equipment or plant failure by inspecting to discover problems, replacing worn parts before failure, lubricating, cleaning, and adjusting equipment, and so on.

TRUE/FALSE QUESTIONS

1. Preventive maintenance eliminates breakdowns during operation.

2. Decision makers have two basic maintenance options: breakdown maintenance and predictive maintenance.

3. The age and condition of equipment is an important consideration in how much preventive maintenance is desirable.

4. The optimum level of preventive maintenance occurs when the cost of preventive maintenance equals the cost of breakdown and repair.

5. Predictive maintenance is an attempt to determine when to perform preventive maintenance.

MULTIPLE-CHOICE QUESTIONS

1. Breakdown programs include all of the following except:

    a. inventories of spare parts.
    b. backup equipment.
    c. periodic inspections.
    d. operators who can perform minor repairs.
    e. repair people.

2. Preventive maintenance is not usually scheduled by:

    a. operating time.
    b. calendar time.
    c. planned inspections.
    d. historical breakdown records.
    e. irregularly, as breakdowns occur.

3. The degree of preventive maintenance that is desirable is influenced by all of the following except:

    a. the age and condition of facilities.
    b. breakdown cost.
    c. salvage value of equipment.
    d. the degree of technology involved.
    e. the cost of preventive maintenance.

16 - Project Management

KEY IDEAS

1. A project is a set of activities or specialized functions all directed toward achieving a unique objective or goal.

2. A network diagram is a graphic representation of the project and its elements. It consists of directed arrows representing activities or subprojects, each node denoting completion of all preceding activities. The leftmost node is the source representing beginning of the project and the rightmost terminal is the end, denoting completion. Nodes are shown as numbers 1, 2t 3, etc. Arrows are either given alphabetic designations *a, b, c,* etc.; or else they are identified by their beginning and ending nodes 1-2, 2-3, etc., numbering makes it easier to identify predecessors and successors.

3. Any connected set of nodes and events headed in the general direction from left to right is called a sequence. A sequence that includes both the start and the end is a path. The path that takes a longer time than any other path is called the critical path and its activities are critical activities. The critical path is the path that determines the length of time for the project. Any hope for shortening project time depends on the ability of the project manager to shorten the time for critical activities. That can sometimes be accomplished by applying more resources to them.

4. Zero-completion-time dummy activities are in A-0-A (activity-on-arrow) diagrams. Dashed arrows are used in certain situations where it is necessary to uniquely identify a path. These are for the most part cases where two activities are parallel, that is, they both begin and end at the same node. Other cases requiring dummies are where two activities have some but not all predecessors in common.

5. The algorithm for finding the critical path involves two passes through the data: first, a forward pass to find the early start (ES) and early finish (EF) times for each activity, and then a backward pass to find the late finish (LF) and late start (LS) times. The critical path is the path for which ES = LS and EF = LF for every member of that path. The slack time is the difference between LS and ES. Thus the activities on the critical path all have zero slack. The critical path is also the path that takes the same amount of time to complete as the project does.

   For the forward pass, assign the time zero to the starting node. This is the ES of every activity emanating from the source; the EF is the time t of completion. The general formula for ES is

   ES = largest early completion *time, EF, of* all immediately *preceding activities*

   The early finish for an activity is EF = ES + t, where t is the activity time. The forward pass computes both ES and EF for every activity.

   The time it takes to get to the final node is the estimated time for the project. This will show up as the LF for all activities ending at the final node.

   The backward pass is reverse of the forward pass. Start the backward pass at the final nodeat LF time.

For every activity ending at the final node, *LS= LF - t.* Then LS becomes the LF for all preceding activities; the formula is

LF = smallest late completion *time, LS, of* all *immediate successors.*

When you are through with the backward pass, all critical activities will show up as having zero slack.

6. Probabilistic PERT introduces uncertainty into a PERT model. For each activity there are three time estimates:

(1) o: optimistic, or shortest estimated completion time
(2) *m*: most likely time
(3) *p*: pessimistic, or longest average completion time

The average time t_e for completing an activity is a weighted average of *o, m,* and *p; o* and *p* both have relative weights of 1 and m has a relative weight of 4. Hence

$$t_e = \frac{o+ 4m+p}{6}$$

The variance of activity completion time is

$$\sigma^2 = \frac{(b-a)^2}{36}$$

t_e and σ^2 are respectively the mean and variance of activity completion time under a beta probability distribution.

Assuming there is just a single critical path and there are no parallel critical paths, the expected time for completion of the project is the sum of times t, for the critical path activities. The variance of project completion time is the sum of the variances for critical path activities. The standard deviation of project completion time is the square root of the sum of the variances.

The distribution of completion times can be represented by a normal distribution with mean equal to the sum of expected times for the activities on the path, and a standard deviation equal to the square root of the sum of the variances of the activities on the path. The objective is to find the probability of completing the project in any specified time. The way to do so is to determine how far the expected path time is from the specified time in terms of number of standard deviations of the path. This is accomplished using the following formula to obtain z for that path:

$$z_{path} = \frac{specified\ time\ -\ expected\ path\ time}{path\ standard\ deviation}$$

Then look up the probability in the table of areas under the normal curve. For example, if z = 1.96, the probability of completion is 97.5 percent (look up z = 1.96 in Appendix Table B).

If there are multiple independent paths with probabilistic time estimates, use the approach described in Examples 5 and 6. and Solved Problem 3 in the text.

7. Shortening the time for completion can reduce costs and enhance profitability in several ways:

   (1) Indirect, or supervision, costs are reduced.
   (2) Bonuses are frequently earned for early completion.
   (3) Resources are freed to be used for other projects.

   Under these conditions, it is worthwhile to incur some increases in direct costs to attain the benefits of reducing the total time by crashing the project. Give priority to those critical path activities that have the lowest cost per day in crashing.

   For each activity, obtain both regular and crash time estimates, in days, and the cost per day of crash*. The number of days available to crash is the difference between regular time and crash time. Rank the critical activities in order of lowest per day crashing cost. Assign funds available for crashing successively to the lowest cost per day until either those funds are all used up or the desired schedule is obtained.

   Crashing can reduce slack time on noncritical activities. Therefore, it frequently happens that as you begin to crash, the slack times for activities on noncritical paths reduce to a point where they become critical too. This results in parallel critical paths. You can continue crashing beyond this point, but only by crashing all parallel paths.

8. PERT has the advantage of forcing managers to organize and quantify the decision-making process. The graphs, tables, and critical path calculations are helpful in showing up how the organization fits together and where to move resources around to achieve the best possible results. For large projects, PERT must be computerized.

TIPS FOR SOLVING PROBLEMS

Computing Algorithm

It can be helpful in working with the computing algorithm to think of nodes with multiple entering or exiting arrows (branches) as being analogous to airports or train stations, and the arrows as arriving or leaving planes or trains.

For instance, in a forward pass (see diagram), think of A and B as arriving trains and C as a leaving train. Train C cannot leave (according to policy) until both A and B have arrived. Consequently, the train that has the latest arrival time (B in this example), establishes the earliest starting time for train C (1 2 in this example). Hence, the rule is: Use the largest EF time of entering arrows (e.g., A = 7, B = 12) for the ES of the leaving arrow.

For a backward pass, when LS and LF times are being determined. the most complex case is when a node has multiple leaving arrows (see diagram below). The question is how to determine the LF for the entering arrow (D in this example). The rule is, use the smaller of the LS times (E = 10, F = 18, so use 10) of the leaving arrows. Again, think of trains E and F leaving a train station. But this time, think of the trains as leaving according to a set schedule: E must leave at 10 and F must leave at 18. Therefore, the latest that D can arrive (LF) so that its passengers can make either train, is 10, the earliest of the leaving (LS) times.

Computing Probabilistic Completion Times

1. Always determine the probability of finishing before the specified time (i.e., the area under the normal curve to the left of the specified time), even for problems that call for the probability of crashing after. In the latter case, find P(before) and subtract from 1.00 to find P(after).

2. Compute a z-value for every path in the network. If z is greater than +2.50, treat the probability of that path finishing by the specified time at 100 percent. Use Appendix Table(B to obtain normal probabilities.

3. Multiply all path probabilities together to obtain P(crash by specified time). Note that because the normal distribution is continuous, so that the probability of finishing exactly at the time specified is theoretically equal to zero, P(finish before) is equivalent to P(finish by) and to P(finish on or before).

Crashing

Only consider crashing activities that are on the critical path. After each crash, redetermine the critical path(s), and include any new critical activities in the next round of crashing.

GLOSSARY

activity: a task.

A-0-A: activity-on-arrow.

A-0-N: activity-on-node.

arrow: indicates the direction of flow in the precedence diagram.

beta distribution: in PERT with three time estimates for completion of an activity, the distribution form governing the calculation of the means and variances of activity completion times.

CPM (Critical Path Method): PERT and CPM were both developed separately at about the same time in the late 1950s. Both techniques are concerned with integrating and managing a project consisting of a number of different tasks.

crash time: in PERT/COST, the completion-time estimate resulting from crashing it.

crashing: accelerating a project by speeding up those critical path activities which have the lowest ratio of incremental cost to incremental time saved.

critical path: the path in a network diagram that takes the longest time for completion.

critical activity: an activity on the critical path.

deterministic time estimate: a single time estimate for an activity, with no alternative estimates or probability distribution of estimates.

dummy activity: an artificial activity on an A-0-A network diagram, to facilitate distinguishing between two or more activities that both begin and end at the same node.

early finish (EF): for an activity, the early start, plus the time required for completion of the activity.

early start (ES): for an activity, the latest early finish of any predecessor.

event: a node in a precedence diagram, showing both the completion of one or more activities and the start of another task or set of tasks.

Gantt chart: visual aid used for scheduling simple projects.

late finish (LF): for an activity, the earliest late finish of any successor.

late start (LS): for an activity, the late finish minus the time required for completion of the activity.

matrix organization: a type of organization chart that shows both the tasks to be performed, and the units in the project or organization to which these tasks are assigned, in the form of a matrix table; the columns, for example, are the tasks, and the rows are the organizations that perform them.

network: a graph that shows the interconnections between all the elements of a system. See also precedence diagram.

node: see precedence diagram.

normal distribution: in PERT with three time estimates for completion of an activity, the distribution obtained by summing the means and variances of the activity completion times is a normal distribution.

path: an unbroken set of arcs and nodes from the source to the terminal.

PERT (Program Evaluation and Review Technique): see CPM.

precedence diagram: a type of directed network graph used in CPM showing the start of the project at one end and the completion at the other end, with every activity displayed as an arc, and with every node joining two or more arcs showing which activities precede others.

predecessor: for two activities joined at a node, the predecessor is the one that precedes, and the successor is the one that follows.

project: a set of diverse tasks, organized to achieve a single objective.

sequence: the order in which tasks are to be performed.

slack: for an activity, the additional time, over and above completion time, that could be used for the activity, without delaying the project.

standard deviation: the square root of the variance.

successor: see predecessor.

time-cost trade-off: **see** crashing.

variance: in PERT with three time estimates for completion of an activity, the variance is the square of the difference between optimistic time and pessimistic time, divided by 6. for a project, the variance is the sum of the variances of completion times for all of the activities on the critical path.

work breakdown structure: a hierarchical listing of what must be done during a project.

z-statistic: the random variable of the standard normal distribution, with mean zero and variance one.

TRUE/FALSE QUESTIONS

1. Because a Gantt chart is a scheduling technique, it should not be used for project management.

2. The early start of an activity is the latest early finish of any immediately preceding activity.

3. The late finish of an activity is the earliest late start of any immediately preceding activity.

4. There can be two or more parallel critical paths, all having exactly the same completion time.

5. The term "work breakdown structure" refers to a failure in the work structure.

6. The estimated means and variances of project completion times are respectively, the sum of the means and variances for the beta distributions of the activities on the critical path.

7. One use of a dummy activity is when two activities would otherwise have the same starting and ending nodes.

8. In crashing it may be necessary to shorten noncritical activities in order to accelerate the project.

9. Activity A has an ES of 8, an EF of 12, an LS of 13, and an LF of 17; the slack time is 4.

10. If two paths are tied for the longest duration, both would be considered to be critical paths.

11. The activity-on-node method of representing a network diagram makes it possible to draw the diagram without any dummy activities.

12. The critical path in a network always has zero slack.

13. In PERT, if the scheduled project completion time and sum of the average completion times for critical path activities are the same, the probability of completing the project on schedule is estimated at 50 percent, assuming no other paths are near-critical.

MULTIPLE-CHOICE QUESTIONS

For the background information on the first group of three questions, refer to the table that follows.

Activity	Immediate follower	Estimated time
A	E	6
B	F	5
C	D, G	8
D	F	4
E	end	5
F	end	10
G	end	10

1. The critical path is:

   a. B, F.   b. C, D, F.   c. C, G.   d. A, E.

2. The time for the critical path is:

   a. 20 days.
   b. 1 1 days.
   c. 18 days.
   d. 19 days.
   e. none of the above.

3. The path with the greatest slack time is:

   a. 1-3-5.
   b. 1-2-5.
   c. 1-4-3-5.
   d. 1-4-5.

4. A major limitation of Gantt charts in project management is that they do not:

    a. indicate the major activities involved.
    b. show activity times.
    c. show the timing of activities.
    d. show precedence relationships.
    e. give a visual portrayal.

5. Which is not a feature of PERT/CPM?

    a. An estimate of how long a project will take.
    b. A graphical display of project activities.
    c. An indication of critical activities.
    d. An indication of slack time.
    e. All are features.

6. Which of these may require the use of a dummy activity?

    a. Gantt chart.
    b. Activity-on-arrow network.
    c. Activity-on-node network.
    d. Both b and c.
    e. None of these.

7. Using the computing algorithm, activity slack can be computed as:

    a. $LF - LS$.   b. $LS - LF$.   c. $LS - ES$.   d. $LF - EF$.   e. c or d.

8. The standard deviation of project completion time Is computed as:

    a. the sum of the standard deviations of critical activities.
    b. the sum of the standard deviations of all project activities.
    c. the square root of the variance of all project activities.
    d. the square root of the sum of the variances of critical activities.
    e. none of these.

9. An important assumption in PERT calculations is:

    a. activity times are normally distributed.
    b. activity times are independent.
    c. a computer will be available to do the calculations.
    d. a and b.
    e. a and c.

PROBLEMS

1. A project consists of 10 activities, lettered A through J, as shown in the accompanying precedence diagram, with the activities on the arrows. For each activity, the deterministic time estimate in weeks is shown in the following table.

Activity	Time	Activity	Time
A	2	F	3
B	4	G	4
C	3	H	3
D	5	I	3
E	6	J	1

a. List all of the paths through the network.
b. What is the duration of each of the paths?
c. N"at is the critical path?
d. What is the critical path?
e. What is the slack time for each activity?
f. Calculate the ES, EF, LS and LF times for the network.

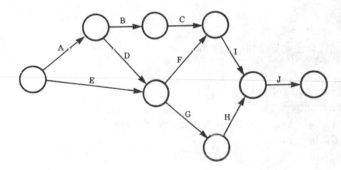

2. A project consists of 11 activities, lettered A through K, below. For each activity, the preceding activity is given, and a deterministic estimate of the length of time required to complete it.

Activity	Time	Preceding Activity
A	1	-
B	3	A
C	2	A
D	4	C
E	2	-
F	3	E
G	4	E
H	6	F
I	2	G
J	1	H, I
K	1	B, D, J

a. Draw the precedence network for this project, with the activities on the arrows.
b. List all of the paths through the network.
c. What is the duration of each of the paths?
d. What is the critical path?
e. What is the slack time for each activity?
f. The materials required to accomplish activity F have been delayed for two weeks by a strike at the supplier's plant. What effect wfll this have on the length of time required to complete the project?
g. An equipment breakdown has delayed activity B for one week. What effect will this have on the length of time required to complete the project?

3. A project consists of 8 activities, lettered A through H. below. For each activity, the preceding activity is given, and a probabilistic estimate of the time required to complete it. Times are in days.

Activity	Preceding Activity	Optimistic Time	Most Likely Time	Pessimistic Time
A	-	2	4	6
B	A	3	6	9
C	A	2	5	11
D	-	2	10	12
E	C, D	4	8	15
F	B, E	2	4	12
G	D	3	4	11
H	F, G	1	1	1

a. Determine the expected time for each activity.
b. Determine the variance for each activity
c. Draw the PERT network for this project, with the activities on the arrows.
d. List all of the paths through the network.
e. What is the duration of each path?
f. What is the variance of each path?
g. What is the critical path?
h. What is the second-most critical path?
i. Activity D was delayed three days by an earthquake in the area. What effect does this have on the length of time required to complete the project?

4. Refer to Problem 3 and the original critical path before the earthquake.

a. What is the mean of the probability distribution for the completion time?
b. What is the standard deviation of the probability distribution for the completion time?
c. What is the probability of finishing the project within 24 days?
d. What is the probability of finishing the project within 22 days?
e. What is the probability that the project will take longer than 28 days?

5. After the earthquake, in Problem 3, management faced the problem of how to make up the lost time, and how much it would cost. Estimates of crash times and costs for each activity are given below.

Activity	Crash Time	Cost per Day
A	not possible	-
B	3 days	$200 per day
C	not possible	-
D	not possible*	-
E	5 days	$300 per day
F	2 days	$500 per day
G	not possible	-
H	not possible	-

*(because of the earthquake)

a. Which activity should be crashed?
b. How many days should it be crashed?
c. How much will it cost?

6. Construct the PERT network for Problem 3 with the activities on the nodes.

7. (One step beyond) Use the time estimates and the network for Problem 2 for solving this problem. Today is Monday, May 1, and work on the project is just beginning. The project is scheduled to be finished on Friday, August 11. Use this information to calculate the ES, EF, LS, and LF.

17 - Waiting Lines

KEY IDEAS

1. Waiting lines are an important consideration in capacity planning. Waiting lines tie up additional resources (waiting space, time, etc.); they decrease the level of customer service: and they require additional capacity to reduce them.

2. Waiting lines occur whenever demand for service exceeds capacity (supply). Even in systems that are underloaded, waiting lines tend to form if arrival and service patterns are highly variable because the variability creates temporary imbalances of supply and demand.

3. All of the waiting line models presented in the chapter (except the constant service time model) assume, or require, that the arrival rate can be described by a Poisson distribution and that the service time can be described by a negative exponential distribution. Equivalently, we can say that the arrival and service rates must be Poisson, and the interarrival time and the service time must be exponential. In practice, one would check for this using a statistical Chi Square test: for problems provided here and in the textbook, assume that these distributions hold. Note that if these assumptions are not met, alternate approaches (e.g., intuition, simulation, other models) should be considered.

4. Much can be learned about the behavior of waiting lines by modeling them. A wide variety of models are presented in the text, different models pertain to different system characteristics.

5. A major distinction in waiting line models relates to whether the number of potential arrivals to the system is limited (finite) or unlimited (infinite). Perhaps the classic example of a finite source system is the machine, repairperson problem, wherein the server or servers handle calls for repairs on a small, fixed number of machines. Note that the definition of terms in Table 17-6 in the text follows this somewhat (e.g., average number running). Other examples of finite source systems include passengers on a plane who might request assistance or information from a steward or stewardess, a sales rep who handles a small set of customers, and a telephone operator who places outgoing calls for residents of a small hotel. Examples of infinite-source systems are plentiful: service stations, banks, post offices, restaurants, theaters, supermarkets, libraries, stop signs, and telephone switchboards.

6. Once a situation has been modeled and the relevant data gathered (e.g., an-arrival rate, service time, number of servers, etc.), formulas and/or tables can be used to obtain information about the system such as the expected number waiting for service, the expected waiting time, the maximum line length, system utilization, and so on. This information can be used to compare various system alternatives (e.g., one server versus two servers, different equipment possibilities, and so on) with respect to cost and impact on waiting times, etc.

7. The goal in queuing analysis is to develop a system in which the sum of capacity costs and waiting costs is minimized. Sometimes this goal may be taken in an absolute sense or the goal

may be to minimize total costs given a minimum level of customer service specified by management.

8. Most of the models described in the chapter assume arrivals are processed on a first-come, f-first-served basis (FCFS). Many examples of FCFS exist. Sometimes, however, customers are processed on a priority basis rather than FCFS. That is, late arriving customers may be processed ahead of those already waiting. A hospital emergency room is an example; seriously ill or injured persons are attended to while less seriously ill persons wait. A key difference in the multiple priority model compared to other models is computation of average waiting times, and average number waiting, for each of the classes or categories of waiting customers.

STUDY TIPS

Much of the material is highly mathematical. Do not to let this overwhelm you. Note that many of the problems can be solved using tables rather than formulas, and that many of the formulas do not involve extensive computation.

The chapter presents two kinds of queuing models, one for infinite source (unrestricted entry) systems, and another for finite source systems. There are four infinite source models and one finite source model. Instead of trying to absorb the entire chapter at once (or even a major portion of it), begin with the general discussion of waiting lines, and then focus on a few infinite source models (e.g., single channel and single channel with constant service, which represent the first two infinite source models), leaving other models to another time. This can be reinforced by attempting some problems at the end of the chapter which relate to the models you have focused on. Moreover, if you have done a good job in studying a particular model, you should be able to ascertain whether or not a given problem can be solved using the model.

TIPS FOR SOLVING PROBLEMS

1. A key element of infinite source models is the number of channels. Generally, there is one channel for every server. The exception would be if the servers work in teams; then there is one channel for every team.

2. Key measures for infinite source problems are the arrival and service rates. The formulas and tables require rates, although times may be given, necessitating a conversion to a rate. Moreover, arrival and service rates must be in the same units (e.g., both in customers per hour, both in customers per minute). Consider these examples for arrivals:

   a. 10 units per hour. This is okay, it is a rate.
   b. Customers arrive at an average of one every 20 seconds. This gives the time between arrivals. To find the arrival rate, use the information to determine the number of customers, say, per minute. Thus,

$$\frac{60 \text{ seconds/minute}}{20 \text{ seconds}} = 3 \text{ customers per minute.}$$

c. The interarrival time is 90 seconds. Again, we have the time between arrivals. Dividing this into 60 seconds per minute, we get .667 customers per minute. Multiplying this by 60 minutes will give us the rate per hour: .667/minute *x* 60 minutes/hour = 40 customers per hour.

Now consider these examples relating to service:

a. Three customers per hour. This is okay, it is expressed as a rate.
b. Four customers can be served in an hour. Thus, the service rate is 4 customers/hour.
c. Service time is 15 minutes. This means that four customers can be served in an hour:

$$\frac{60 \text{ minutes/hour}}{15 \text{ minutes/customer}} = 4 \text{ customers per hour.}$$

d. The service time is 12 minutes. The service rate is 1/12 per minute. Multiplying by 60 gives us the hourly rate: 60 (1/12) = 5 customers/hour.

3. When a problem refers to the average number waiting in line, check to see if it pertains to all arrivals, or just those that actually wait, since customers that arrive when the service facility is idle would not have to wait, thereby lowering the average waiting time of all arrivals. Use the formula or table for W_q if the average for all customers is required; and use W_a if the average waiting time only for those that wait is required. Note that in a heavily loaded system, most customers will have to wait, in which case the two averages, W_q and W_a, will be approximately equal. More generally, W_a will be greater than W_q.

GLOSSARY

channels: "avenues" for service (e.g., a bank with one teller is a single-channel system, a bank with more than one teller is a multiple-channel system). The terms "server" and "channel" are synonymous.

customer: a unit an-arriving for service (e.g., a person, an order, an item in need of repair). finite population source: a system that has a limited number of potential customers.

finite population source: a system that has a limited number of potential customers.

infinite population source: a system that has a potential number of customers that is very large relative to the capacity of the system.

multiple-channel system: a system with more than one possible avenue of customer service (e.g., a bakery counter with more than one server).

multiple-priority model: a waiting line model that has more than one category of customers; arriving customers are assigned to a category and then processed according to priority category rather than first-come, first-served.

queue: a waiting line.

queue discipline: the order in which customers are processed or served. First-come, first served is service in order of arrival.

server: attendant, machine, etc., that handles customer service or processing.

service time: processing time: the time a customer is in the system minus time spent waiting in line for service.

steady-state conditions: a system operating under stable conditions (i.e.. arrival and service patterns are not changing over time).

system: consists of customers waiting in line plus those being served.

system utilization: the proportion of time a service facility is busy with customer processing.

waiting time in line: the usually nonproductive time customers wait before being served or processed.

waiting time in the system: time in line plus processing time.

TRUE/FALSE QUESTIONS

1. A waiting line tends to form when service capacity exceeds demand.

2. Queuing systems tend to be overloaded and highly variable.

3. A finite source model is appropriate when the potential number of arrivals is relatively small.

4. Service time is the reciprocal of service rate.

5. If the average time between customer arrivals is five minutes, the arrival rate is twenty per hour.

6. The terms "server" and "channel" are used interchangeably to mean the number of possible service routes available to customers.

7. As system utilization increases, the expected number of customers waiting for service increases.

8. For infinite source systems, the average number of customers being served is equal to the arrival rate divided by the service rate.

9. In a finite-source system, the arrival rate is dependent on the number waiting for service.

MULTIPLE-CHOICE QUESTIONS

1. A three-step repair service with one server at each step would be an example of a:

    a. multiple-phase, multiple-channel system.
    b. single-phase, multiple-channel system.
    c. multiple-phase, single-channel system.
    d. none of these.

2. A system with an arrival rate of two per hour, a service time of 20 minutes, and one server, would have a utilization of.

    a. 10%
    b. 33%
    c. 40%
    d. 67%
    e. none of these

3. The term "queue discipline" refers to:

    a. customers waiting in a single line for service.
    b. processing order.
    c. the willingness of customers to wait in line.
    d. well-behaved customers.

4. As the system utilization increases, the average number waiting:

    a. doesn't change.
    b. increases.
    c. decreases.
    d. impossible to say.

5. Waiting lines tend to form in underloaded systems because:

    a. capacity always exceeds demand.
    b. capacity sometimes exceeds demand.
    c. demand always exceeds supply.
    d. demand sometimes exceeds supply.
    e. none of these.

6. Which of these would not increase system utilization?

    a. a decrease in the number of servers
    b. a decrease in the service rate
    c. a decrease in the arrival rate
    d. an increase in the arrival rate

7. For an infinite-source system with an arrival rate of 6 per hour (Poisson) and service time of 6 minutes per customer (exponential), the average number being served is:

    a. .10
    b. .60
    c. 1.0
    d. none of these

8. Which one of these would illustrate a finite-source system?

    a. Supermarket
    b. Bakery
    c. Drug store
    d. One-lane bridge
    e. None of these

PROBLEMS

1. A bank has a drive-in window, which is open from 10 a.m. to 3 p.m. on business days. Customers drive up at a mean rate of 12 per hour, according to a Poisson distribution. The teller requires a mean of 2.4 minutes to serve each customer. service times have a negative exponential distribution.

    a. How many channels are there?
    b. Do the customers come from a finite source or from an infinite source?
    c. Which queue model is appropriate here?
    d. What is the value of λ?
    e. What is the interpretation of λ?
    f. What is the value of μ?
    g. What is the interpretation of μ?
    h. What is the utilization rate? Is this a feasible system?
    i. What is the proportion of idle time?
    j. What is the expected number of customers waiting for service?
    k. What is the expected duration of the wait?
    l. What is the mean number of customers in the system?
    m. What is the mean time that a customer spends in the system?
    n. What is the probability that the system will be idle?
    o. What is the probability that there will be one car in the system?
    p. What is the probability that there will be three cars in the system?

2. In a factory, the parts to be copper-plated must be immersed in an electrolytic solution so that copper ions will be deposited on the part. The company has one electrolytic bath, in which each part is submerged for 20 minutes. Parts to be copper-plated arrive at a mean rate of 16 per 8-hour shift, according to a Poisson distribution.

    a. How many channels are there?
    b. Do the parts come from a finite source or from an infinite source?

   c. Which queue model is appropriate here?
   d. What is the value of λ?
   e. What is the interpretation of λ?
   f. What is the value of μ?
   g. What is the interpretation of μ?
   h. What is the utilization rate? Is this a feasible system?
   i. What is the proportion of idle time?
   j. What is the expected number of parts waiting for copper-plating?
   k. What is the expected duration of the wait?
   l. What is the mean number of parts in the system?
   m. What is the mean time that a part spends in the system?

3. A bank has an array of five drive-in windows, some or all of which may be open from 10 a.m. to 3 p.m. on normal business days. At each window, the teller requires a mean of 2.4 minutes to serve each customer; service times have a negative exponential distribution. Customers arrive at a mean rate of 65 per hour, according to a Poisson distribution. (Use Table 17-4)

   a. Do the customers come from a finite source or from an infinite source?
   b. What is the value of λ?
   c. V*rhat is the interpretation of λ?
   d. What is the value of μ?
   e. What is the interpretation of μ?
   f. What is the n-mininum number of drive-in windows which should be open to have an underloaded system?
   g. What is the expected number of customers waiting for service with three drive-in windows open?
   h. What is the expected duration of the wait if all three open windows are busy.?
   i. What is the probability that the system will be idle?
   j. What is the probability that an arrival will have to wait for service with three drive-in windows open?

4. Rework Problem 3 with five drive-in windows open.

   a. What is the expected number of customers waiting for service?
   b. What is the expected duration of the wait if all five windows are busy?
   c. What is the probability that the system will be idle?
   d. What is the probability that an arrival will have to wait for service?

5. The bus company in a small city has a fleet of 10 buses and a single mechanic to service the buses as needed. Buses break down or require periodic maintenance at a mean rate of one every other day, seven days a week. The mechanic works five days per week (40 hours), and the mean time required to service one bus is four hours, with a negative exponential distribution. Buses which break down on Saturday or Sunday are parked until the mechanic can attend to them in the following week.

   a. How many channels are there?
   b. Should the bus arrivals be treated as coming from a finite source or from an infinite source?

c. Which waiting line model is appropriate here?
d. What is the number of potential customers, N?
e. What is the value of the mean service time, T
f. What is the value of the mean time between service calls, U?
g. What is the value of the service factor, X?
h. What is the value of the efficiency factor, F?
i. What is the expected number of buses running, J?
j. What is the mean number of buses being serviced, H?
k. What is the mean number of buses waiting for the mechanic, L?
l. Check to see that $N = J + L + H$.

6. A typing pool for a large corporation consists of six typists, each of whom can type at the rate of 12 pages per hour, on the average, with a Poisson distribution. The pool receives various kinds of typing jobs from a very large number of executives and managers. Thejobs are classified into four priority levels as they arrive. Each level is shown below, with the mean of its particular arrival rate. Typing jobs arrive according to Poisson distributions:

first priority: correspondence with customers (to be typed first); $\lambda_1 = 9$ pages per hr.
second priority: correspondence with suppliers; $\lambda_2 = 8$ pages per hr.
third priority: correspondence with federal, state, and local governments (other than that dealing with sales); $\lambda_3 = 6$ pages per hr.
fourth priority: internal memoranda and conununications and miscellaneous correspondence; $\lambda_4 = 31$ pages per hr.

a. Which set of waiting line formulas should be used here?
b. What is s?
c. What is the value of λ?
d. What is $1/\lambda$?
e. What is the value of μ?
f. What is $1/\mu$?
g. What is the utilization?
h. On the average, how many pages are being typed at any one time?
i. Determine the value of L_q.
j. Determine the value of A.
k. Determine these values:
   B_0 .
   B_1 .
   B_2 .
   B_3 .
   B_4 .
l. Determine these values:
   W_1 .
   W_2 .
   W_3 .
   W_4 .
m. Find the average time in the system for pages in each priority class.
n. Find the average number of pages in the queue for each priority class.
o. Discuss the results of the above analysis.

17S - Simulation

KEY IDEAS

1. Simulation is a tool managers can use to describe the behavior of a system under specified conditions. A major feature of simulation is the ability to answer "what if" questions by describing how a system will behave given certain changes.

2. Simulation is especially useful in situations that are too complex to be analyzed mathematically.

3. Monte Carlo simulations involve the use of random numbers to incorporate randomness in models of system behavior.

4. Simulations that use random numbers must be run a sufficient number of times to enable a decision maker to separate the "real" aspects of behavior from the random aspects.

5. In developing simulation models, it is important to thoroughly test the models to assure that their results are consistent with reality.

6. Simulation applications are found throughout production and operations management. Examples include product design, facilities layout, aggregate planning, scheduling, and project management.

7. The advantages of simulation include:

   a. It is useful when situations are too complex for analytical models.
   b. It can be used to answer "what if" questions for a variety of conditions.
   c. Time is compressed; simulations of a year's experience can be run in a matter of seconds.
   d. Simulations can serve as training exercises for managers and others.

8. Among the limitations of simulation are:

   a. It is descriptive, it does not provide an optimal solution to a problem.
   b. The construction of large-scale simulations can be very costly and time consuming.
   c. Monte Carlo simulation is only appropriate when randomness is a factor.

9. When a random event can be described by a theoretical distribution, simulation models should incorporate that; empirical distributions can be used for situations not adequately described by a theoretical distribution.

TIPS FOR SOLVING PROBLEMS

A frequently asked question is: "How can I tell which distribution type (normal, Poisson, etc.) to use in solving a simulation problem?"

The answer is that (1) if a theoretical distribution such as the uniform, normal Poisson, or exponential is appropriate, this will be specified in the problem, (2) if an empirical distribution is called for, the frequencies will be given in the problem (see, for instance, Example S - I in the textbook). In a few instances, the distribution will be given in a more subtle way, such as: "The four outcomes are equally likely." The implication is that each of the four outcomes has a probability of 1/4, or .25.

Another question that often comes up is: "Which random number table should I use?" Use Table 17S-1 for all problems except when a distribution is normal. In the normal case, use Table 17S-2.

Finally, the question of how to obtain the simulated values. Here is a summary of the methods used:

Distribution Type	*Get Simulated Values by*
Empirical	matching RN with cumulative empirical ranges.
Poisson	matching RN with cumulative probabilities using Appendix Table C.
Uniform	a + .RN(b - a), where a is the lower end and b is the upper end of a uniform distribution.
Exponential	$-(1/\chi) \ln(.RN)$
Normal	mean + RN (standard deviation).

GLOSSARY

experiment: a simulation run or trial.

Monte Carlo method: a type of simulation involving the use of random numbers to incorporate randomness in models of system behavior.

random: chance; having no discernible pattern.

random number table: a table of numbers which, if read systematically, will not exhibit discernible pattern.

simulation: a descriptive technique used to portray the behavior of a system.

validation: step in the process of model development intended to assure that the model will produce meaningful (realistic) results.

TRUE/FALSE QUESTIONS

1. Managers can use simulation to obtain optimal answers for a wide range of problems.

2. Monte Carlo simulations are deterministic.

3. In many real-life applications, computers are used to conduct simulations.

4. Simulation is a descriptive tool.

5. Simulation is especially useful for situations too complex to be analyzed using mathematical models.

6. When using a random number table, it is important to avoid always starting to read numbers in the same spot.

7. Simulation is useful for estimating the mean of a probability distribution, given the distribution.

8. Monte Carlo simulations produce approximate results rather than exact results.

9. Simulation is often the first choice of decision makers instead of analytic models.

MULTIPLE-CHOICE QUESTIONS

1. Which of the following would not generally be listed as a reason for the popularity of simulation as a managerial tool?

    a. Ability to provide optimal solutions
    b. Useful as a training device
    c. Ability to conduct experiments
    d. Extensive software packages are available
    e. All are reasons for its popularity

2. Given this probability distribution, the random number, 22, would be interpreted as a demand of:

Demand	Frequency
0	38
1	22
2	22
3	18

   a. 0   b. 1   c. 2   d. 1 or 2   e. 3

3. Which one of the following is not a simulation language?

    a. SIMSCRIPT
    b. GPSS
    c. GASP
    d. DYNAMO
    e. SIMSUM

4. The main reason that a large number of runs of a simulation would be made is:

    a. It is a form of sampling, and large samples give more accurate results than small samples.
    b. Computers are usually used, and they can easily handle large runs.
    c. It is part of the scientific approach.
    d. Large run sizes are more apt to provide optimal answers.
    e. None of these.

5. Which one of the following would not be a probable reason for choosing simulation as a decision-making tool?

    a. An intuitive approach doesn't seem applicable and the situation is too complex for a mathematical model.
    b. There is a limited time in which to obtain results.
    c. Good results have been obtained in the past using simulation.
    d. Users are able to understand the model.
    e. All of these are probable reasons for choosing simulations.

PROBLEMS

1. The Orange Octagon Discount Department Store sells snowblowers during the winter months. Snowblowers cost $175.00 each and sell for $395.00. The manager knows that the volume of sales is not large, as indicated by the following data on the number of snowblowers that were sold in each week during the past two selling seasons, which contained 20 weeks each: 0, 1, 3, 1, 2, 0, 3, 4, 2, 1, 4, 2, 0, 2, 0, 0, 2, 0, 1. 3, 1, 1, 1, 3, 3, 2, 2, 0, 4, 1, 1, 0, 2, 2, 0, 1, 3, 1, 3 snowblowers. The manager has decided to start the season with four snowblowers on hand. Only snowblowers on hand at the beginning of the week can be sold. Additional snowblowers can be ordered from the supplier, with a two-week lead time, and the manager plans to order two of them whenever the quantity on hand falls to two or less at the end of the week. Use the random numbers that follow to simulate this policy for 10 weeks: 491, 631, 139, 502, 006, 856, 904, 91, 821, 757.

    a. What is the empirical probability distribution for the weekly sales of snowblowers?
    b. What random numbers go with each value of the random variable?
    c. Construct a table in the style of Example 17S-2b(2) in your textbook, showing the history of the inventory of snowblowers for the 10-week period.
    d. How many snowblowers were sold? How much gross margin was made?

e. How many sales were lost? What was the dollar amount of the loss?

f. What is your evaluation of the policy?

2. The number of ambulance calls can be represented by a Poisson distribution with a mean of four per day. Obtain the Poisson distribution from Table C in the Appendix of your textbook and use the following random numbers to simulate six days of ambulance calls: 005, 820, 471, 187, 177, 341.

a. Which random numbers go with each value of the random variable?

b. Construct a table in the style of Solved Problem I in your textbook to show the history of the six days.

3. The daily sales of unleaded gasoline at the self-serve pump can be represented by a normal curve with a mean of 300 gallons and a standard deviation of 30 gallons. Use row 8, columns 1, 2, 3, 4, in Table 17S-2 in your textbook to simulate four days of gasoline sales.

4. The length of time which a customer spends pumping gasoline at the self-serve pump can be represented by a negative exponential distribution with a mean of 2 minutes. Use these four random numbers to simulate four customers pumping gasoline: 84275, 07523, 33362, 64270.

a. What is the value of λ?

b. What are the four times?

5. (One step beyond) The plant manager knows that in the production of fluorescent light tubes, 6 percent will turn out to be defective; the remainder will be satisfactory. Use rows 10-12 in Table 17S-1 in your textbook to simulate the production of 36 fluorescent light tubes.

a. Which random numbers go with each type of fluorescent light tube?

b. What is the sequence of satisfactory (S) and defective (D) tubes?

c. What percent of the 36 tubes are defective?

d. Is the plant manager mistaken in the 6 percent figure?

ANSWERS TO TRUE-FALSE AND MULTIPLE-CHOICE QUESTIONS

CHAPTER 1 INTRODUCTION

True/False

Question	Answer	Glossary/ Key Idea	Textbook ref. page
1	F		5
2	F		23
3	T	1	6
4	T	1	6-7
5	T	2, 3	6-7
6	F	1	6-7
7	F		14
8	F		14
9	F		10, 11
10	F		11
11	T	G	21
12	F	9	26-32

Multiple-Choice

Question	Answer	Glossary/ Key Idea	Textbook ref. page
1	b		6-7, 11
2	e		11
3	c		22-23
4	d	9	26-32
5	a-2		27
	b-5		
	c-1		
	d-6		
	e-4		
	f-3		
	g-7		

CHAPTER 2 PRODUCTIVITY, COMPETITIVENESS, AND STRATEGY

True/False

Question	Answer	Glossary/ Key Idea	Textbook ref. page
1	F	G	47
2	F	G, 3	40
3	T	6	58-59
4	T	6	58-59
5	T	6	58-59

Multiple-Choice

Question	Answer	Glossary/ Key Idea	Textbook ref. page
1	e		42
2	b		42-43
3	e	1	49
4	c	G, 2	40
5	b		51-52
6	e	6	53, 58
7	d	4	45-46

CHAPTER 2S   DECISION MAKING

True/False

Question	Answer	Glossary/ Key Idea	Textbook ref. page
1	F	G, 4	72
2	T	G	72
3	T	G, 5c	78
4	T	G, 5c	78
5	T	G, 6	74-75
6	F		72
7	T		76-77
8	T	5b	75-76
9	T	6	74

Multiple-Choice

Question	Answer	Glossary/ Key Idea	Textbook ref. page
1	a	6	74, 78
2	c		75-76
3	a		74-75
4	b		74-75
5	c		75-76
6	a	7	70
7	e		71

CHAPTER 3   QUALITY MANAGEMENT

True/False

Question	Answer	Glossary/ Key Idea	Textbook ref. page
1	T	G, 3	95
2	F		100
3	T		100
4	T	7	101
5	T	1	98
6	T		108
7	T	G	103
8	F		98
9	T		100

Multiple-Choice

Question	Answer	Glossary/ Key Idea	Textbook ref. page
1	e		98
2	b	6	99-101
3	e		101
4	c		101
5	b		101
6	e		109
7	a	7	98, 103
8	a		95
9	e		97-98

CHAPTER 3S CONTINUOUS IMPROVEMENT

True/False

Question	Answer	Glossary/ Key Idea	Textbook ref. page
1	T		123
2	T		130
3	F	G, 2	130
4	T	G	119
5	T	·	120
6	F	G	120
7	T	G	122

Multiple-Choice

Question	Answer	Glossary/ Key Idea	Textbook ref. page
1	b	G	126
2	d	G, 2	119
3	d	G	119
4	b	G	123

CHAPTER 4 PRODUCT AND SERVICE DESIGN

True/False

Question	Answer	Glossary/ Key Idea	Textbook ref. page
1	T	3, 4	144, 146
2	F		146
3	F	6	146
4	F	G	146-47
5	T	G, 3	148
6	T		151
7	T	5	149
8	F		153
9	T	G	154
10	T	G, 10	141

Multiple-Choice

Question	Answer	Glossary/ Key Idea	Textbook ref. page
1	d	6	145
2	c	11	154
3	d	5	149
4	e		141
5	a		153
6	c		155

CHAPTER 4S   RELIABILITY

True/False

Question	Answer	Glossary/ Key Idea	Textbook ref. page
1	T		166
2	T	6	167
3	T	4	169
4	F	G	172
5	T		167
6	T		171

Multiple-Choice

Question	Answer	Glossary/ Key Idea	Textbook ref. page
1	c	3	167-68
2	c		167-68
3	c		169-70
4	235		169
5	.8749		170-71

CHAPTER 5   PROCESS SELECTION AND CAPACITY PLANNING

True/False

Question	Answer	Glossary/ Key Idea	Textbook ref. page
1	T		197
2	F	3	184-85
3	F		188
4	T		184
5	T	3	185
6	T	G, 11	194-95
7	T	11	195, 197
8	T	13	202-204
9	F		193-94
10	F		195

Multiple-Choice

Question	Answer	Glossary/ Key Idea	Textbook ref. page
1	a	G, 11	195
2	c		196-97
3	a		197
4	e	14	206
5	b		202-204
6	a		185
7	a		185

CHAPTER 5S   LINEAR PROGRAMMING

True/False

Question	Answer	Glossary/ Key Idea	Textbook ref. page
1	T		218
2	T	1	217
3	T	3	225
4	F	1, 3	225
5	T	1, 3	221-23
6	T		225
7	F	5	218
8	F	5	228
9	F	G, 5	235-36
10	F	G	242
11	T	G, 6	240-41

Multiple-Choice

Question	Answer	Glossary/ Key Idea	Textbook ref. page
1	b		222-23
2	c		224-25
3	d		225,228
4	d	3	242
5	d		227
6	c		218
7	a		217

CHAPTER 6   FACILITIES LAYOUT

True/False

Question	Answer	Glossary/ Key Idea	Textbook ref. page
1	T		264
2	T	G	269-70
3	F		273
4	T	G, 8	272-73
5	F	8, 9	272-73
6	F	12	283
7	F	G, 10	274
8	T	G, 10	275
9	T		266
10	T	9	273

Multiple-Choice

Question	Answer	Glossary/ Key Idea	Textbook ref. page
1	d	G	274
2	c		272-73
3	e		262
4	e	3	272
5	c		272-74
6	c		264

CHAPTER 7   DESIGN OF WORK SYSTEMS

True/False

Question	Answer	Glossary/ Key Idea	Textbook ref. page
1	T		330
2	F		330
3	F		326
4	F	G	325
5	F	G	305-307
6	T	G	321
7	T	G, 3	303
8	T		321
9	T		319-20

Multiple-Choice

Question	Answer	Glossary/ Key Idea	Textbook ref. page
1	a		306-307
2	d	G	309
3	f		325
4	b	G	321
5	b		302
6	d		302
7	c		330
8	b		330
9	c		304

CHAPTER 7S   LEARNING CURVES

True/False

Question	Answer	Glossary/ Key Idea	Textbook ref. page
1	F	3	345
2	T		345
3	T	1	344
4	F	2	344
5	T	3	345

Multiple-Choice

Question	Answer	Glossary/ Key Idea	Textbook ref. page
1	c	3	345-46
2	d	5	347-49
3	e		361
4	a	3	346-47

CHAPTER 8   LOCATION PLANNING

True/False

Question	Answer	Glossary/ Key Idea	Textbook ref. page
1	F		370
2	T	2	359
3	F		370
4	T		368-69
5	T	4	360
6	T		364-65
7	T		370
8	F		370-73

Multiple-Choice

Question	Answer	Glossary/ Key Idea	Textbook ref. page
1	d		358-59
2	d		365
3	c		365
4	d		359-60
5	a	6	362
6	c		370-71

CHAPTER 8S   THE TRANSPORTATION MODEL

True/False

Question	Answer	Glossary/ Key Idea	Textbook ref. page
1	T		364
2	T	1	383
3	T		387-89
4	F	G, 3	396-98
5	F		389
6	T		393

Multiple-Choice

Question	Answer	Glossary/ Key Idea	Textbook ref. page
1	d		397
2	c		393-95
3	a		393-95
4	c		393-95
5	b		397

CHAPTER 9   QUALITY CONTROL

True/False

Question	Answer	Glossary/ Key Idea	Textbook ref. page
1	T		417
2	T	4	416
3	F	4	426
4	T	G, 1	426
5	T		430
6	T		427
7	T		426-27
8	T		426
9	T		422
10	F	2	417

Multiple-Choice

Question	Answer	Glossary/ Key Idea	Textbook ref. page
1	b		420-21
2	d		421, 425
3	c	4	432, 433
4	b	4	430, 433
5	d	G	433
6	b		435
7	c		435, 445
8	c	4	426
9	b	G	433
10	c	7	440

CHAPTER 9S   ACCEPTANCE SAMPLING

True/False

Question	Answer	Glossary/ Key Idea	Textbook ref. page
1	T	4	454
2	T	G, 1	455
3	F	3	454
4	F		455
5	F	G, 5	456
6	F	5	456
7	T	G, 6	461

Multiple-Choice

Question	Answer	Glossary/ Key Idea	Textbook ref. page
1	b	3	454
2	e		454
3	d	G	456
4	b		454-55

CHAPTER 10   FORECASTING

True/False

Question	Answer	Glossary/ Key Idea	Textbook ref. page
1	F	4	
2	T	4	469
3	T	8	
4	F	4	469
5	T		486
6	F	G, 3	472
7	T	G, 5	482
8	F	G	497
9	T		498
10	F		498
11	F	G	497
12	T		499
13	T	5	482
14	F		
15	T		473
16	F	9	488-90

Multiple-Choice

Question	Answer	Glossary/ Key Idea	Textbook ref. page
1	e		480-85
2	c		497
3	a		499
4	d	9	488-90
5	c		497
6	b		500
7	e		481

CHAPTER 11   INVENTORY MANAGEMENT

True/False

Question	Answer	Glossary/ Key Idea	Textbook ref. page
1	T	G	545
2	T	5	542
3	F	6	550-51
4	T	G, 6	533
5	T		543
6	T		548
7	T	6	550
8	F	6	551
9	F		561
10	T		561
11	T		561-63
12	T		561

Multiple-Choice

Question	Answer	Glossary/ Key Idea	Textbook ref. page
1	d	9	551-54
2	e		550-51
3	d	6	551
4	b		550-51
5	e	2	531
6	d	3	532
7	e	5	534-35
8	e		538
9	a	5	542
10	a		547
11	c		561-62
12	e		561-62
13	d		561-62
14	c		561-62

CHAPTER 12   AGGREGATE PLANNING

True/False

Question	Answer	Glossary/ Key Idea	Textbook ref. page
1	F	G, 1	590
2	T		593
3	F	8	595
4	F		596-97
5	T		600
6	T		604-607
7	T		608-609
8	T	G	596
9	T	G	610
10	T	G	609, 610

Multiple-Choice

Question	Answer	Glossary/ Key Idea	Textbook ref. page
1	d	7	
2	a	9	593-94
3	d		598-608
4	d	G	608-609
5	d	4	594-96
6	d		593-94
7	c	1	608-609
8	b		610
9	c		610

CHAPTER 13   MATERIAL REQUIREMENTS PLANNING

True/False

Question	Answer	Glossary/ Key Idea	Textbook ref. page
1	F		624
2	T	G, 1	625
3	T		630
4	F	G, 3	628
5	F	G	628
6	F		638
7	F	G	634-35
8	F	10	641-42
9	T		638
10	F	5	624
11	T	5	629-30
12	F		646
13	T		625
14	T		630-32
15	T	9	640-41

Multiple-Choice

Question	Answer	Glossary/ Key Idea	Textbook ref. page
1	a	5	624
2	a	G, 6	630
3	d		
4	b	G, 6	633
5	e	G	626
6	d	G, 2	626
7	c		630

CHAPTER 14   JUST-IN-TIME SYSTEMS

True/False

Question	Answer	Glossary/ Key Idea	Textbook ref. page
1	T	4	678
2	T		678
3	T	2	671
4	F		687
5	T		666
6	T		669
7	T	G	677

Multiple-Choice

Question	Answer	Glossary/ Key Idea	Textbook ref. page
1	c	4	678
2	d		671-76
3	b		684
4	c		687
5	e		677

CHAPTER 14S   MATERIALS MANAGEMENT AND PURCHASING

True/False

Question	Answer	Glossary/ Key Idea	Textbook ref. page
1	F	G, 1	696
2	T	2	696
3	F	2	697
4	F	G	698
5	F		700
6	T		700
7	T		700
8	T		704
9	T	8	702

Multiple-Choice

Question	Answer	Glossary/ Key Idea	Textbook ref. page
1	e		699
2	e	5	700
3	d		700
4	c	2	696
5	b		701

CHAPTER 15   SCHEDULING

True/False

Question	Answer	Glossary/ Key Idea	Textbook ref. page
1	T	1	712
2	T	11	722
3	F	6, 9	712
4	T	10	714-15
5	F	8	717
6	T	G, 8	717
7	T	9	715-17
8	T	3	712
9	F		725-26
10	T	10, 12	721-27
11	T	G	722
12	F	10	722-23
13	F		725-27
14	T		725-27

Multiple-Choice

Question	Answer	Glossary/ Key Idea	Textbook ref. page
1	b	5	717
2	a	6	712
3	a	G	715
4	b	6	717
5	b		725-26
6	a	2	727
7	d		727
8	c		730

CHAPTER 15S   MAINTENANCE

True/False

Question	Answer	Glossary/ Key Idea	Textbook ref. page
1	F	G, 2	751
2	F	2	750
3	T	3	750
4	F		750-51
5	T	G, 4	751

Multiple-Choice

Question	Answer	Glossary/ Key Idea	Textbook ref. page
1	c	6	752
2	e	5	751
3	c		750

CHAPTER 16   PROJECT MANAGEMENT

True/False

Question	Answer	Glossary/ Key Idea	Textbook ref. page
1	F		761-62
2	T	5	770
3	F	5	773
4	T	7	783
5	F	G	761
6	T		775-77
7	T		782-3
8	F	3	782
9	F	5	773
10	T		
11	T		778, 781
12	T	5	773
13	T		778-79

Multiple-Choice

Question	Answer	Glossary/ Key Idea	Textbook ref. page
1	b	3	768
2	e	3	768
3	a		768
4	d		762-63
5	e		763
6	b		766-67
7	e	5	773
8	d	6	775
9	b		776-77

CHAPTER 17   WAITING LINES

True/False

Question	Answer	Glossary/ Key Idea	Textbook ref. page
1	T	2	809
2	F		809
3	T	3	810
4	T		816
5	F		813
6	T	G	811
7	T		815
8	T		816
9	T		829

Multiple-Choice

Question	Answer	Glossary/ Key Idea	Textbook ref. page
1	c		812
2	d		816-17
3	b	G	814
4	b		815
5	d	2	809
6	c		816
7	b		816-17
8	e	5	810-11

CHAPTER 17S   SIMULATION

True/False

Question	Answer	Glossary/ Key Idea	Textbook ref. page
1	F	8	842
2	F	G, 3	844
3	T		853
4	T	G, 1,8	842
5	T	2	842
6	T		845
7	F		
8	T		847
9	F	8	854

Multiple-Choice

Question	Answer	Glossary/ Key Idea	Textbook ref. page
1	e	8	842
2	a		845-46
3	e		854
4	a	4	847
5	b		842

SOLUTIONS TO STUDY GUIDE PROBLEMS

CHAPTER 2 PRODUCTIVITY, COMPETITION, AND STRATEGY

1. Productivity $\quad = \quad \dfrac{\text{Number of window fans}}{\text{Direct labor hours}}$

    $\quad = \quad \dfrac{1728 \text{ window fans}}{(12 \text{ emp.})*(9 \text{ days})*(8 \text{ hrs.})}$

    $\quad = \quad$ 2 fans/hour.

2. Productivity $\quad = \quad \dfrac{\text{Number of window fans}}{\text{Direct labor hours}}$

    $\quad = \quad \dfrac{1872 \text{ window fans}}{(12)\,(10)\,(8) + (10)\,(1)\,8}$

    $= 1.8$ fans/hour.

    b. The productivity of the window fans is higher.

3. a. Multi-factorProductivity $\quad = \quad \dfrac{\text{Standard price of fans}}{\text{Labor cost} + \text{Material cost} + \text{Overhead cost}}$

    $\quad = \quad \dfrac{(1728)*(30) + (1872)*(20)}{(864 + 1040)*(16) + (1728)*(6) + (1872)*(4) + 9500}$

    $= 1.54.$

    b. A dollar's worth of inputs produces \$1.54 worth of outputs.

CHAPTER 2S DECISION THEORY

1. a. The maximax criterion involves selecting the best payoff for each alternative and then selecting the best payoff in that set.

Alternative	Best Payoff
A	$500
B	700 (best)
C	600

Implement Alternative B.

b. The maximin criterion involves selecting the worst payoff for each alternative and then selecting the best payoff in that set.

Alternative	Worst Payoff
A	$300 (best)
B	100
C	(300)

Implement Alternative A.

c. The LaPlace criterion involves selecting the best mean payoff.

Alternative	Mean Payoff
A	$400* (tie)
B	400 (tie)
C	150

Implement Alternative A or Alternative B.

*Note: (500 + 300)/2 = 400.

d. Find the regret for each cell by subtracting each entry in the state of nature <u>column</u> from the maximum entry in the column

State of Nature

Alternative	1	2
A	200	300
B	0	500
C	1,000	0

e. The minimax regret criterion involves selecting the worst regret for each alternative, and then selecting the best of that set.

Alternative	Worst Regret
A	$300 (best)
B	500
C	1,000

Implement Alternative A.

2.

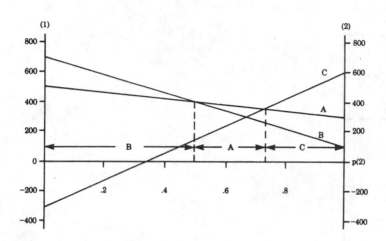

At the points where the lines in the diagram intersect the y coordinates are equal; y = a + bx, where a is the intercept on the (1) column and b = payoff #2 - payoff #1.

A line: $y = 500 + (300 - 500)x = 500 - 200x$.
B line: $y = 700 + (100 - 700)x = 700 - 600x$.
C line: $y = -300 + (600 - (-300))x = -300 + 900x$.

The A line and the B line intersect.

$500 - 200p(2) = 700 - 600p(2)$
$-200 = -400p(2)$

$p(2) = 0.5$
$p(1) = 1 - p(2) = 1 - 0.5 = 0.5$.

The A line and the C line intersect.

$$500 - 200p(2) = -300 + 900p(2)$$
$$800 = 1100p(2)$$

$$p(2) = 0.727$$
$$p(1) = 1 - p(2) = 1 - 0.727 = .273.$$

a. Choose A for $0.5 < p(2) < 0.727$.
b. Choose B for $0 < p(2) < 0.5$.
c. Choose C for $0.727 < p(2) < 1.0$.

3. a.

Alternative	Best Payoff
Large Order	$5,000 (best)
Medium Order	3,000
Small Order	1,000

Place a large order.

b.

Alternative	Worst Payoff
Large Order	($5,000)
Medium Order	(2,000)
Small Order	500 (best)

Place a small order.

c.

Alternative	Meant Payoff
Large Order	$667*
Medium Order	1,000
Small Order	667

Place a medium order.
*Note: $(5000 + 1000 - 4000)/3 = 667$.

d. Find the regret for each cell in the payoff matrix by subtracting each entry in the state of nature <u>column</u> from the maximum payoff in the column. For the Heavy Snow column, the best payoff is $5,000, and the regrets are 0, $3,000, and $4,500.

	State of Nature		
Alternative	Heavy Snow	Medium Snow	Light Snow
Large Order	0	2,000	5,000
Medium Order	3,000	0	3,000
Small Order	4,500	2,500	0

e.

Alternative	Worst Regret
Large Order	$5,000
Medium Order	3,000 (best)
Small Order	4,500

Place a medium order.

4. a.

State of Nature

Alternative	Heavy Snow .10	Medium Snow .50	Light Snow .40	Expected Value
Large Order	5,000	1,000	(4,000)	(600)*
Medium Order	2,000	3,000	(2,000)	900 (best)
Small Order	500	500	1,000	(100)

Place a medium order.
*Note: 5000(.10) + 1000(.50) - 4000(.40) = -600.

b.

State of Nature

Alternative	Heavy Snow .10	Medium Snow .50	Light Snow .40	Expected Loss
Large Order	0	2,000	5,000	3,000*
Medium Order	3,000	0	3,000	1,500 (best)
Small Order	4,500	2,500	0	1,700

*Note: 0(.10) + 2000(.50) + 5000(.40) = 3000.

Place a medium order. The strategy which is selected by the least expected loss criterion will always be the same as the one selected by the best expected value criterion.

c. EVPI = least expected loss = $1,500.

d. $1,500 is the absolute maximum which might be spent to obtain information about the states of nature. The manager might, for example, hire a weather forecaster to forecast next winter's snowfall.

5. a. Set E(A) = E(B); solve for X.

.20(500) + .80(1200) = .20X + .80(400)

X = $3,700.

b. Since E(B) > E(A) at X = $4,000, the decision maker would prefer alternative B.

CHAPTER 3S CONTINUOUS IMPROVEMENT

1. a.

Piece	Total
Back- panel	8
Top shelf	10
1 Middle shelf	31
2 Middle shelves	6
1 Side panel	35
2 Side panels	7
Screws	21
Carton	0
Total	118

Weekday	Total
Monday	23
Tuesday	26
Wednesday	23
Thursday	22
Friday	24
Total	118

b. 1 side panel.
c. Perhaps a worker could be delegated to tape the panels together in sets of two, so that the packer must pick up both of them. You may be able to think of something better.
d. 1 middle shelf.
e. Perhaps a worker could be delegated to tape the panels together in sets of two.
f. The day totals are all about the same, and no day appears to be particularly error prone.
g. No action is needed.

2. Percent

3. a. The rate of missing pieces has been reduced from 118 per week to 41, which is an improvement of 77 pieces, or 65%.
    b. The package of screws.
    c. Perhaps a brightly colored tag could be attached to the package, to make it noticeable. You may be able to think of something better.

CHAPTER 4S RELIABILTY

1. a.

b. Let p(A) be the probability that component A does not work.

   $p(A) = 1 - p(A) = 1 - .90 = .10.$
   $p(B) = 1 - p(B) = 1 - .70 = .30.$
   $p(C) = 1 - p(C) = 1 - .95 = .05.$
   $p(D) = 1 - p(D) = 1 - .60 = .40.$

c. p(system works) = p(A)p(B)p(C)p(D) = (.90)(.70)(.95)(.60) = .3591.

d. 1) A works; B works; C works; D works.
   2) A works; B fails; B-B works; C works; D works.
   3) A works; B works; C works; D fails; D-B works.
   4) A works; B fails; B-B works; C works; D fails; D-B works.

e. The probability will be the sum of the probabilities for each of the four cases above.

1) p(A)p(B)p(C)p(D) = .3591.
2) p(A)p(B)p(B-B)p($\overline{C}$)p(D) = .1077.
3) p(A)p(B)p($\overline{C}$)p(D)p(D-B) = .1436.
4) p(A)p(B)p(B-B)p($\overline{C}$)p(D)p(D-B) = .0431.

The probability that the system will work is .6535.

f. The improvement is .6535 - .3591 = .2944. The backups have nearly doubled the reliability of the system, but it is still very low. Even with the backups, the system can be expected to fail about 1 time in 3.

2. a.   p(system works) = p(A)p(B)p(C) = .7351.
    b.   For one additional C:

    p(works)   .7351
    p($\overline{A}$)p(B)p(C)p(C) =   .1838
    p(works)   .9189

For 2 additional C's:

    p(works) =   .9189
    p(A)p($\overline{B}$)p($\overline{C}$)p(C)p(C) =   .0460
                                .9649 (> .95; stop)

Two additional C's will be required.

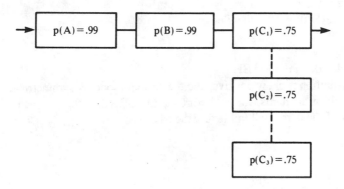

    d.   Two C's will cost $12,000.

3. a.   p(T < 3200 hrs) = 1 - exp(-T/MTBF) = 1 - exp(-3200/4000) = 1 - .4473 = .5507.

    b.   p(T > 6400) = exp(-T/MTBF) = exp(-6400/4000) = .2019.

    c.   p(failure before time, T) = .02.
         1 - exp(-T/4000) = .02
         exp(-T/4000) = .98
         ln(exp(-T/4000)) = -T/4000; ln(.98) = -.02
         T/4000 = .02
         T = 80 hours.

    d.   No; over half of the area falls to the left of the MTBF.

205

4. a. Convert from the T scale to the z scale.

$z = (T - MTBF)/s = (22000 - 20000)/800 = 2.50$.
$p(T < 22000) = p(z < 0) + p(0 < z < 2.50) = .5000 + .4938 = .9938$.

b. Convert from the T scale to the z scale.

$z = (T - MTBF)/s = (19000 - 20000)/800 = -1.25$.
$p(T > 19000) = p(-1.25 < z < 0) + p(z > 0) = .3944 + .5000 = .8944$.

c. Let T' = the warranted service live. Then,
$p(T < T') = .01$; $p(T' < T < MTBF) = .5000 - .0100 = .4900$.   Find the area of .4900 in the table of the standardized normal curve, read the z value, and convert to the T scale.
$p(T' < T < MTBF) = p(z' < z < 0)$; $z' = -2.33$.
$T' = MTBF - z's = 20000 - 2.33(800) = 18,100$ miles.

d. Yes; half of the area is on each side of the MTBF.
e. The negative exponential distribution is skew positive, and the normal model is symmetrical. The normal model indicates that half of the items will fail before the MTBF, while the exponential model indicates that over half of the items will fail before the MTBF.

5. a. MTBF = 20 days.
    b. MTR = 2 days.
    c. Availability = $\dfrac{MTBF}{MTBF + MTR} = \dfrac{20}{20 + 2} = .909$.
    d. The copier is operational about 90% of the time.

6. a. MTBF = 25 days.
    b. MTR = 3 days.
    c. Availability = .893.
    d. No; the new machine has less operational time than the old one.

CHAPTER 5 PROCESS SELECTION AND CAPACITY PLANNING

1. a. Design capacity = 8 hrs. x 400 tumblers = 3,200 tumblers per 8-hour shift.
    b. Effective capacity = Design capacity - Nonproductive activities.

Design capacity	8.0 hrs.
Less: Breaks	.5 hrs.
Heat-up	.5 hrs.
Net productive time	7.0 hrs.

    Effective capacity = 7 hrs. x 400 tumblers = 2,800 tumblers.
    Effective capacity percent = (100)(2800)/3200 = 87.5%.

    c. Actual output = 10,000/5 = 2,000 tumblers per 8-hour shift. (This is a mean output. In reality there will be variation; some shifts will exceed 2,000 tumblers and some will fall short.)
    d. Efficiency = Actual output/Effective capacity = (100)(2000)/2800 = 71.43%.
    e. Utilization = Actual output/Design capacity = (100)(2000)/3200 = 62.50%.

2. a. Design capacity = 160 frying pans x 2 shifts x 20 working days = 6,400 frying pans per four weeks.
    b. 160/8 = 20 frying pans per hour.
        8 hrs. x 2 shifts x 20 working days = 320 hrs. available.
    Less)
    Breaks: (12 min. x 2 per shift x 2 shifts x 20 working days)/60 = 16 hrs.
    Cleaning:: 2 hrs. x 4 weeks   8 hrs.
                Quality Circle   4 hrs.

    Therefore, Net productive time is:
    Available time   320 hours
    Less 16 + 8 + 4 =   28 hours
                           292 hours

    Effective capacity = 292 hrs. x 20 frying pans = 5,840 frying pans per four weeks.
    Effective capacity percent = (100)(5840)/6400 = 91.25%

    c. Actual output = 3,500 frying pans.
    d. Efficiency = Actual output/Effective Capacity = (100)(3500)/5840 = 59.93%.
    e. Utilization = Actual output/Design capacity = (100)(3500)/6400 = 54.69%.
    f. In terms of one 8-hour shift: Design capacity = 160 frying pans.
        Effective capacity = 146 frying pans.
    The percentage answers will be the same as above.

3. a. Total Revenue = R x Q = 199.95Q.
   b. Total cost = FC + VC x Q = 300000 + (60.25 + 25.70 + 21.50 + 17.50)Q = 300000 + 124.95Q.
   c. Profit per year = R x Q - (VC x Q + FC) = 199.95Q - (124.95Q - 300000) = 75Q - 300000.
   d. Q_{BEP} = FC/(R - VC) = 300000/75 = 4,000 units.
   e. Revenue at the break-even point = 4000(199.95) = $799,800.
   f. Income at the break-even point = $0.
   g. Profit at 9,000 units = 75(9000) - 300000 = $375,000.
   h. Number of units = (SP + FC)/(R - VC) = (900000 + 300000)/75 = 16,000 units.

4. a. Total revenue = R x Q = 99.75Q.
   b. Total cost = FC + VC x Q = 94400 + 49.75Q.
   c. Profit per year = R x Q - (VC x Q + FC) = 99.75Q - (49.75Q + 94400) = 50Q - 94400.
   d. Q_{BEP} = FC/(R - VC) = 94400/50 = 1,888 chairs.
   e. Revenue at the break-even point = 99.75(1888) = $188,328.
   f. Income at the break-even point = $0.
   g. Profit at 1,500 chairs = 50(1500) - 94400 = -$19,400, which is a net loss.
   h. Number of chairs = (SP + FC)/(R - VC) = (94400 + 75000)/50 = 3,388 chairs.

5. a. It is necessary to estimate the total cost of each possible number of calls under each billing plan.
   Plan a) The cost will be $20, regardless of the number of calls.
   Plan b) The cost will be $16 + (number of calls - 50) x $0.08, when there are more than 50 calls.
   Plan c) The cost will be $12 + (number of calls - 20) x $0.10, when there are more than 20 calls.

   The payoff table will be:

   | | State of Nature | | | |
Alternative	60 calls	90 calls	120 calls	160 calls
Plan a	20.00	20.00	20.00	20.00
Plan b	16.80	19.20	21.60	24.80
Plan c	16.00	19.00	22.00	26.00

   b. Select the best payoff for each state of nature; they are 16.00, 19.00, 20.00, and 20.00. Subtract every entry in the <u>column</u> from the best entry. The differences are the regrets.

   | | State of Nature | | | |
Alternative	60 calls	90 calls	120 calls	160 calls
Plan a	4.00	1.00	0	0
Plan b	.80	.20	1.60	4.80
Plan c	0	0	2.00	6.00

   Pick the worst regret for each alternative:

Alternative	Worst Regret
Plan a	4.00 (best)
Plan b	4.80
Plan c	6.00

The subscriber should select Plan a.

    c.   It is improper to use the maximax criterion here because the payoffs are expenses rather than incomes.

    d.   Incorporate the probabilities into the payoff table and calculate the expected value of each plan.

State of Nature

Probability	.40	.30	.20	.10
Alternative	60 calls	90 calls	120 calls	160 calls
Plan a	20.00	20.00	20.00	20.00
Plan b	16.80	19.20	21.60	24.80
Plan c	16.00	19.00	22.00	26.00

The subscriber should select Plan c.
*Note: $(16.80)(.40) + (19.20)(.30) + (21.60)(.20) + (24.80)(.10) = 19.28$.

    e.   The subscriber should select Plan c.

6. a.   Capacity = 4 disks/hr. x 15 hrs./day x 250 days/yr = 15,000 disks/yr.
    b.   Depreciation = cost/service life = \$80,000/5 yrs. = \$16,000.
    c. Q_{BEP} = FC/(R - VC) = 4(\$16,000)/(\$19 - \$7) = 5,333disks.
    d.   Capacity = 6 disks/hr. x 15 hrs./day x 250 days/yr. = 22,500 disks/yr.
    e.   Capacity = 4(15,000) + 1(22,500) = 82,500 disks/yr.
    f.   VC = [\$7(60,000) + \$6(22,500)]/82,500 = \$6.727.
    g. Q_{BEP} = FC/(R - VC) = [4(\$16,000) + 1(\$17,000)]/(\$19 - \$6.727) = 6,600 disks.
    h.   Capacity = 4(15,000) + 2(22,500) = 105,000 disks/yr.
    i.   VC = [\$7(60,000) + \$6(45,000)]/105,000 = \$6.571.
    j. Q_{BEP} = FC/(R - VC) = [4(\$16,000) + 2(\$17,000)]/(\$19 - \$6.571) = 7,885 disks.

1.   a,b,c.

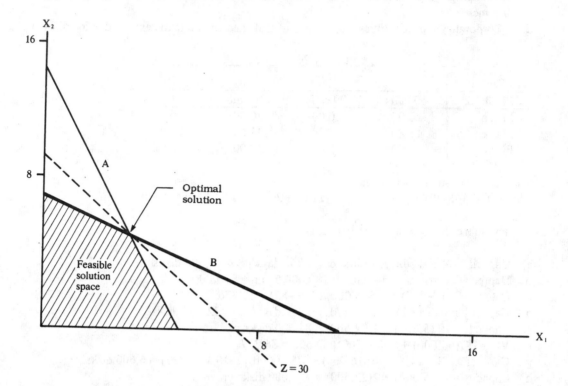

d. $x_1 = 4$; $x_2 = 4.67$.

e. $Z = 4(4) + 3(4.67) = \$30.00$.

2. a. The initial tableau is:

C		4	3	0	0	
Variables in solution		x_1	x_2	s_1	s_2	Quantity
0	s_1	14	6	1	0	84
0	s_2	7	12	0	1	84
	Z	0	0	0	0	0
	C-Z	4	3	0	0	

The first pivot point is 14.

b. The final tableau:

C		4	3	0	0	
Variables in solution		x_1	x_2	s_1	s_2	Quantity
4	x_1	1	0	1	0	4
3	x_2	0	1	0	1	14/3
	Z	4	3	3/14	1/7	30
	C-Z	0	0	-3/14	-1/7	

c. $x_1 = 4$; $x_2 = 4.67$.
d. Nothing is left over in either constraint.

3. a,b,c.

d. $x_1 = 35$; $x_2 = 15$.
e. $Z = 5(35) + 8(15) = \$295.00$.

4. a.   The initial tableau:

C		5	8	0	0	0	99	99	99	
Variables in solution		x_1	x_2	s_1	s_2	s_3	a_1	a_2	a_3	Quantity
99	a_1	2	2	-1	0	0	1	0	0	100
99	a_2	10	35	0	-1	0	0	1	0	700
99	a_3	0	1	0	0	-1	0	0	1	15
	Z	1188	3762	-99	-99	-99	99	99	99	0
	C-Z	-1183	-3754	99	99	99	0	0	0	

The pivot is 1 (at a_3 and x_2).

b.   The final tableau:

C		5	8	0	0	0	99	99	99	
Variables in solution		x_1	x_2	s_1	s_2	s_3	a_1	a_2	a_3	Quantity
99	s_2	0	0	-5	1	-25	1	0	0	175
99	x_1	1	0	-1/2	0	1	1/2	0	-3/2	35
99	x_2	0	1	0	0	-1	0	0	1	15
	Z	5	8	-5/2	0	-3	5/2	0	1/2	295
	C-Z	0	0	4	5/2	0	3	193/2	99	197/2

c. $x_1 = 35$; $x_2 = 15$.
d. $s_1 = 0$; $s_2 = 175$; $s_3 = 0$.

5. a. Because the problem contains information about the selling price, it will involve maximization.
    b. The items under managerial control are the number of checker sets and the number of chess sets to be produced next week. Use mnemonic symbols; we suggest H = the number of checker sets and K = the number of chess sets.
    c. The coefficients of the objective function must be the contribution per unit. The contribution per checker set is $7.95 - $3.95 = $4.00. The objective function is maximize Z = 4H + 9K.
    d. The limitations on production are the supply of pine rods, the operating time of the power saw, and the operating time of the turning machine. Be sure that you use the same units of measurement within each constraint.

    Pine Rods) $2H + 7K \leq 350$ board feet
    Power Saw) $(1/2)H + K \leq 30$ hours
    Turning Machine) $(1/2)H + (3/2)K \leq 36$ hours
    Non-negativity constraints) $H \geq 0$; $K \geq 0$.

e.

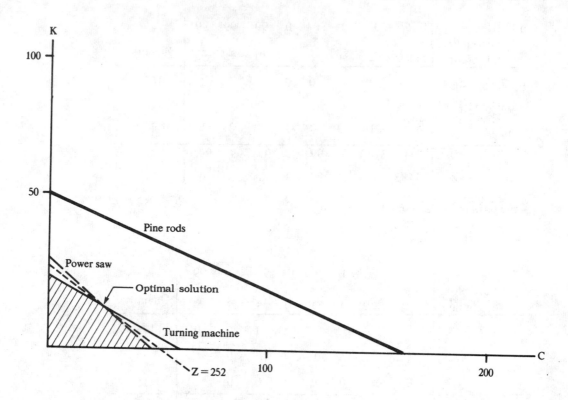

f.   H = 36 checker sets; K = 12 chess sets.
g.   Z = 4(36) + 9(12) = $252.00

6. Solve these problems by substituting the values of the decision variables into the constraints.

   a. $2H + 7K \leq 350$
      $2(36) + 7(12) = 156$
      $350 - 156 = 194$ board feet left over.

   b. There will be no idle time on the saw.
   c. There will be no idle time on the turning machine.
   d. These are the values of the slack variables:
      $s_1 = 194$ for the pine rods
      $s_2 = 0$ for the saw
      $s_3 = 0$ for the turning machine

   e. Additional production will require additional saw time and additional turning time.

7. a. Here is the initial tableau:

C		4	9	0	0	0	
	Variables in solution	H	K	s_1	s_2	s_2	Quantity
0	s_1	2	7	1	0	0	350
0	s_2	1/2	1	0	1	0	30
0	s_3	1/2	3/2	0	0	1	36
	Z	0	0	0	0	0	0
	C-Z	4	9	0	0	0	

The first pivot point is 3/2.

   b. Here is the final tableau:

C		4	9	0	0	0	
	Variables in solution	H	K	s_1	s_2	s_2	Quantity
0	s_1	0	0	1	2	-6	194
0	H	1	0	0	6	-4	36
0	K	0	1	0	-2	2	12
	Z	4	9	0	6	2	252
	C-Z	0	0	0	-6	-2	

   c. The shadow price for the saw is -6.

d. If one more hour of sawing time was available, the value of the objective function would increase by $6.

8. a. Since the problem contains information about the cost of the ingredients, it will involve minimization.
    b. The dietician can decide how much of each ingredient to use in the recipe. Use P and Q as symbols.
    c. Minimize Z = 5P + 3Q.
    d. The food must provide certain quantities of vitamins.

    A)   2000P + 6000Q ≥ 500 units
    B)   3000P + 3000Q ≥ 500 units
    C)   5000P + 0Q   ≥ 1000 units

e.

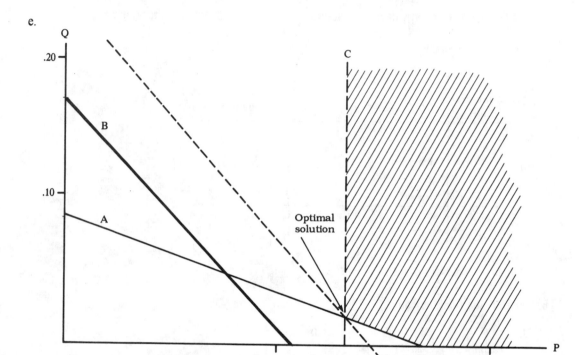

f. P = .20 kg; Q = .017 kg.
g. One serving will be .20 + .017 = .217 kilograms, or about 7.6 ounces.
h. Z = 5(.20) + 3(.017) = $1.05.

9. Substitute the values of the decision variables into the constraints.

    a. 2000P + 6000Q ≥ 500
        2000(1/5) + 6000(1/60) = 500

216

$500 - 500 = 0$ excess units of vitamin A.

b. There will be 150 excess units of vitamin B.
c. There will be no excess units of vitamin C.
d. These are the surplus variables.

    $s_1 = 0$ units of vitamin A

    $s_2 = 150$ units of vitamin B

    $s_3 = 0$ units of vitamin C

e. Reducing the requirements for vitamin A or for vitamin C will reduce the cost of the food.

10. a. Here is the initial tableau:

C		5	3	0	0	0	99	99	99	
	Variables in solution	P	Q	s_1	s_2	s_3	a_1	a_2	a_3	Quantity
99	a_1	2000	6000	-1	0	0	1	0	0	500
99	a_2	3000	3000	0	-1	0	0	1	0	500
99	a_3	5000	0	0	0	-1	0	0	1	1000
	Z	990000	891000	-99	-99	-99	99	99	99	0
	C-Z	-989995	-890997	99	99	99	0	0	0	

The first pivot will be the 3000 in the P column.

b. Here is the final tableau:

C		5	3	0	0	0	99	99	99	
	Variables in solution	P	Q	s_1	s_2	s_3	a_1	a_2	a_3	Quantity
3	Q	0	1	-1/6000	0	1/15000	1/6000	0	-1/15000	1/60
5	P	1	0	0	0	-1/5000	0	0	1/5000	1/5
0	s_2	0	0	-1/2	1	-2/5	1/2	-1	2/5	150
	Z	5	3	-1/2000	0	-1/1250	1/2000	0	1/1250	21/20
	C-Z	0	0	1/2000	0	1/1250	-	99	-	

c. 1/1250
d. If the requirements for vitamin C could be reduced by one unit, the value of the objective function would be *decreased* by \$.0008.

11. a. Since the problem contains information about the selling price, it will involve maximization.
  b. The management can decide how many hockey sticks, hockey pucks, and baseball bats to produce next week. We suggest using H, P, and B.
  c. Maximize $Z = 12H + 7P + 8B$.
  d. Oak: $4H + 2P + 3B \le 600$ board feet

    Saw: $.05H + .025P + .025B \le 3.6$ hours

    Finishing: $H + .5P + 1.5B \le 160$ hours

12. Here is the printout of the solution to problem #11, using LINDO software:

```
LP OPTIMUM FOUND AT STEP    2

      OBJECTIVE FUNCTION VALUE

1)     1096.0000000


  VARIABLE          VALUE     REDUCED COST
      H            .000000       2.000000
      P          55.999990        .000000
      B          88.000000        .000000


  ROW   SLACK OR SURPLUS     DUAL PRICES
   2)       224.000000          .000000
   3)          .000000       260.000000
   4)          .000000         1.000000

NO. ITERATIONS  = 2
```

REDUCED COST: the values in the C - Z row of the decision variable columns. These are the amounts that the respective objective function coefficients would have to be increased in order to bring that variable into solution. For variables that are in solution, the amount is zero.

DUAL PRICES: the values in the C - Z row of the surplus variable columns. LINDO prints all of these as positive numbers although they are negative in the final tableau of a linear programming problem in maximization.

a. Produce: H = 0 hockey sticks; P = 56 pucks and B = 88 baseball bats. (The 55.999990 is caused by the computer's internal representation of decimal fractions and should be read to the nearest whole number.)
b. $Z = 12H + 7P + 8B = 12(0) + 7(56) + 8(88) = \$1,096$. (Find this number in 1), above.)
c. Use the Oak constraint, $4H + 2P + 3B \leq 600$
   $4(0) + 2(56) + 3(88) = 376$.
   $s_1 = 600 - 376 = 224$ board feet (in row 2)).
d. There will be no idle time on the saw.
e. There will be no idle time in the finishing department.
f. Additional production will require additional time on the saw and additional time in the finishing department.
g. Add a constraint to the problem: $H \geq 30$.
h. The shadow price of oak is 0.
i. An additional supply of oak will have no effect on the value of the objective function, since there is a surplus of oak under this manufacturing schedule.

CHAPTER 6 FACILITIES LAYOUT

1. a. The operating time (OT) is (8)(60) - 20 - 40 = 420 minutes per shift. One work station would require 9.1 minutes to produce one widget. In one shift it could produce 420/9.1= 46 widgets, and the objective cannot be achieved.

    b. With 14 workstations, the output is limited by the station with the longest time, which is station k with 1.2 minutes. In eight hours, fourteen stations could produce 420/1.2 = 350 widgets, which is more than adequate.

    c.

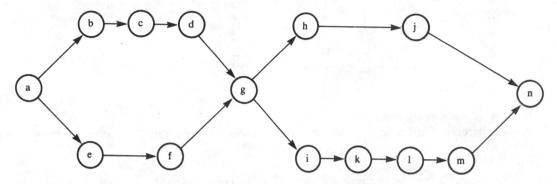

    d. The minimum number of work stations = DΣt/OT = 300(9.1)/420 = 6.5 work stations.

2. a. Count the tasks which follow a particular task on a path through the precedence diagram which was obtained in #1c.

Task	Number Following
a	13
b	10
c	9
d	8
e	9
f	8
g	7
h	2
i	4
j	1
k	3
l	2
m	1
n	0

The cycle time (CT) = OT/D = 420/300 = 1.4 minutes. Each work station can spend a maximum of 1.4 minutes accomplishing a set of tasks.

Here is a set of feasible assignments. (It may not be the only one.) The idle time per station is the maximum total time (1.4 minutes) - the total station time.

Station	Tasks	Total time (minutes)	Idle time (minutes)
1	a,b,c	1.1	0.3
2	d,e	1.4	0
3	f	0.5	0.9
4	g	1.1	0.3
5	h,j	1.1	0.3
6	I	0.8	0.6
7	k	1.2	0.2
8	l	0.9	0.5
9	m,n	1.0	0.4
			3.5

b. 9 work stations are required.

c. The percent of idle time = (Idle Time per Cycle)/(number of stations)×(maximum station time)

$$= 3.5/[(9)(1.4)] \approx 27.78\%.$$

3. a. The positional weight of a task is the sum of its own time and the times of all following tasks on the precedence diagram (#1 - c).

Task	Positional Weight
a	9.1 minutes
b	7.4
.	.
.	.
m	1.0
n	0.4

The assignment of tasks to work stations will be identical with Problem #2a. Because there must be a high correlation between the number of following tasks and the sum of the task times, these two rules must produce very similar layouts.

b. 9 work stations will be required.

c. The same as #3c.

4. a. 5! = 5(4)(3)(2)(1) = 120 possible layouts.

    b. The distance matrix.

	From				
To	A	B	C	D	E
A	0	18	36	54	24
B	18	0	18	36	42
C	36	18	0	18	60
D	54	36	18	0	78
E	24	42	60	78	0

    c. One layout is shown in the diagram below. This one starts with departments 3 and 4, since they
        have the heaviest traffic.

    d. Find the products of the loads and distances for every pair of departments.

Departments	Loads	Areas	Distances	Products
3 to 4	140	D, C	18'	2,520
3 to 5	10	D, B	36'	360
.	.	.	.	.
.	.	.	.	.
1 to 5	30	E, B	42'	1,260
1 to 2	100	E, A	24'	2,400
Total (The Load-Distance Index)				30,600

    e. It is not known whether this is the minimum possible value among all of the 120 values of the
        load-distance index.

5. a. In the traffic matrix, the rows represented "from" and the columns represented "to." In the distance matrix, the rows will represent "to" and the columns will represent "from." Use the diagram in #4c to align the elements of the distance matrix with the elements of the traffic matrix. Thus, column 1 of the distance matrix must be "from E," since department 1 is in area E. Row 3 of the distance matrix must be "to D," since department 3 is in area D. Here is the rearranged distance matrix:

	From				
To	E	A	D	C	B
E	0	24	78	60	42
A	24	0	54	36	18
D	78	54	0	18	36
C	60	36	18	0	18
B	42	18	36	18	0

   b. Each element on the principal diagonal of the product matrix will be the sum of the products of the traffic from each department and the distances from each department to all of the other departments.

6. a. One assignment of departments to areas is shown in the diagram.

   b. The Load-Distance Index = 36,000. Compare this value with the value in #4d. The constraints on the locations of the departments have caused the value to increase.

CHAPTER 7 DESIGN OF WORK SYSTEMS

1. a. $p = 100(60)/300 = 20\%$.

    b. $s_p = \ddot{O}\sqrt{p(1-p)/n} = \sqrt{20(100-20)/300} = 2.31\%$.

    c.   Lower Confidence Limit $= p - z(s_p) = 20 - 1.96(2.31 = 15.47\%$.
         Upper Confidence Limit $= p + z(s_p) = 20 + 1.96(2.31) = 24.53\%$.

    d.   There is a .95 probability that the true percent of idle time in the packaging department lies between 15.47% and 24.53%.

    e.   The loss due to idle time will be the total of the loss due to the foreman's idle time and the loss due to the workers' idle time:

         Foreman) .20(40 hrs.)($12.00)   = $96.00
         Workers) .20(40 hrs.)($5.00)(3 workers) = <u>120.00</u>
                   Total weekly loss $216.00

    f. $n = z^2(p)(100 - p)/e^2 = (1.96)^2(20)(100 - 20)/2^2 \approx 1{,}537$. Therefore, 1,237 additional observations will be required.

    g.   The new value of p cannot be calculated until the additional observations are obtained.

2. a.   The population mean is unknown.

    b.   The Observed Time (OT) $= \Sigma x/n = 141.1/16 = 8.82$ min.

    c. $\Sigma(x - \bar{x})^2 = \Sigma x^2 - (\Sigma x)^2/n = 1252.27 - (141.1)^2/16 = 7.94$.

         $s^2 = \Sigma(x - \bar{x})^2/(n - 1) = 7.94/(16 - 1) = .5293$.

         $s = \sqrt{.5293} = .7277$ min.

    d. $s = s/\sqrt{n} = .7277/\sqrt{16} = .1819$ min.

    e.   The Lower Confidence Limit $= OT - z(s) = 8.82 - 1.96(.1819) = 8.46$ min.
         The Upper Confidence Limit $= OT + z(s) = 8.82 + 1.96(.1819) = 9.18$ min.

    f. $n = z^2(s^2)/e^2 = (1.96)^2(.5293)/(.15)^2 \approx 91.00$. 75 additional repetitions of the task of installing the off-on switch.

3. a.   Normal Time (NT) $= OT \times PR = 8.82(1.25) = 11.025$ min.

    b.   Because a performance rating of 125% is greater than 100%, the worker was working rapidly.

    c.   The allowance percent (A) $= 100$(total allowance time)/(job time) $= 100(20 + 20 + 30 + 20)/[(8(60) - 90] = 23.08\%$ of job time.

    d.   Standard Time (ST) $= NT(1 + A) = 11.025(1 + .2308) = 13.57$ minutes per installation.

4. a.   Number of installations $= 8(60)/13.57 \approx 35$ switches.

    b.   The standard labor cost $= (13.57/60)(9)(1.35) = \$2.75$.

5. a.   The allowance percent (A) $= 100$(total allowance time)/(working time) $= 100(90)/[8(60)] = 18.75\%$

    b.   Standard time (ST) $= NT/(1 - A) = 11.025/(1 - .1875) = 13.57$ minutes per installation. (Compare to #3-d)

1. a.   .477(2000) = 954 direct labor hours.
   b.   6.315(2000) = 12,630 direct labor hours.
   c.   .663(3000) = 1,989 direct labor hours.
   d.   5.101(3000) = 15,303 direct labor hours.

2. a.   Every time the output doubles, the time required to produce one unit is 85% as large as it was before the doubling occurred.

   b.   .686(25000) = 17,150 direct labor hours.
   c.   Direct Labor) 17,150 hrs.($9.00) = \$154,350.00
        Fringe Benefits) 154,350.00(.30) =   46,305.00
        Direct Materials)   200,000.00
                Total   \$400,655.00

   d.   12.402(25000) = 310,050 direct labor hours.
   e.   Direct Labor) 310,050 hrs.($9.00) = \$2,790,450.00
        Fringe Benefits) 2 790 450.00(.30) =   837,135.00
        Direct Materials) 20($200,000) =   4,000,000.00
                Total Cost   \$7,627,585.00

   f.   The mean direct cost per tanker is estimated at 7,627,585/20 » \$381,380.00. The price per tanker would be 381380 x (2.50) = \$953,450.00.

3. a.   Ln 2 = 0.6931.

   b.   Ln .85 = -0.1626.
   c.   b = Ln .85/Ln 2 = -0.1625/0.6931 = -0.2345.
   d. $T_4 = T_1 \times n^b = 5000(4^{-0.2345}) = 5000(.7225) = 3,612$ hrs.

4. a.   Ln .82 = -0.1985.
   b.   b = Ln .82/Ln 2 = -0.1985/0.6931 = -0.2863.
   c. $T_5 = T_1 \times n^b = 7000(5^{-0.2863}) = 7000(.6308) = 4,415$ hrs.

CHAPTER 8 LOCATION PLANNING

1. a. A) $C_A = 1,500,000 + 1.25x$

   B) $C_B = 1,250,000 + 1.75x$

b, c.

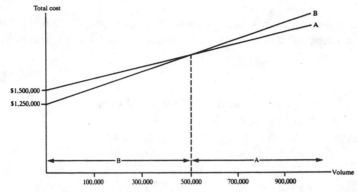

d. For 400,000 batteries, location B is less expensive. For 800,000 batteries, location A is less expensive.

e. At the cutoff point (Q), the total costs will be equal at both locations.

$$C_A = C_B$$

$$1,500,000 + 1.25Q = 1,250,000 + 1.75Q$$

$$Q = 500,000 \text{ batteries.}$$

2. a. A) $C_A = 3,500,000 + 600x$
      B) $C_B = 3,000,000 + 800x$
      C) $C_C = 4,000,000 + 500x$
      D) $C_D = 4,500,000 + 400x$

b, c.

d. For 4,000 chips, location A is the least expensive. For 12,000 chips, location D is the least expensive.

e. $C_B = C_A$

$3,000,000 + 800Q = 3,500,000 + 600Q$
$Q = 2,500$ microchips.

At a lower volume, B is superior; at a higher volume, A is superior. The cutoff point between A and C is 5,000 microchips. The cutoff point between C and D is 10,000 microchips.

3. a.

		Score		Weighted score	
Factor	Weight	A	B	A	B
1. Public Transportation	.20	9	2	1.80	0.40
2. Parking lot	.40	3	7	1.20	2.80
3. Property taxes	.25	6	4	1.50	1.00
4. Electricity rates	.15	5	8	0.75	1.20
				5.25	5.40

b. The condominium should be built in suburb B, since it has the higher composite score.

4. a.

b. $\bar{x} = \dfrac{\Sigma Qx}{\Sigma Q} = \dfrac{1(2) + 3(5) + 2(3) + 6(10) + 2(6)}{1 + 3 + 2 + 6 + 2} = 6.78$

c. $\bar{y} = \dfrac{\Sigma Qy}{\Sigma Q} = \dfrac{1(3) + 3(2) + 2(6) + 6(4) + 2(5)}{1 + 3 + 2 + 6 + 2} = 3.93$

d.

e. The partners should build a new warehouse at $\bar{x} = 6.78$ and $\bar{y} = 3.93$, since shipping expenses should be lower from the new warehouse.

227

1. a, b.

To: From:	A	B	Dummy	Supply
1	12 250	10	0	250
2	14 350	11 50	0	400
3	9	12 450	0	450
4	8	7 200	0 150	350
Demand	600	700	150	1450

c.

From - To	Quantity	Cost	Product
1 - A	250	$12	$3,000
2 - A	350	14	4,900
2 - B	50	11	550
3 - B	450	12	5,400
4 - B	200	7	1,400
4 - DUMMY	150	0	0
		Total Cost	$15,250

d.

To: From:	A	B	Dummy	Supply
1	12 250	10 (+1)	0 (-2)	250
2	14 350	11 50	0 (-4)	400
3	9 (-6)	12 450	0 (-5)	450
4	8 (-2)	7 200	0 150	350
Demand	600	700	150	1450

e.

To: From:	A	B	Dummy	Supply
1	12 (+1)	10 250	0 (+1)	250
2	14 (+2)	11 250	15 0 150	400
3	9 450	12 (+4)	0 (+3)	450
4	8 150	7 200	0 (+4)	350
Demand	600	700	150	1450

Here is the total cost of the optimum shipping schedule.

From - To	Quantity	Cost	Product
1 - B	250	$10	$2,500
2 - B	250	11	2,750
2 - DUMMY	150	0	0
3 - A	450	9	4,050
4 - A	150	8	1,200
4 - B	200	7	1,400
Total Cost			$11,900

f. Because 150 units are to be sent to the dummy destination, they willnot be produced. Factory #2 will have idle time.

2. a. For occupied cells, use the formulas:
   column index =cell cost - row index; or row index = cell cost - column index.
   Begin with the cost for the first row, and let the first row index, R_1, be 0.

Cell	Cell Cost	Row/column Index	Cell/column Index
1-A	12	$R_1 = 0$	$C_1 = 12$
2-A	14	$C_1 = 12$	$R_2 = 2$
2-B	11	$R_2 = 2$	$C_2 = 9$
3-B	12	$C_2 = 9$	$R_3 = 3$
4-B	7	$C_2 = 9$	$R_4 = -2$
4-D	0	$R_4 = -2$	$C_3 = 2$

b. For unoccupied cells, use the formula: cell index = cell cost - row index - column index.

229

Cell	Cell Cost	Row Index	Column Index
1-B	10	0	1
1-Dummy	0	0	-2
2-Dummy	0	2	-4
3-A	9	3	-6
3-Dummy	0	3	-5
4-A	8	-2	-2

Compare the cell indexes with the circled numbers in the matrix for #1-b. Because some of the cell indexes are negative, a cheaper shipping schedule exists.

c. Solve this problem by finding the plus-minus path for the cell with the most negative index and reallocating the quantities to be shipped. At each iteration, find the indexes for the occupied cells by using the technique of #2a; find the indexes for the unoccupied cells by using the technique of #2b. The answer will be the same as #1d.

d. Same as #1e.

3. a, b.

To: From:	A	B	C	D	Dummy	Supply
1	15 300	13 200	13 (-1)	10 (-8)	0 (-2)	500
2	9 (-4)	11 ε	12 400	16 200 15 0	0 300	900
Demand	300	200	400	200	300	1600

c.

From - To	Quantity	Cost	Product
1 - A	300	$15	$4,500
1 - B	200	13	2,600
2 - C	400	12	4,800
2 - D	200	16	3,200
2 - DUMMY	300	0	0
		Total Cost	$15,100

d.

To: From:	A	B	C	D	Dummy	Supply
1	15 / (+6)	13 / ε	13 / (+1)	10 / 200	0 / 300	500
2	9 / 300	11 / 200 + ε	12 / 400	16 / (+6) 15 0	0 / (+2)	900
Demand	300	200	400	200	300	1600

e.

From - To	Quantity	Cost	Product
1 - D	200	$10	$2,000
1 - DUMMY	300	0	0
2 - A	300	9	2,700
2 - B	400	11	2,200
2 - C	300	12	4,800
	Total Cost		$11,700

f. Factory #1 will have idle time.

4. a. Min $Z = 15x_{1A} + 13x_{1B} + 13x_{1C} + 10x_{1D} + 0x_{1E} + 9x_{2A} + 11x_{2B} + 12x_{2C} + 16x_{2D} + 0x_{2E}$

ST:

1) $x_{1A} + x_{1B} + x_{1C} + x_{1D} + x_{1E} = 500$

2) $x_{2A} + x_{2B} + x_{2C} + x_{2D} + x_{2E} = 900$

A) $x_{1A} + x_{2A} = 300$

B) $x_{1B} + x_{2B} = 200$

C) $x_{1C} + x_{2C} = 400$

D) $x_{1D} + x_{2D} = 200$

E) $x_{1E} + x_{2E} = 300$

b,c Here is the LINDO printout.

```
LP OPTIMUM FOUND AT STEP    6

      OBJECTIVE FUNCTION VALUE

1)          11700.0000                    º

VARIABLE      VALUE        REDUCED COST
   X1A        .000000       5.000000
   X1B        .000000       1.000000
   X1C        .000000        .000000
   X1D      200.000000       .000000
   X2A      300.000000       .000000
   X2B      200.000000       .000000
   X2C      400.000000       .000000
   X2D        .000000       7.000000
   X1E      300.000000       .000000
   X2E        .000000       1.000000

ROW   SLACK OR SURPLUS    DUAL PRICES*
 2)        .000000      -13.000000
 3)        .000000      -12.000000
 4)        .000000        3.000000
 5)        .000000        1.000000
 6)        .000000         .000000
 7)        .000000        3.000000
 8)        .000000       13.000000

NO. ITERATIONS =     6                 º
```

*NOTE: Because all of the constraints are equalities, the dual prices are meaningless. LINDO always calculates the reduced costs and the dual prices.

CHAPTER 9 QUALITY ASSURANCE

1. a. Use the p chart. This is attribute data with the categories of satisfactory and defective bushings.

    b. CL = $\bar{p}$ = 100(15 + 13 + . . . + 45)/(125 + 125 + . . . + 125) = 100(202)/1250 = 16.16%.

    c. $s_p = \sqrt{\bar{p}(100-\bar{p})/n} = \sqrt{16.16(100-16.16)/125} = 3.29\%$.

    LCL = $\bar{p}$ - 3s_p = 16.16 - 3(3.29) = 6.29%.

    UCL = $\bar{p}$ + 3s_p = 16.16 + 3(3.29) = 26.03%.

    d.

Sample No.	Statistic (p)	Sample No.	Statistic (p)
1	16/125 = 12%	6	11.2%
2	10.4	7	16.0
3	12.8	8	20.0
4	8.8	9	24.0
5	10.4	10	36.0

    e.

    f. No. Sample #10 falls above the UCL.
    g. He should look for an assignable cause for sample #10.

2. a. The revised center line will be obtained by deleting sample #10 and recalculating the value of $\bar{p}$ on the basis of the remaining nine samples.

    Revised $\bar{p}$ = 100(202 - 45)/(1250 - 125) = 13.96%.

    b. Revised $s_p = \sqrt{\bar{p}(100-\bar{p})/n} = \sqrt{3.96(100-13.96)/125} = 3.10\%$

    Revised LCL = $\bar{p}$ - 3s_p = 13.96 - 3(3.10) = 4.66%

    Revised UCL = $\bar{p}$ + 3s_p = 13.96 + 3(3.10) = 23.26%.

233

c. The revised control limits have lower values than the original control limits, and they are slightly closer to the center line.

3. a. Use the x-bar chart; this is measurement data.

   b. CL = $\Sigma x/k$ = (4.99 + 4.87 + . . . + 5.05)/16 = 5.06 v.
      (k = the number of samples)

   c. Because the value of the population standard deviation is unknown, use $\overline{R}$ and the A_2 control chart factor.

      $\overline{R}$ = $\Sigma R/k$ = (0.41 + 0.57 + . . . + 0.33)/16 = 0.53

      LCL = CL − $A_2 \overline{R}$ = 5.06 - .48(.53) = 4.81 v.

      UCL = CL + $A_2 \overline{R}$ = 5.06 + .48(.53) = 5.31 v.

   d. The sample mean.

   e.

   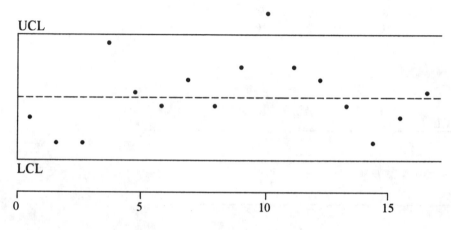

   f. No, sample #11 is out of control.

   g. He should look for an assignable cause for sample #11.

4. a. Because s is unknown, use $\overline{R}$ and the factors, D_3 and D_4 from the Table of Control Chart Factors.

      LCL = $D_3 \overline{R}$ = 0(.53) = 0.

      UCL = $D_4 \overline{R}$ = 2.00(.53) = 1.06 v.

   b. The sample ranges.

c.

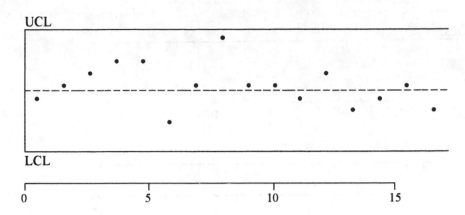

d. Yes.

e. No action is needed.

5. a. CL = (80.98 - 5.60)/(16 - 1) = 5.03 v.

   b. LCL = 5.03 − .48(.53) = 4.78 v.
      UCL = 5.03 + .48(.53) = 5.28 v.

   c. The new control limits are lower but are still the same distance from the center line.

6. a. Use the x-bar chart; this is measurement data.

   b. CL = ΣΣx/Σn = (2.47 + 2.41 + . . . + 2.47)/(5 + 5 + . . + 5) = .4974 k

   c. Because the value of the population standard deviation is known, find the standard deviation of the sample means and use z = ±3s.
      $$\sigma_{\bar{x}} = \sigma/\sqrt{n} = .016/\sqrt{5} = .007$$

      LCL = CL − 3s- = .497 − 3(.007) = .476 k.
      UCL = CL + 3s- = .497 + 3(.007) = .518 k.

   d. The sample mean. Here are the first few.

Sample No.	Mean
1	$\bar{x}$ = Σx/n = 2.47/5 = .494 k.
2	$\bar{x}$ = Σx/n = 2.41/5 = .482
.	
.	
.	

e.

f. Yes.

g. No action is necessary.

7. a. Because s is known, use the factors, D_1 and D_2, from the Table of Control Chart Factors in this Study Guide.

$$LCL = D_1 s = 0(.016) = 0.$$
$$UCL = D_2 s = 4.916(.016) = .078 \text{ k}.$$

b. Plot the ranges. Here are the first few of them.

Sample No.	Range (R)
1	$R = x_{largest} - x_{smallest} = .51 - .47 = .04.$
2	$R = x_{largest} - x_{smallest} = .50 - .47 = .03.$
.	
.	
.	

c.

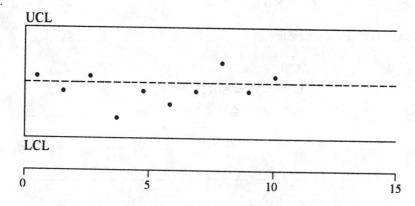

    d.   Yes.

    e.   No action is necessary.

8.   a.   Use a c-chart, because the data consists of the number of defects per unit; a unit is a towel.

    b. $CL = C = \Sigma c/k = 21/12 = 1.75$ defects per unit

    c. $LCL = CL - 3\sqrt{c} = 1.75 - 3\sqrt{1.75} = -2.22 \rightarrow 0.$

         $UCL = CL + 3\sqrt{c} = 1.75 + 3\sqrt{1.75} = 5.72.$

    d.   The number of defects per towel.

    e.

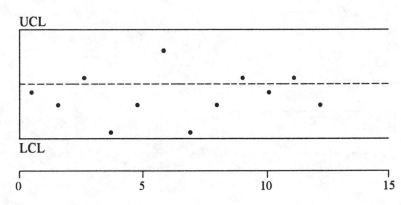

    f.   Yes.

    g.   No action is necessary.

9.   a. $E(r)_{med} = (k/2) + 1 = (20/2) + 1 = 11$ runs.

       (k = the number of samples)

    b. $s_{med} = (k - 1)/4 = (20 - 1)/4 = 2.18.$

    c. $r = 5$ runs.

    d. $z_{test} = (r - E(r))/s = (5 - 11)/2.18 = -2.75.$

    e. $z = \pm 1.96.$

    f.   No; $-2.75 < -1.96.$

1 a. Use the binomial distribution. This is attribute data with the categories of satisfactory and defective fuses, and the sample size is small.

   b. Use Table D in your textbook.

Assumed Percentage of Defective Fuses	$P(x \leq 1)$
0%	1.0000
5%	0.7358
10%	0.3917
15%	0.1756
20%	0.0692
100%	0.0

   c. Operating Characteristic Curve
   P(accepting batch)

   d. A Type I sampling error, consisting of rejecting a satisfactory batch of fuses.
   e. p(Type I sampling error) = α = 1 - .7358 = .2642.
   f. A Type II sampling error, consisting of accepting an unsatisfactory batch of fuses.
   g. p(Type II sampling error) = ß = .1756.

2. a. Use the Poisson distribution. This is attribute data with the categories of satisfactory and defective indicator lights, and the sample size is large.

   b. Use Table C in your textbook, or in this Study Guide, with a mean, $\mu = np$.

Assumed Percentage of Defective Items	Mean $= np$	$P(x \leq 5)$
0%	0	1.000
1%	1.5	.996
2%	3.0	.916
4%	6.0	.446
6%	9.0	.116
100%	150.0	0

c.

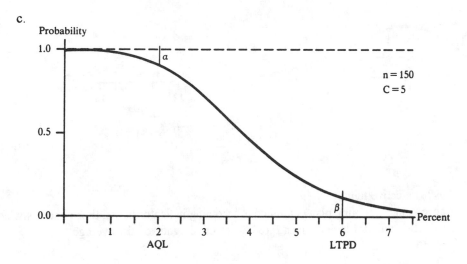

d. A Type I sampling error, consisting of rejecting a satisfactory batch of indicator lights.
e. p(Type I sampling error) = α = 1 - .916 = .084.
f. A Type II sampling error, consisting of accepting an unsatisfactory batch of indicator lights.
g. p(Type II sampling error) = ß = .116.

3. Use the formula, AOQ = p×p(accepting the lot), since the batch size is large compared to the sample size.

Assumed Percent of Defective Items	p(accepting the lot)	AOQ
0%	1.000	0
1%	.996	.996%
2%	.916	1.832%
3%	.703*	2.109%
4%	.446	1.784%
5%	.242	1.210%
100%	0	0

a.

b. AOQL = 2.109% defective lights.
c. Because this acceptance sampling plan is applied to incoming indicator lights, those batches which are used in production will not include over 2.109% defective lights, on the average.

CHAPTER 10 FORECASTING

1. a. A forecast for t = 9 will require the last five prices.

$$MA_5 = (23.250 + 23.250 + 23.875 + 23.875 + 24.500)/5 = \$23.750$$

   b. Error = Actual - Forecast = 24.125 - 23.750 = 0.375.

   c. $MA_5 =(23.250 + 23.875 + 23.875 + 24.500 + 24.125) /5 = \$23.925$

2. a. The size will be the independent variable (X) and the cost will be the dependent variable (Y).

   b.

   c. $\Sigma x = 660$; $\Sigma y = 55.9$; $\Sigma x^2 = 63,600$, $\Sigma y^2 - 439.11$; $\Sigma xy = 5,264$.

$$b = \frac{n(\Sigma xy) - (\Sigma x)(\Sigma y)}{n(\Sigma x^2) - (\Sigma x)^2} = \frac{9(5264) - (660)(55.9)}{9(63600) - (660)^2} = 0.0766.$$

   e. It is estimated that each additional piece in a batch costs $.0766(10^3) = \$76.60.\$76.60$.

   f. $a = \bar{y} -- bx\,\bar{x} = 6.211 - .0766(73.333) = 0.5937.$

   g. It is estimated that the cost of setting up to produce a batch is $0.5937(10^3) = \$593.70$.

   h. $y_c = a + bx = 593.70 + 76.60(125) = \$10,168.70.$

   i. $r = (n\Sigma xy - \Sigma x\Sigma y)/[(n\Sigma x^2 - (\Sigma x)^2)(n\Sigma y^2 - (\Sigma y)^2)]^{1/2}$

$$= \frac{9(5264) - (660)(55.9)}{[(9(63600) - (660)^2)(9(439.11) - (55.9)^2)]^{1/2}} = 0.9854.$$

   This high value confirms the impression given by the scatterplot and indicates a strong linear relationship.

3. a.

b. $\Sigma t = 55$; $\Sigma t^2 = 385$; $\Sigma y = 10,670$; $\Sigma ty = 61187$.

c. $b = (n\Sigma ty - (\Sigma t)(\Sigma y))/(n\Sigma t^2 - (\Sigma t)^2) = (10(61187) - 55(10670))/(10(385) - (55)^2) = 30.33$.

d. It is estimated that the enrollment increases by 30.33 FTE per year, on the average.

e. $a = \bar{y} - b\bar{t} = 1067 - 30.33(5.5) = 900.20$.

f. It is estimated that the enrollment at t = 0 was 900.2 FTE.

g. $y_c = a + bt = 900.2 + 30.33(11) = 1,233.83$ FTE.

4. a. The first 12-month total is: $6.7 + 6.2 + ... + 11.6 = 141.8$ and the average is 11.82. The second total is 143.0 and the average is 11.92. The last 12-month total is 239.9 and the average is 19.99.

b. The first centered 12-month moving average is $(11.82 + 12.01)/2 = 11.87$. Here is the complete set:

	1	2	3	4
January		12.43	14.32	19.09
February		12.48	14.66	19.24
March		12.57	15.34	19.56
April		12.74	16.03	19.71
May		12.82	16.54	19.74
June		12.84	16.97	19.87
July	11.87	12.89	17.12	
August	12.0	13.01	17.36	
September	12.23	13.31	17.89	
October	12.42	13.59	18.52	
November	12.51	13.81	18.96	
December	12.46	14.12	19.07	

c. The first ratio is $6.4/11.87 = .5392$. The last ratio is $10.4/19.87 = .5234$. Each month has three ratios.

d, e. Here are the totals of each month's ratios and the seasonal indexes:

	Total	Mean	Index
January	1.6377	.5459	.5459
February	2.2801	.7600	.7600
March	3.8656	1.2885	1.2886
April	3.6768	1.2256	1.2257
May	2.7308	.9103	.9103
June	1.4820	.4940	.4940
July	1.6487	.5496	.5496
August	3.2254	1.0751	1.0752
September	5.2906	1.7635	1.7636
October	3.8122	1.2707	1.2708
November	3.6886	1.2295	1.2296
December	2.6600	.8867	.8867
		11.9994	12.0000

The adjustment factor = 12.0000/11.9994 = 1.00005; multiply each mean by this factor.

f. Advertising for apparel and accessories is highest in the spring and fall months and lowest in the winter and summer months. It is, perhaps, surprising that advertising is low in December.

5. a. F_{Jan} = \$19,800,000.
    b. F_{Jan} = \$7,400,000.

6. a. $F_t = F_{t-1} + a(A_{t-1} - F_{t-1})$
       $F_2 - A_1 - 6.7.$
       $F_3 = F_2 + a(A_2 - F_2) = 6.7 + .20(6.2 - 6.7) = 6.60.$

Here is the complete table:

Month	t	A_t	F_t	$(A_t - F_t)$
January	1	6.7	-	-
February	2	6.2	6.7	-5.5
March	3	12.1	6.6	5.5
April	4	14.4	7.7	6.7
May	5	11.1	9.04	2.06
June	6	7.4	9.45	-2.05
July	7	6.4	9.04	-2.64
August	8	12.9	8.51	4.39
September	9	21.1	9.39	11.71
October	10	15.4	11.73	3.67
November	11	16.5	12.46	4.04
December	12	11.6	13.27	1.67

b.

7. a,b,d. Here is a portion of the table:

t	A	F	$A - F$	$(A-F)^2$	$\lvert A-F \rvert$
1	6.7				
2	6.2	6.70	-0.50	0.25	0.50
3	12.1	6.60	5.50	30.25	5.50
.	.	.	.	.	.
.	.	.	.	.	.
12	11.6	13.27	-1.67	2.79	1.67
				279.77	44.93

c. $\text{MSE} = \Sigma(A - F)^2/(n - 1) = 279.77/(11 - 1) = 27.98$.

e. $\text{MAD} = \Sigma\lvert A - F \rvert /n = 44.93/11 = 4.08$.

f, g. Here are the calculations for the first few rows.

$\text{MAD}_2 = 0.50$

$\text{TS}_2 = \Sigma(A - F)/\text{MAD}_2 = -0.50/0.50 = 1.00$

$\text{MAD}_3 = \text{MAD}_2 + \alpha(\lvert A - F \rvert_3 - \text{MAD}_2) = 0.50 + .20(5.50 - 0.50) = 1.50$

$\text{TS}_3 = \Sigma(A - F)/\text{MAD}_3 = 5.00/1.50 = 3.33$.

$\text{MAD}_4 = \text{MAD}_3 + \alpha\lvert A - F \rvert_4 - \text{MAD}_3 = 1.50 + .20(6.70 - 1.50) = 2.54$.

$\text{TS}_4 = \Sigma(A - F)/\text{MAD}_4 = 11.70/2.54 = 4.61$.

Here is the beginning and ending of the table.

t	$A - F$	$\Sigma(A - F)$	$A - F$	MAD	TS
2	-0.50	-0.50	0.50	0.50	1.00
3	5.50	5.00	5.50	1.50	3.33
4	6.70	11.70	6.70	2.54	4.61
12	-1.67	31.21	1.67	3.81	8.19

h.

CONTROL CHART   PROBLEM NO. 7-h
☼ = A STATISTIC

i. Since the tracking signal is seldom within the limits, the value of $\alpha = .20$ is a poor choice. In fact, the use of single-factor smoothing may be inappropriate with this time series. Two-factor smoothing may be preferable, since a trend appears to be present.

8. a. $T_4 = (14.4 - 6.7)/3 = 2.57$.

b. $TAF_5 = 14.4 + 2.57 = 16.97$.

c. Here are the calculations for the first two rows of the table.

$S_5 = TAF_5 + \alpha_1(A_5 - TAF_5) = 16.97 + .20(11.1 - 16.97) = 15.80$.

$T_5 = T_4 + \alpha_2(TAF_5 - TAF_4 - T_4) = 2.57 + .20(0) = 2.57$.

$TAF_6 = S_5 + T_5 = 15.80 + 2.57 = 18.37$.

$S_6 = TAF_6 + \alpha_1(A_6 - TAF_6) = 18.37 + .20(7.4 - 18.37) = 16.18$.

$T_6 = T_5 + \alpha_2(TAF_6 - TAF_5 - T_5) = 2.57 + .20(18.37 - 16.97 - 2.57) = 2.34.$

$TAF_7 = S_6 + T_6 = 16.18 + 2.34 = 18.52.$

Here is the complete table.

t	A	TAF	$(A - TAF)$
5	11.1	16.97	-5.87
6	7.4	18.37	-10.97
7	6.4	18.52	-12.12
8	12.9	18.00	-5.10
9	21.1	18.40	2.70
10	15.4	20.16	-4.76
11	16.5	20.97	-4.47
12	11.6	21.65	-10.05

d.

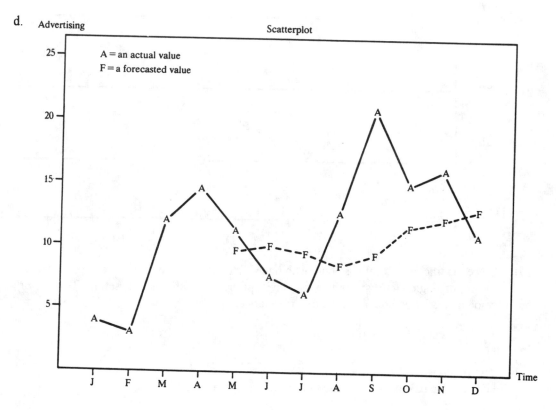

CHAPTER 11   INVENTORY MANAGEMENT

1. a. Use the instantaneous model.
    b. The annual carrying cost = HQ/2 = 3(12)Q/2 = 18Q.
    c. The annual ordering cost = DS/Q = 60000(25)/Q = 1500000/Q.
    d. The annual total cost = 18Q + 1500000/Q.
    e. $Q = \sqrt{\dfrac{2DS}{H}} = \sqrt{\dfrac{2(60,000)25}{36}} \approx 289$ pairs of bumpers.
    f. Every time the company places an order, it should order 289 pairs of bumpers.
    g. The annual total expense = (Q/2)H + (D/Q)S = (289/2)36 + (60,000/289)25 = $10,392.00 per year.
    h. The number of orders = D/Q = 60000/289 ≈ 208 per year.
    i. The annual total expense = 18(600) + 1500000/600 = $13,300. The annual savings are $13,300 − $10,392 = $2,908.00.

2. a. Use the noninstantaneous model.
    b. The annual carrying cost = (HQ/2)[(P-U)/P] = (2.50(12)Q/2)[(400 - 60000/240)]/400 = 5.625Q.
    c. The annual setup cost = DS/Q = 60000(250)/Q = 15000000/Q.
    d. The annual total cost = 5.625Q + 15000000/Q.
    e. $EOQ = \sqrt{\dfrac{2DS}{H}} \sqrt{\dfrac{p}{p-u}} = \sqrt{\dfrac{2(6000)250}{30}} \times \sqrt{\dfrac{400}{400-250}} = 1,633$ pairs of bumpers.
    f. The company should place a production order for 1,633 pairs of bumpers every time.
    g. The annual total cost = 5.625EOQ + 15000000/EOQ = 5.625(1633) + 15000000/1633 ≈ $18,371.00 per year.
    h. The number of production runs = D/EOQ = 60000/1633 = 36.74 runs per year.
    i. The annual total cost = 5.625(3000) + 15000000/3000 = $21,875.00. The annual savings are $21,875.00 - $18,371.00 = $3,504.00.

3. a. Use the quantity discount model.
    b. The annual total cost = 18Q + 1500000/Q + 150D.
    c. The net price = 150(1 - d) = 150(1 - .04) = $144.00. The annual total cost = 18Q + 1500000/Q + 144D.
    d. The net price = 150(1 - d) = 150(1 - .10) = $135.00. The annual total cost = 18Q + 1500000/Q + 135D.

e. Total cost

f. The EOQ is the minimum feasible point, which is 500 pairs of bumpers.
g. The annual total cost = 18(500) + 1500000/500 + 135(500) = $79,500.00

4. a. Use the fixed lead time and variable demand model.
   b. The mean usage during lead time = $\bar{d}$ (LT) = 30(5) = 150 floppy disks.
   c. The standard deviation = $\sigma_d \sqrt{LT}$ = $4\sqrt{5}$ = 8.94 floppy disks.
   d. ROP = $\bar{d}$ (LT) + z(standard deviations) = 150 + 2.58(8.94) = 173.08 floppy disks.

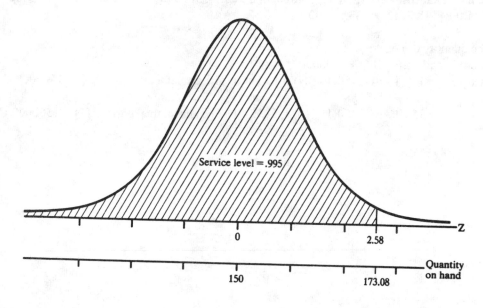

e. When the quantity of floppy disks on hand falls to 173.08 disks (or fewer) place an order for the economic order quantity.

f. The safety stock = ROP - mean usage = 173.08 - 150 = 23.08 floppy disks.

5. a. Use the fixed demand and variable lead time model.

b. The mean usage during lead time = $d \overline{LT}$ = 50(10) = 500 pencils.

c. The standard deviation = $d(\sigma_{LT})$ = 50(2) = 100 pencils.

d. ROP = $\overline{d}$ (LT) + z(standard deviations) = 500 + 1.65(100) = 665 pencils.

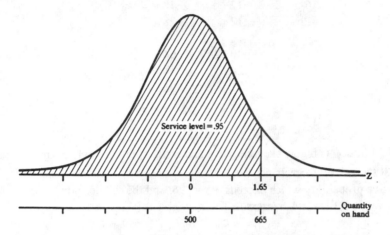

e. When the quantity of pencils on hand falls to 665 (or fewer), place an order for the economic order quantity.

f. The safety stock = ROP – the mean usage – 665 – 500 = 165 pencils.

6. a. Use the variable demand and variable lead time model.

b. The mean usage during lead time = $\overline{d}$ (LT) = 200(25) = 5,000 sheets.

c. The standard deviation = $\sqrt{LT \sigma_d^2 + \overline{d}^2 \sigma_{LT}^2}$ = $\sqrt{25(169) + 40000(4)}$

$$= \sqrt{4225 + 160000} = 405.25 \text{ Sheets.}$$

d. ROP = The mean usage + z(standard deviations) = 5000 + 2.33(405.25) = 5,944.23 sheets.

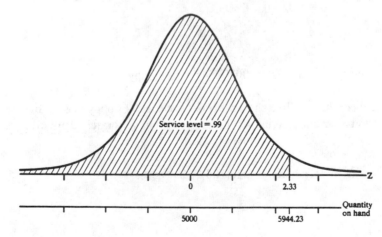

e. When the quantity of letterhead paper on hand falls to 5,944.23 sheets (or fewer) place an order for the Economic Order Quantity.

f. The safety stock = ROP - the mean usage = 5,944.23 - 5,000 = 944.23 sheets.

7. a,c,d.

Freezer Sales (x)	f	fx	p	Cumulative p
0	2	0	.04	.04
1	6	6	.12	.16
2	6	12	.12	.28
3	8	24	.16	.44
4	10	40	.20	.64
5	12	60	.24	.88
6	4	24	.08	.96 ←
7	2	14	.04	1.00
	50	180	1.00	

The frequency distribution is highly skew negative and is not approximately normal.

b. $\bar{x} = \Sigma fx/\Sigma f = 180/50 = 3.60$ freezers per week.

e. The first cumulative probability which exceeds .95 is .96, and the reorder point is 6 freezers.

f. The safety stock = 6 - 3.6 = 2.4 freezers.

8. a. Use the fixed order interval and variable quantity model.

b. The expected demand = $\bar{d}$ (OI + LT) = 6 sets.

The safety stock = $z(\sigma_d)(\sqrt{OI + LT}$ = 1.28(1.5) = 1.92 sets.

The order quantity = the expected demand + the safety stock - the quantity on hand
$$= 6 + 1.92 - 5 \approx 3 \text{ sets.}$$

c. The ending inventory on April 30 will be 5 + 3 - 4 = 4 sets.

d. The order quantity = the expected demand + the safety stock - the quantity on hand
$$= 6 + 1.92 - 4 \approx 4 \text{ sets.}$$

e. The ending inventory on May 31 will be 4 + 4 - 8 = 0 sets.

f. The order quantity = the expected demand + the safety stock - the quantity on hand
$$= 6 + 1.92 - 0 \approx 8 \text{ sets.}$$

9. a. E(z) = E(2.58) = .002

E(n) = E(z)(standard deviations) = .002(8.94) = .02 floppy disks.

b. The mean number which will be short per order cycle is .02 floppy disks. In other words, no shortage should be experienced in most order cycles, but very rarely there may be a shortage of one disk.

c. E(z) = E(1.65) ≈ .020.
E(n) = E(z)(standard deviations) = .020(100) = 2 pencils.

d. The mean number which will be short per order cycle is 2 pencils. In other words, sometimes there will be a shortage of around 2 pencils (e.g., 1, 2, 3, or 4, but probably not more, pencils).

10. a.

Item	Annual Dollar Value
a	$20,800*
b	6,000
.	.
.	.
n	22,500
o	64,800
Total	$372,050

* (800 x $26.00)

b. Rearrange the items in the order of decreasing annual dollar value. Calculate the cumulative totals and the cumulative percents. Here are the first few items:

Item	Annual Dollar Value	Cumulative Dollar Value	Cumulative Percent
o	$64,800	$ 64,800	17.41%
c	63,000	127,800	34.35*
m	47,500	175,300	47.11
g	42,000	217,300	58.41
d	35,000	252,300	67.81

*34.35% = 100(127,800)/372,050. Classification A will contain items o, c, m, and g. B will contain items d, n, a, l, e, and h. C will contain items f, i, j, b, and k.

11. a. Use the single period model.
    b. C_s = Revenue per unit - cost per unit = $1.49 -$0.80 = $0.69 per pound.
    c. C_e = Cost per unit = salvage value per unit = $0.80 - 0 = $0.80.
    d. The service level = $C_s/(C_s + C_e)$ = .69/(.69 + .80) = .46.
    e. The value of z for the service level = -0.04. The batch size = the mean demand + z(standard deviations) = 60 - 0.04(16) = 59.36 pounds of potato salad.

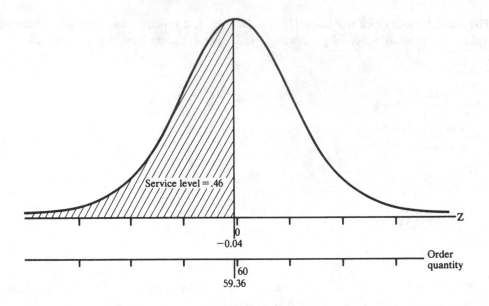

Service level = .46

−0.04

Order quantity

60
59.36

12. a. The single-period model, since the t-shirts are salable only at one event.
   b. The Poisson distribution displays decreasing probabilities as the value of the random variable increases.
   c. C_s = revenue per unit - cost per unit = 25(144) - 864(.97) = 3600 - 838.08 = $2761.92.
   d. C_e = cost per unit - salvage value per unit = 864(.97) - .02(144) = 838.08 - 2.88 = $835.20.
   e. The service level = $C_s/(C_s + C_e)$ = 2761.92/(2761.92 + 835.20) = .7678.
   f. Use the cumulative Poisson distribution with μ = 3, in Table C to obtain these values:

x	$P(x)$
0	.050
1	.199
2	.423
3	.647
4	.815 ←
5	.916
6	.966
7	.988
8	.996
9	.999
10	1.000

   Because $P(x)$ = .815 is the lowest probability to exceed .7678, Ms. White should prepare 4 gross of t-shirts.
   g. Profits = revenues - expenses = 4(3600) − 4(838.08) = 4(2761.92) = $11,047.68. It is improper to count Ms. White's labor as an expense.

CHAPTER 12 AGGREGATE PLANNING

1. a,b.

Month	J	A	S	O	N	D	6 Month Total
Forecast	125	150	300	350	400	600	1925
Production	320	320	320	320	320	320	1920
Inventory							
Beginning Balance	50	245	415	435	405	325	
Ending Balance	245	415	435	405	325	45	
Average Balance	147.5	330	425	420	365	185	
Lost Sales (Pairs of Skis)							

Month	J	F	M	A	M	J	12 Month Total
Forecast	500	450	200	150	50	25	3300
Production	320	320	320	320	320	320	3840
Inventory							
Beginning Balance	45	0	0	120	290	560	
Ending Balance	0	0	120	290	560	855	
Average Balance	22.5	0	60	205	425	707.5	
Lost Sales (Pairs of Skis)	135	130					265

c.

Month	J	A	S	O	N	D	6 Month Total
Sales Volume	125	150	300	350	400	600	1925
Sales Dollars	$18750	22500	45000	52500	60000	90000	$288750
Cost of Goods Sold	7500	9000	18000	21000	24000	36000	115500
Cost of Storage	295	660	850	840	730	370	3745
Total Costs	7795	9660	18850	21840	24730	36370	119245
Gross Margin	$10955	12840	26150	30660	35270	53630	$169505

Month	J	F	M	A	M	J	12 Month Total
Sales Volume	365	320	200	150	50	25	3035
Sales Dollars	$54750	48000	30000	22500	7500	3750	$455250
Cost of Goods Sold	21900	19200	12000	9000	3000	1500	182100
Cost of Storage	45	0	120	410	850	1415	6585
Total Costs	21945	19200	12120	9410	3850	2915	188685
Gross Margin	$32805	28800	17880	13090	3650	835	$266565

d,e.

Month	J	A	S	O	N	D	6 Month Total
Forecast	125	150	300	350	400	600	1925
Production (Day)	320	320	320	320	320	320	1920
Production (Night)							
Total Production							
Inventory							
Beginning Balance	50	245	415	435	405	325	
Ending Balance	245	415	435	405	325	45	
Average Balance	147.5	330	425	420	365	185	
Lost Sales (Pairs of Skis)							

Month	J	F	M	A	M	J	12 Month Total
Forecast	500	450	200	150	50	25	3300
Production (Day)	320	320	320	320	320	320	3840
Production (Night)	160	160	80	—	—	—	400
Total Production	480	480	400	320	320	320	4240
Inventory							
Beginning Balance	45	25	55	255	425	695	
Ending Balance	25	55	255	425	695	990	
Average Balance	35	40	155	340	560	842.5	
Lost Sales (Pairs of Skis)							

f.

Month	J	A	S	O	N	D	6 Month Total
Sales Volume	125	150	300	350	400	600	1925
Sales Dollars	$18750	22500	45000	52500	60000	90000	$288750
Cost of Goods Sold (Day)	7500	9000	18000	21000	24000	36000	115500
Cost of Goods Sold (Night)							
Cost of Storage	295	660	850	840	730	370	3745
Total Cost	7795	9660	18850	21840	24730	36370	119245
Gross Margin	$10955	12840	26150	30660	35270	53630	$169505

Month	J	F	M	A	M	J	12 Month Total
Sales Volume	500	450	200	150	50	25	3300
Sales Dollars	$75000	67500	30000	22500	7500	3750	$495000
Cost of Goods Sold (Day)	20400	17400	7200	9000	3000	1500	174000
Cost of Goods Sold (Night)	11200	11200	5600				28000
Cost of Storage	70	80	310	680	1120	1685	7690
Total Cost	31670	28680	13110	9680	4120	3185	209690
Gross Margin	$43330	38820	16890	12820	3380	565	$285310

g. The day shift might be reduced to half-time during the spring months, to reduce the inventory build-up.

h. Peak demand might be met by obtaining skis from a supplier. Or the night shift might be scheduled to begin earlier, say in December, to anticipate the winter demand for skis.

2. X = Calendar Time

Y = The cumulative demand or production from July 1 up to date.

The month's initial refers to the last day of the month. Graph the following points:

Month	Production	Demand	Month	Production	Demand
O	0	0	J	2240	2425
J	320	125	F	2560	2875
A	640	275	M	2880	3075
S	960	575	A	3200	3225
O	1280	925	M	3520	3275
N	1600	1325	J	3840	3300
D	1920	1925			

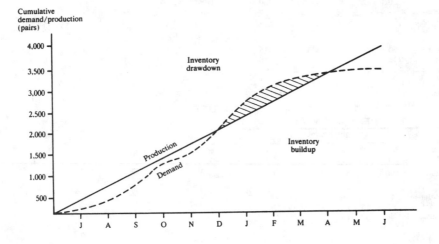

3. Place the months in the columns; the column totals will be the monthly demand. A dummy column will be needed. Place the day shifts and the night shifts in the rows; the row totals will be the monthly capacities of each shift. A different row will be needed for each shift for each month. The costs will be the variable cost per pair of skis plus the cost of storage. Thus, skis produced by the day shift in July and stored until September will cost $60 + $2 + $2= $64. Because it is not possible to produce skis in November for sale in October, enter a large cost ($100) in the October column and November row, in order to exclude those cells from the solution.

	Months					
	Oct.	Nov.	Dec.	Jan.	Dummy	Capacity
Day shift October	60	62	64	66	0	320
Night shift October	70	72	74	76	0	320
Day shift November	100	60	62	64	0	320
Night shift November	100	70	72	74	0	320
Day shift December	100	100	60	62	0	320
Night shift December	100	100	70	72	0	320
Day shift January	100	100	100	60	0	320
Night shift January	100	100	100	70	0	320
Demand	350	400	600	500	710	2560

4. a.

60	May			
	6	13	20	27
Forecast	500	500	500	500
Customer Orders	400	450	450	1,000
Projected Inventory	760	260	960	1,160
MPS	1,200		1,200	1,200

	June			
	3	10	17	24
Forecast	550	550	600	600
Customer Orders	500	500	600	650
Projected Inventory	610	60	660	10
MPS			1,200	

b. Six-packs will produced in the weeks of May 6, May 20, May 27, and June 17.

1. a.

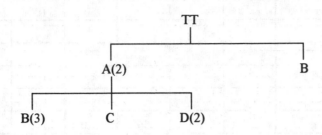

b.   The master schedule calls for 150 units of product TT.

Subassembly/component	Quantity
Product TT	
Subassembly A	300 (150 x 2)
Component B	150
Subassembly A	
Component B	900 (300 x 3)
Component C	300
Component D	600 (300 x 2)

The list may be condensed by combining the quantities for Component B:

Subassembly/component	Quantity
Product TT	
Subassembly A	300
Component B	1050
Component C	300
Component D	600

c.

Subassemby A LT = 1 wk.	1	2	3	4	5	6
Gross requirements				50	100	150
Scheduled receipts						
Projected on hand						
Net requirements				50	100	150
Planned-order receipts				50	100	150
Planned-order releases			50	100	150	

Component B LT = 2 wk.	1	2	3	4	5	6
Gross requirements			150	325	500	75
Scheduled receipts						
Projected on hand	100	100	100			
Net requirements			50	325	500	75
Planned-order receipts			50	325	500	75
Planned-order releases	50	325	500	75		

Component C LT = 1 wk.	1	2	3	4	5	6
Gross requirements			50	100	150	
Scheduled receipts						
Projected on hand						
Net requirements			50	100	150	
Planned-order receipts			50	100	150	
Planned-order releases		50	100	150		

Component D LT = 1 wk.	1	2	3	4	5	6
Gross requirements			100	200	300	
Scheduled receipts						
Projected on hand						
Net requirements			100	200	300	
Planned-order receipts			100	200	300	
Planned-order releases		100	200	300		

2. a. The delay in producing component D will cause a one-week delay in producing subassembly A and the last 75 units of product TT will be delayed one week beyond that time, or two weeks, in total.

Week	4	5	6	7	8
Quantity	25	50			75

b.

Assembly A LT = 1 wk.	4	5	6	7	8
Gross requirements	50	100			150
Scheduled receipts					
Projected on hand					
Net requirements	50	100			150
Planned-order receipts	50	100			150
Planned-order releases	100		150		

Component B LT = 2 wk.	4	5	6	7	8
Gross requirements	325	50		450	75
Scheduled receipts					
Projected on hand			450	450	
Net requirements	325	50			75
Planned-order receipts	325	50			75
Planned-order releases			75		

Component C LT = 1 wk.	4	5	6	7	8
Gross requirements	100		150		
Scheduled receipts					
Projected on hand					
Net requirements	100		150		
Planned-order receipts	100		150		
Planned-order releases		150			

259

Component D LT = 1 wk.	4	5	6	7	8
Gross requirements	200		300		
Scheduled receipts					
Projected on hand					
Net requirements	200		300		
Planned-order receipts	200		300		
Planned-order releases		200			

3. a. The cumulative usage schedule.

Period	1	2	3	4	5	6
Quantity	60	110	190	260	290	340

b. EPP = (Setup Cost)/(Unit Holding Cost) = 500/2 = 250.
c. Calculate cumulative part-periods based on the cumulative quantities.

Period	Lot size	Inventory	Periods carried	Part-periods	Cumulative Part-periods
1	60	0	0	0	0
	110	50	1	50	50
	190	80	2	160	210*
	260	70	3	210	420

*210 is closest to the EPP of 250; produce 190 units.

The 190 units will satisfy the requirements of the first three periods. Repeat the calculation for the next three periods.

Period	Lot size	Inventory	Periods carried	Part-periods	Cumulative Part-periods
4	70	0	0	0	0
	100	30	1	30	30
	150	50	2	100	130

The final entry of 130 does not seem to be close to the EPP of 250. Obtain the requirements for component K for later weeks and continue the calculation.

CHAPTER 14   JUST-IN-TIME SYSTEMS

1. a. $D = 160/8 = 20$ sunglasses per hour.
   b. $T = 12(3.0) + 15 + 15 = 66$ min. $= 1.1$ hrs.
   c. $X = .20$.
   d. $C = 12$ sunglasses.
   e. $N = DT(1 + X)/C = 20(1.1)(1.2)/12 = 2.2 \rightarrow 3$ kanban cards.

2. a. $D = 6(7.5 \text{ hrs.})/(.75 \text{ hrs}) = 60$ woven heads per day.

   b. $T = 1 + 3 = 4$ days.
   c. $X = .05$.
   d. $C = 72$ heads.
   e. $N = DT(1 + X)/C = 60(4)(1.05)/72 = 3.50 \rightarrow 4$ kanban cards.
   f. N will increase to 5.
   g. N will decrease to 3.
   h. N will decrease to 3.
   i. Using the information in 2-h, N remains at 3.

CHAPTER 15 SCHEDULING

1. a.   Runout Time = (Production available + Current Inventory)/Demand Rate.

Type of Pencil	Production	Inventory	Demand	Runout Time (days)
2B	12,000	2,000	500	28
3B	9,000	3,000	600	20
4B	27,000	0	1,200	22.5
5B	18,000	3,000	1,000	21
6B	5,000	6,000	500	22

   b. Produce the pencils in the order of small to large runout times: 3B, 5B, 6B, 4B, 2B.
   c.   It is assumed that there are no priority or rush orders for any of the pencils. A rush order for
       4Bpencils, for example, would require that 4B pencils be produced first, rather than fifth.

2. List the calendar working days, and count them off, starting with May 6. The count numbers will lie
    on the x-axis: May 6 = 1; July 12 = 47.

a.

262

b.

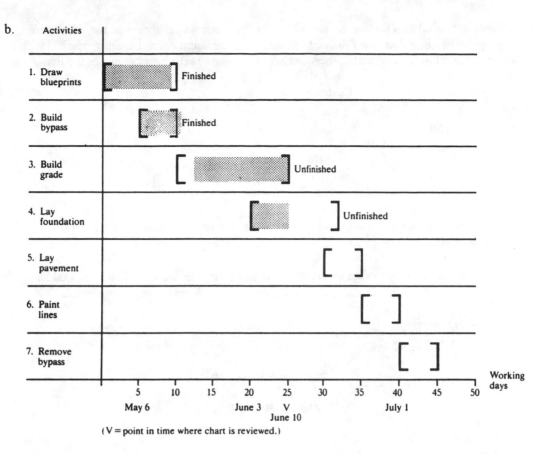

Activities		
1. Draw blueprints	▨ Finished	
2. Build bypass	▨ Finished	
3. Build grade	[▨] Unfinished	
4. Lay foundation	[▨] Unfinished	
5. Lay pavement	[ ]	
6. Paint lines	[ ]	
7. Remove bypass	[ ]	

Working days: 5 10 15 20 25 30 35 40 45 50

May 6   June 3   V   July 1
                   June 10

(V = point in time where chart is reviewed.)

3. a. Because the tableau is not square, a dummy Bureau will be required.

Customer

Bureau	1	2	3	4	5
A	200	[50]	500	100	60
B	100	200	80	[40]	600
C	90	300	400	[60]	200
D	700	100	200	400	[90]
Dummy	0	0	0	0	0

b. Subtract the minimum number in each row, marked with brackets above, from every entry in the row. Subtract the minimum number in each column (0) from every entry in the column. The result is:

Customer

Bureau	1	2	3	4	5
A	150	0	450	[50]	10
B	60	160	40	0	560
C	[30]	240	340	0	140
D	610	10	110	310	0
Dummy	0	0	0	0	0

263

The zeroes in this tableau may be covered with four lines; one way is shown above. There are other ways. The algorithm is not finished. Subtract the minimum unlined number, marked with brackets, from all of the unlined numbers and add it to values at the intersections of the lines. The result is:

| | | | Customer | | |
Bureau	*1*	*2*	*3*	*4*	*5*
A	150	0	450	[80]	10
B	30	130	10	0	530
C	0	210	310	0	110
D	610	10	110	340	0
Dummy	0	0	0	30	0

In the above tableau, a minimum of five lines is required to cover all of the zeroes, and the algorithm is finished.

c,d One assignment of a technician to a customer must be made in each row of the final tableau. Start with rows with only one zero, and check off a row and a column for each assignment.

Assignment	*One-way Distance*
A-2	50k
B-4	40
C-1	90 (Customer #4 was taken by B)
D-5	90
Dummy-3	0 (The only customer left)
Total	270
Round trip	x 2
Total	540

e. Because the dummy is assigned to Customer #3, Customer #3 will not receive a service call.

4. a. Replace the 90 in cell #C-1 with 1,000.
    b. Replace the 80 in cell #B-3 with 0.

    c.

| | | | Customer | | |
Bureau	*1*	*2*	*3*	*4*	*5*
A	200	50	500	100	60
B	100	200	0	40	600
C	1000	300	400	60	200
D	700	100	200	400	90
Dummy	0	0	0	0	0

d. Perform the algorithm explained in 3b. The final tableau is:

			Customer		
Bureau	1	2	3	4	5
A	150	0	450	50	10
B	100	200	0	40	600
C	940	240	340	0	140
D	610	10	110	310	0
Dummy	0	0	0	30	0

e,f.

Assignment	One-way Distance
A-2	50k
B-3	40
C-4	90
D-5	90
Dummy-1	0
Total	280
Round trip	x 2
Total	560

g. Customer #1 does not receive a service call.

5. a. The FCFS sequence is the order of arrival: 1, 2, 3, 4, 5, 6.
   b. The SPT rule is the order of processing times: 1, 6, 3, 5, 2, 4.
   c. The DD rule is the order of due dates: 3, 6, 2, 4, 5, 1.
   d. The runout rule should be used in intermediate volume plants, in which there are relatively few large production runs per time period. The FCFS, SPT, and DD rules should be used in job shops in which there are many small orders per time period.

6. a. The first few steps in the algorithm are:
   1) The shortest processing time is 8 minutes for job B in work center A. Schedule B first.
   2) The next shortest time is 9 minutes for job C in work center B. Schedule C last.
   3) The next shortest time is 10 minutes for job A in work center A. Schedule A second.
      Proceeding in this manner produces this sequence: B, A, D, F, G, E, C.

b.

c. The throughput time is the length of time from beginning the first job to finishing the last job. It is 108 minutes on the diagram for 6b.

d. Jobs A and G have waiting time. The total waiting time is: (23 - 18) + (68 - 66) = 7 minutes.

e. Work center B has 5 idle periods. The total idle time is: 8 + (38 - 35) + (55 - 49) + (84 - 82) + (99 − 94) = 24 minutes. It is customary to ignore the idle time of work center A while work center B is finishing up.

CHAPTER 16 PROJECT MANAGEMENT

1. a, b.

Path	Duration (weeks)
A-B-C-I-J	$2 + 4 + 3 + 3 + 1 = 13$
A-D-F-I-J	$2 + 5 + 3 + 3 + 1 = 14$
A-D-G-H-J	$2 + 5 + 4 + 4 + 1 = 16$
E-F-I-J	$6 + 3 + 3 + 1 = 13$
E-G-H-J	$6 + 4 + 4 + 1 = 15$

c. The critical path is #3.

d. The second-most critical path is #5.

e. The slack is the difference between the duration of the critical path and the duration of each alternative path. When an activity appears on more than one path, the slack is the smallest difference.

Activity	Path	Slack (wk.)
A	3	0
B	1	3
C	1	3
D	3	0
E	5	1
F	2	2
G	3	0
H	3	0
I	2	2
J	3	0

f.

Activity	ES	EF	LS	LF	Slack (wk.)
A	0	2	0	2	0
B	2	6	5	9	3
C	6	9	9	12	3
D	2	7	2	7	0
E	0	6	1	7	1
F	7	10	9	12	2
G	7	11	7	11	0
H	11	15	1	15	0
I	10	13	2	15	2
J	15	16	5	16	0

2. a.

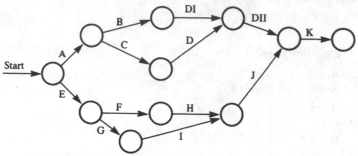

DI = a dummy activity
DII = a dummy activity

It is possible to draw this network without dummy activities.

b,c.

Path	Duration (weeks)
A-B-DI-DII-K	1 + 3 + 0 + 0 + 1 = 5
A-C-D-DI-K	1 + 2 + 4 + 0 + 1 = 8
E-F-H-J-K	2 + 3 + 6 + 1 + 1 = 13
E-G-I-J-K	2 + 4 + 2 + 1 + 1 = 10

d. The critical path is #3, with a duration of 13 weeks.

e.

Activity	Path	Slack (wk.)
A	2	5
B	1	8
C	2	5
D	2	5
DI	1	8
DII	2	5
E	3	0
F	3	0
G	4	3
H	3	0
I	4	3
J	3	0
K	3	0

f. It will delay the completion of the project by 2 weeks.

g. It will have no effect on the completion of the project.

3. a,b. The expected time, t_e, for an activity $= (a + 4m + b)/6$.
   For activity A: $t_e = [2 + 4(4) + 6]/6 = 4$ days. Repeat for each activity.

   The variance, σ^2, for an activity $= (b - a)^2/36$.
   For activity A: $\sigma^2 = (6 - 2)^2/36 = .4444$. Repeat for each activity.

Activity	Expected time (days)	Variance
A	4	.4444
B	6	1.0000
C	5.5	2.2500
D	9	2.7778
E	8.5	3.3611
F	5	2.7778
G	5	1.7778
H	1	0

c.

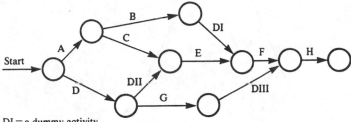

DI = a dummy activity
DII = a dummy activity
DIII = a dummy activity

It is possible to draw this network without DI and DIII. DII, however, is indispensable, since activity E must be preceded by C and D, while activity G is preceded only by D.

d,e. There are four paths through the network.

Path	Duration (days)
A-B-DI-F-H	$4 + 6 + 0 + 5 + 1 = 16$
A-C-E-F-H	$4 + 5.5 + 8.5 + 5 + 1 = 24$
D-DII-E-F-H	$9 + 0 + 8.5 + 5 + 1 = 23.5$
D-G-DII-H	$9 + 5 + 0 + 1 = 15$

f. The variance for each path is obtained by adding the variances of the activities on the path. For Path #1) Variance $= .4444 + 1.0000 + 0 + 2.7778 + 0 = 4.2222$. Repeat for each path.

Path	Variance
1)	4.2222
2)	8.8333
3)	8.9167
4)	4.5556

g. The critical path is #2, with a duration, D of 24 days.

h. The second-most critical path is #3, with a duration of 23.5 days.

i. The duration along the path, D - DII - E - F - H, is increased to 26.5 days. Because this total is larger than 24 days, this constitutes a new critical path.

4. a. The mean is the longest duration: D = 24 days.

b. The standard deviation is the square root of the variance: $\sigma_{path} = \sqrt{8.8333} = 2.9721$.

c. Find the value of z in order to read the table of the areas of the standardized normal curve:

$$z = (x - D)/\sigma_{path} = (24 - 24)/2.9721 = 0. \quad P(z < 0) = .50.$$

d. $z = (x - D)/\sigma_{path} = (22 - 24)/2.9721 = -0.67. \quad P(z < -0.67) = .2514.$

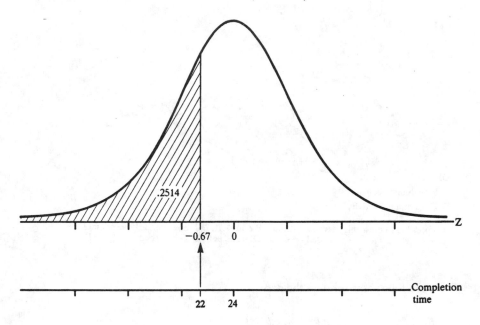

e. $z = (x - D)/\sigma_{path} = (28 - 24)/2.9721 = 1.35. \quad P(z > 1.35) = .0885.$

270

$z = (x - D)/\sigma_{path} = (28 - 24)/2.9721 = 1.35.$
$P(z>1.35) = .0885.$ See figure below.

5. a. Activity E should be crashed because it is on the critical path and crashing it would be less expensive than crashing activity F.
   b. Activity E should be crashed for 3 days to make up for the earthquake.
   c. The expense will be: 3 days x $200 = $600.

6.

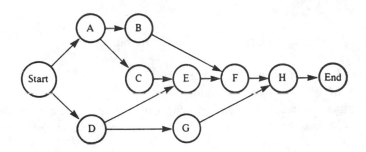

7. From Monday, May 1 to Friday, August 11 is 15 work weeks; set the last LS equal to 15.

Activity	ES	EF	LS	LF	Slack (wk.)
A	0	1	7	8	7
B	1	4	1	14	10
C	1	3	8	10	7
D	3	7	0	14	7
DI	4	4	4	14	10
DII	7	7	4	14	7
E	0	2	2	4	2
F	2	5	4	7	2
G	2	6	7	11	5
H	5	11	7	13	2
I	6	18	1	13	5
J	11	12	3	14	2
K	12	13	4	15	2

271

1. a. $M = 1$ channel.
   b. An infinite source.
   c. Single channel, single phase, Poisson arrivals, negative exponential service times.
   d. $\lambda = 12$ cars per hour.
   e. λ is the mean number of customers who demand service every hour.
   f. $1/\mu = 2.4$ minutes and $\mu = 60/2.4 = 25$ cars per hour.
   g. μ is the mean number of cars which the teller can handle in one hour.
   h. $\rho = \lambda/M\mu = 12/[1(25)] = .48$, which is less than 1. The system is feasible.
   i. The proportion of idle time $= 1 - \rho = 1 - .48 = .52$.
   j. $L_Q = \lambda^2/[\mu(\mu - \lambda)] = 12^2/[25(25 - 12)] = .44$ cars in the queue.
   k. $W_Q = L_Q/\lambda = .44/12 = .03669$ hrs. or 2.2 min.
   l. $L_S = L_Q + \lambda = .44 + .48 = .92$ cars.
   m. $W_S = W_Q + 1/\mu = 2.2 + 2.4 = 4.6$ min.
   n. $p(0 \text{ cars}) = 1 - \lambda/\mu = 1 - .48 = .52$.
   o. $p(1 \text{ car}) = p(0)(\lambda/\mu)^1 = .52(.48) = .2496$.
   p. $p(3 \text{ cars}) = p(0)(\lambda/\mu)^3 = .52(.48)^3 = .0575$.

2. a. $M = 1$ channel.
   b. An infinite population.
   c. Single channel, single phase, Poisson arrivals, constant service times.
   d. $\lambda = 16$ parts per shift or 2 per hour.
   e. λ is the mean number of parts which arrive per time period.
   f. $1/\mu = 20$ min. and $\mu = 8(60)/20 = 24$ parts per shift.
   g. μ is the maximum number of pieces which can be electro-plated per shift. (Compare this with 1g.)
   h. $\rho = \lambda/\mu = 16/24 = .6667$. The electrolytic bath is in use 67% of the time and system is feasible.
   i. The proportion of idle time $= 1 - \rho = 1 - .67 = .33$.
   j. $L_Q = \lambda^2/[2(\mu)(\mu - \lambda)] = 16^2/[2(24)(24 - 16)] = .6667$ parts.
   k. $W_Q = L_Q/\lambda = .6667/16 = .0417$ of an 8-hour shift, or $.0417(8) = .3333$ hrs. or 20 minutes.
   l. $L_S = L_Q + \lambda/\mu = .6667 + .6667 = 1.3334$ parts.
   m. $W_S = W_Q + 1/\mu = 20 + 20 = 40$ min.

3. a. An infinite source.
   b. $\lambda = 65$ customers per hr.
   c. λ is the mean number of customers who demand service at the array of drive-in windows per hour.
   d. At each window, $1/\mu = 2.4$ min. and $\mu = 25$ customers per hr.
   e. μ is the mean number of customers which any one teller can handle in one hour.
   f. ρ must be less than 1; hence $\rho = \lambda/M\mu = 65/25M$ and M must be at least 3.

g. Use Table #17-4 in your textbook. $\lambda/\mu = 65/25 = 2.6$ and $L_Q = 4.933$ cars.

h. $W_Q = 1/(M\mu - \lambda) = 1/[3(25) - 65] = .10$ hrs.

i. Use table 17-4; $p(0) = .035$.

j. $P_w = (\lambda/\mu)^M p(0)/[M!(1 - \lambda/M\mu)] = (2.6)^3(.035)/[3!(1 - .8667)] = .7691$.

4. a. Use Table 17-4; $\lambda/\mu = 65/25 = 2.6$ and $L_Q = .161$ cars.

 b. $W_Q = 1/(M\mu - \lambda) = 1/[5(25) - 65] = .017$ hrs.

 c. Use Table 17-4; $p(0) = .072$.

 d. $P_w = (\lambda/\mu)^M p(0)/[M!(1 - \lambda/M\mu)] = (2.6)^5(.072)/\{5![1 - 65/5(25)]\} = .1485$.

5. a. M = 1 channel, namely the mechanic.

 b. The customers come from the finite fleet of 10 buses.

 c. The finite source model.

 d. N = 10 buses.

 e. T = 4 hrs.

 f. Presumably the buses run 24 hours a day, 7 days a week. U = 168 hrs./3.5 breakdowns = 48 hrs. between breakdowns.

 g. X = T/(T + U) = 4/(4 + 48) = .077.

 h. Use table 17-7 in your textbook. For X = .077 and M = 1, $F \approx .973$.

 i. J = N(F)(1 − X) = 10(.973)(1 - .077) = 8.98 buses.

 j. H = F(N)(X) = .973(10)(.077) = .75 buses.

 k. L = N(1 − F) = 10(1 − .973) = .27 buses.

 l. Check: N = J + L + K = 8.98 + .75 + .27 = 10 buses.

6. a. The multiple-channel, multiple-priority model.

 b. s = 6 typists.

 c. $\lambda = \Sigma_{=1}\lambda_k = 9 + 8 + 6 + 31 = 54$ pages per hr.

 d. $1/\lambda = 1/54 = .0185$ hrs. or about 1.1 min.

 e. $\mu = 12$ pages per hr.

 f. $1/\mu = 1/12$ hrs., or 5 min.

 g. $\rho = \lambda/s\mu = 54/[6(12)] = .75$.

 h. $r = \lambda/\mu = 54/12 = 4.5$ pages.

 i. $L_Q = 1.265$ customers (from Table 17-4).

 j. $A = \lambda/[(1 - \rho)L_Q] = 54/[(1 - .75)1.265] = 170.75$.

 k. $B_0 = 1$.

 $B_1 = 1 - \lambda_1/s\mu = 1 - 9/72 = .8750$.

 $B_2 = 1 - \lambda_1/s\mu - \lambda_2/s\mu = 1 - 9/72 - 8/72 = .7639$.

 $B_3 = 1 - \lambda_1/s\mu - \lambda_2/s\mu - \lambda_3/s\mu = 1 - 9/72 - 8/72 - 6/72 = .6806$.

 $B_4 = 1 - \lambda_1/s\mu - \lambda_2/s\mu - \lambda_3/s\mu - \lambda_4/s\mu = 1 - 9/72 - 8/72 - 6/72 - 31/72 = .2500$.

l. $W_1 = 1/(AB_0B_1) = 1/[170.75(1)(.8750)] = .0067$ hours or about 24 seconds.

$W_2 = 1/(AB_1B_2) = 1/[170.75(.8750)(.7639)] = .0088$ hours or about 32 seconds.

$W_3 = 1/(AB_2B_3) = 1/[170.75(.7639)(.6806)] = .0113$ hours or about 40 seconds.

$W_4 = 1/(AB_3B_4) = 1/[170.75(.6806)(.2500)] = .0344$ hours or about 2.1 minutes.

m.

Priority Class	Average Time in System
1	$W = W_1 + 1/\mu = 0.400 + 5 = 5.400$ minutes.
2	$W = W_2 + 1/\mu = 0.525 + 5 = 5.525$ minutes.
3	$W = W_3 + 1/\mu = 0.675 + 5 = 5.675$ minutes.
4	$W = W_4 + 1/\mu = 2.064 + 5 = 7.064$ minutes.

n.

Priority Class	Average Pages in Queue
1	$L_1 = \lambda_1 W_1 = 9(.0067) \approx .06$ pages
2	$L_2 = \lambda_2 W_2 = 8(.0088) \approx .07$ pages
3	$L_3 = \lambda_3 W_3 = 6(.0113) \approx .07$ pages
4	$L_4 = \lambda_4 W_4 = 31(.0344) \approx 1.07$ pages.

o. This system looks feasible; the jobs in each priority class are typed within a reasonable time, on the average.

CHAPTER 17S SIMULATION

1.a, b.

x	f	p	Cumulative Probability	Random Numbers
0	9	.225	.225	000-224
1	12	.300	.525	225-525
2	9	.225	.750	525-749
3	7	.175	.925	750-924
4	3	.075	1.000	925-999

c.

Week	Random Number	Demand	Sales	Quantity Ordered	Quantity Received
1	491	1*	1	0	0
2	631	2	2	2	0
3	139	0	0	2**	0
4	502	1	1	2	2
5	006	0	0	0	2
6	856	3	3	0	2
7	904	3	3	2	0
8	091	0	0	2	0
9	821	3	0***	0	2
10	757	3	2	2	2
		Total 16		12	

*491 comes between 225 and 524 and designates X = 1.

**Since the inventory contains 1 snowblower at the end of the third week.

***Because the beginning inventory is 0.

Week	Beginning Inventory	Sales	Receipts	Ending Inventory
1	4	1	0	3
2	3	2	0	1
3	1	0	0	1
4	1	1	2	2
5	2	0	2	4
6	4	3	2	3
7	3	3	0	0
8	0	0	0	0
9	0	0	2	2
10	2	2	2	2

d. The total of the sales column is 12 snowblowers. The gross margin = 12(395 - 175) = $2,640.

e. The difference between the total of the demand column and the total of the sales column is 4 snowblowers. The gross margin lost = 4(395 - 175) = $880.

f. While 10 weeks is a very small sample, a tentative hypothesis is that more snowblowers could be sold if the order quantity were increased.

2. a.

Number of Calls	Cumulative Probability	Random Number Range
0	.018	0 - 017
1	.092	018 - 091
2	.238	092 - 237
3	.433	238 - 432
4	.629	433 - 628
5	.785	629 - 784
6	.889	785 - 888
7	.949	889 - 948
8	.979	949 - 978
9	.992	979 - 991
10	.997	992 - 996
11	.999	997 - 998
12	1.000	999

b.

Day	Random Number	Number of Calls
1	005	0*
2	820	6
3	471	4
4	187	2
5	177	2
6	341	3

*005 comes between 0 and 017 and designates X = 0.

3.

Day	Random Number	Sales
1	2.40	372.00*
2	0.38	311.40
3	−0.15	295.50
4	−1.04	268.80

*Sales = Mean + (R.N.)·(standard deviation)
300 + (2.40)·(30) = 372.00 gal.

4. a.   The service time: $1/\lambda = 2$ minutes, and $\lambda = .50$.

b.

Customer	Random Number	ln(.RN)	Pumping Time (min.)*
1	.84275	−0.1711	0.3422
2	.07523	−2.5872	5.1744
3	.33362	−1.0978	2.1958
4	.64270	−0.4421	0.8842

*Pumping Time = $-2 \cdot \ln(.RN)$

5. a.

Type of Tube	Random Number Range
Satisfactory	00-93
Defective	94-99

b.   Reading Table 17S-1 horizontally: S S S S S S S S S S
     S S S S S S S S S S S S S S D S S S S S S S S S S S S.

c.   p − 1/36 = 2.78%.

d.   Not necessarily; the 6% defective tubes will occur over
     the long run but not for any very short period. (For the statistician: the standard error of the
     sample percent, if the true percent of defective tubes is, in fact, 6% is 3.96% and it is easy to draw
     a sample with p = 2.78% from a population with 6% defective items.)

APPENDIX TABLES

z		.00	.01	.02	.03	.04	.05	.06	.07	.08	.09
0.0	. . . . .	.0000	.0040	.0080	.0120	.0160	.0199	.0239	.0279	.0319	.0359
0.1	. . . . .	.0398	.0438	.0478	.0517	.0557	.0596	.0636	.0675	.0714	.0753
0.2	. . . . .	.0793	.0832	.0871	.0910	.0948	.0987	.1026	.1064	.1103	.1141
0.3	. . . . .	.1179	.1217	.1255	.1293	.1331	.1368	.1406	.1443	.1480	.1517
0.4	. . . . .	.1554	.1591	.1628	.1664	.1700	.1736	.1772	.1808	.1844	.1879
0.5	. . . . .	.1915	.1950	.1985	.2019	.2054	.2088	.2123	.2157	.2190	.2224
0.6	. . . . .	.2257	.2291	.2324	.2357	.2389	.2422	.2454	.2486	.2517	.2549
0.7	. . . . .	.2580	.2611	.2642	.2673	.2703	.2734	.2764	.2794	.2823	.2852
0.8	. . . . .	.2881	.2910	.2939	.2967	.2995	.3023	.3051	.3078	.3106	.3133
0.9	. . . . .	.3159	.3186	.3212	.3238	.3264	.3289	.3315	.3340	.3365	.3389
1.0	. . . . .	.3413	.3438	.3461	.3485	.3508	.3531	.3554	.3577	.3599	.3621
1.1	. . . . .	.3643	.3665	.3686	.3708	.3729	.3749	.3770	.3790	.3810	.3830
1.2	. . . . .	.3849	.3869	.3888	.3907	.3925	.3944	.3962	.3980	.3997	.4015
1.3	. . . . .	.4032	.4049	.4066	.4082	.4099	.4115	.4131	.4147	.4162	.4177
1.4	. . . . .	.4192	.4207	.4222	.4236	.4251	.4265	.4279	.4292	.4306	.4319
1.5	. . . . .	.4332	.4345	.4357	.4370	.4382	.4394	.4406	.4418	.4429	.4441
1.6	. . . . .	.4452	.4463	.4474	.4484	.4495	.4505	.4515	.4525	.4535	.4545
1.7	. . . . .	.4554	.4564	.4573	.4582	.4591	.4599	.4608	.4616	.4625	.4633
1.8	. . . . .	.4641	.4649	.4656	.4664	.4671	.4678	.4686	.4693	.4699	.4706
1.9	. . . . .	.4713	.4719	.4726	.4732	.4738	.4744	.4750	.4756	.4761	.4767
2.0	. . . . .	.4772	.4778	.4783	.4788	.4793	.4798	.4803	.4808	.4812	.4817
2.1	. . . . .	.4821	.4826	.4830	.4834	.4838	.4842	.4846	.4850	.4854	.4857
2.2	. . . . .	.4861	.4864	.4868	.4871	.4875	.4878	.4881	.4884	.4887	.4890
2.3	. . . . .	.4893	.4896	.4898	.4901	.4904	.4906	.4909	.4911	.4913	.4916
2.4	. . . . .	.4918	.4920	.4922	.4925	.4927	.4929	.4931	.4932	.4934	.4936
2.5	. . . . .	.4938	.4940	.4941	.4943	.4945	.4946	.4948	.4949	.4951	.4952
2.6	. . . . .	.4953	.4955	.4956	.4957	.4959	.4960	.4961	.4962	.4963	.4964
2.7	. . . . .	.4965	.4966	.4967	.4968	.4969	.4970	.4971	.4972	.4973	.4974
2.8	. . . . .	.4974	.4975	.4976	.4977	.4977	.4978	.4979	.4979	.4980	.4981
2.9	. . . . .	.4981	.4982	.4982	.4983	.4984	.4984	.4985	.4985	.4986	.4986
3.0	. . . . .	.4987	.4987	.4987	.4988	.4988	.4989	.4989	.4989	.4990	.4990

.09	.08	.07	.06	.05	.04	.03	.02	.01	.00	z
.0002	.0003	.0003	.0003	.0003	.0003	.0003	.0003	.0003	.0003	−3.4
.0003	.0004	.0004	.0004	.0004	.0004	.0004	.0005	.0005	.0005	−3.3
.0005	.0005	.0005	.0006	.0006	.0006	.0006	.0006	.0007	.0007	−3.2
.0007	.0007	.0008	.0008	.0008	.0008	.0009	.0009	.0009	.0010	−3.1
.0010	.0010	.0011	.0011	.0011	.0012	.0012	.0013	.0013	.0013	−3.0
.0014	.0014	.0015	.0015	.0016	.0016	.0017	.0018	.0018	.0019	−2.9
.0019	.0020	.0021	.0021	.0022	.0023	.0023	.0024	.0025	.0026	−2.8
.0026	.0027	.0028	.0029	.0030	.0031	.0032	.0033	.0034	.0035	−2.7
.0036	.0037	.0038	.0039	.0040	.0041	.0043	.0044	.0045	.0047	−2.6
.0048	.0049	.0051	.0052	.0054	.0055	.0057	.0059	.0060	.0062	−2.5
.0064	.0066	.0068	.0069	.0071	.0073	.0075	.0078	.0080	.0082	−2.4
.0084	.0087	.0089	.0091	.0094	.0096	.0099	.0102	.0104	.0107	−2.3
.0110	.0113	.0116	.0119	.0122	.0125	.0129	.0132	.0136	.0139	−2.2
.0143	.0146	.0150	.0154	.0158	.0162	.0166	.0170	.0174	.0179	−2.1
.0183	.0188	.0192	.0197	.0202	.0207	.0212	.0217	.0222	.0228	−2.0
.0233	.0239	.0244	.0250	.0256	.0262	.0268	.0274	.0281	.0287	−1.9
.0294	.0301	.0307	.0314	.0322	.0329	.0336	.0344	.0351	.0359	−1.8
.0367	.0375	.0384	.0392	.0401	.0409	.0418	.0427	.0436	.0446	−1.7
.0455	.0465	.0475	.0485	.0495	.0505	.0516	.0526	.0537	.0548	−1.6
.0559	.0571	.0582	.0594	.0606	.0618	.0630	.0643	.0655	.0668	−1.5
.0681	.0694	.0708	.0721	.0735	.0749	.0764	.0778	.0793	.0808	−1.4
.0823	.0838	.0853	.0869	.0885	.0901	.0918	.0934	.0951	.0968	−1.3
.0985	.1003	.1020	.1038	.1056	.1075	.1093	.1112	.1131	.1151	−1.2
.1170	.1190	.1210	.1230	.1251	.1271	.1292	.1314	.1335	.1357	−1.1
.1379	.1401	.1423	.1446	.1469	.1492	.1515	.1539	.1562	.1587	−1.0
.1611	.1635	.1660	.1685	.1711	.1736	.1762	.1788	.1814	.1841	−0.9
.1867	.1894	.1922	.1949	.1977	.2005	.2033	.2061	.2090	.2119	−0.8
.2148	.2177	.2206	.2236	.2266	.2296	.2327	.2358	.2389	.2420	−0.7
.2451	.2483	.2514	.2546	.2578	.2611	.2643	.2676	.2709	.2743	−0.6
.2776	.2810	.2843	.2877	.2912	.2946	.2981	.3015	.3050	.3085	−0.5
.3121	.3156	.3192	.3228	.3264	.3300	.3336	.3372	.3409	.3446	−0.4
.3483	.3520	.3557	.3594	.3632	.3669	.3707	.3745	.3783	.3821	−0.3
.3859	.3897	.3936	.3974	.4013	.4052	.4090	.4129	.4168	.4207	−0.2
.4247	.4286	.4325	.4364	.4404	.4443	.4483	.4522	.4562	.4602	−0.1
.4641	.4681	.4721	.4761	.4801	.4840	.4880	.4920	.4960	.5000	−0.0

2. Areas under the standardized normal curve from $-\infty$ to $+z$

z	.00	.01	.02	.03	.04	.05	.06	.07	.08	.09
.0	.5000	.5040	.5080	.5120	.5160	.5199	.5239	.5279	.5319	.5359
.1	.5398	.5438	.5478	.5517	.5557	.5596	.5636	.5675	.5714	.5753
.2	.5793	.5832	.5871	.5910	.5948	.5987	.6026	.6064	.6103	.6141
.3	.6179	.6217	.6255	.6293	.6331	.6368	.6406	.6443	.6480	.6517
.4	.6554	.6591	.6628	.6664	.6700	.6736	.6772	.6808	.6844	.6879
.5	.6915	.6950	.6985	.7019	.7054	.7088	.7123	.7157	.7190	.7224
.6	.7257	.7291	.7324	.7357	.7389	.7422	.7454	.7486	.7517	.7549
.7	.7580	.7611	.7642	.7673	.7703	.7734	.7764	.7794	.7823	.7852
.8	.7881	.7910	.7939	.7967	.7995	.8023	.8051	.8078	.8106	.8133
.9	.8159	.8186	.8212	.8238	.8264	.8289	.8315	.8340	.8365	.8389
1.0	.8413	.8438	.8461	.8485	.8508	.8531	.8554	.8577	.8599	.8621
1.1	.8643	.8665	.8686	.8708	.8729	.8749	.8770	.8790	.8810	.8830
1.2	.8849	.8869	.8888	.8907	.8925	.8944	.8962	.8980	.8997	.9015
1.3	.9032	.9049	.9066	.9082	.9099	.9115	.9131	.9147	.9162	.9177
1.4	.9192	.9207	.9222	.9236	.9251	.9265	.9279	.9292	.9306	.9319
1.5	.9332	.9345	.9357	.9370	.9382	.9394	.9406	.9418	.9429	.9441
1.6	.9452	.9463	.9474	.9484	.9495	.9505	.9515	.9525	.9535	.9545
1.7	.9554	.9564	.9573	.9582	.9591	.9599	.9608	.9616	.9625	.9633
1.8	.9641	.9649	.9656	.9664	.9671	.9678	.9686	.9693	.9699	.9706
1.9	.9713	.9719	.9726	.9732	.9738	.9744	.9750	.9756	.9761	.9767
2.0	.9772	.9778	.9783	.9788	.9793	.9798	.9803	.9808	.9812	.9817
2.1	.9821	.9826	.9830	.9834	.9838	.9842	.9846	.9850	.9854	.9857
2.2	.9861	.9864	.9868	.9871	.9875	.9878	.9881	.9884	.9887	.9890
2.3	.9893	.9896	.9898	.9901	.9904	.9906	.9909	.9911	.9913	.9916
2.4	.9918	.9920	.9922	.9925	.9927	.9929	.9931	.9932	.9934	.9936
2.5	.9938	.9940	.9941	.9943	.9945	.9946	.9948	.9949	.9951	.9952
2.6	.9953	.9955	.9956	.9957	.9959	.9960	.9961	.9962	.9963	.9964
2.7	.9965	.9966	.9967	.9968	.9969	.9970	.9971	.9972	.9973	.9974
2.8	.9974	.9975	.9976	.9977	.9977	.9978	.9979	.9979	.9980	.9981
2.9	.9981	.9982	.9982	.9983	.9984	.9984	.9985	.9985	.9986	.9986
3.0	.9987	.9987	.9987	.9988	.9988	.9989	.9989	.9989	.9990	.9990
3.1	.9990	.9991	.9991	.9991	.9991	.9992	.9992	.9992	.9993	.9993
3.2	.9993	.9993	.9994	.9994	.9994	.9994	.9994	.9995	.9995	.9995
3.3	.9995	.9995	.9995	.9996	.9996	.9996	.9996	.9996	.9996	.9997
3.4	.9997	.9997	.9997	.9997	.9997	.9997	.9997	.9997	.9997	.9998

Table C

Cumulative Poisson
probabilities

$$P(x \le c) = \sum_{x=0}^{x=c} \frac{\mu^x \cdot e^{-\mu}}{x!}$$

μ \ x	0	1	2	3	4	5	6	7	8	9
0.05	.951	.999	1.000							
0.10	.905	.995	1.000							
0.15	.861	.990	.999	1.000						
0.20	.819	.982	.999	1.000						
0.25	.779	.974	.998	1.000						
0.30	.741	.963	.996	1.000						
0.35	.705	.951	.994	1.000						
0.40	.670	.938	.992	.999	1.000					
0.45	.638	.925	.989	.999	1.000					
0.50	.607	.910	.986	.998	1.000					
0.55	.577	.894	.982	.998	1.000					
0.60	.549	.878	.977	.997	1.000					
0.65	.522	.861	.972	.996	.999	1.000				
0.70	.497	.844	.966	.994	.999	1.000				
0.75	.472	.827	.960	.993	.999	1.000				
0.80	.449	.809	.953	.991	.999	1.000				
0.85	.427	.791	.945	.989	.998	1.000				
0.90	.407	.772	.937	.987	.998	1.000				
0.95	.387	.754	.929	.984	.997	1.000				
1.0	.368	.736	.920	.981	.996	.999	1.000			
1.1	.333	.699	.900	.974	.995	.999	1.000			
1.2	.301	.663	.880	.966	.992	.998	1.000			
1.3	.273	.627	.857	.957	.989	.998	1.000			
1.4	.247	.592	.833	.946	.986	.997	.999	1.000		
1.5	.223	.558	.809	.934	.981	.996	.999	1.000		
1.6	.202	.525	.783	.921	.976	.994	.999	1.000		
1.7	.183	.493	.757	.907	.970	.992	.998	1.000		
1.8	.165	.463	.731	.891	.964	.990	.997	.999	1.000	
1.9	.150	.434	.704	.875	.956	.987	.997	.999	1.000	
2.0	.135	.406	.677	.857	.947	.983	.995	.999	1.000	
2.2	.111	.355	.623	.819	.928	.975	.993	.998	1.000	
2.4	.091	.308	.570	.779	.904	.964	.988	.997	.999	1.000
2.6	.074	.267	.518	.736	.877	.951	.983	.995	.999	1.000
2.8	.061	.231	.470	.692	.848	.935	.976	.992	.998	.999

Table C (concluded)

μ\x	0	1	2	3	4	5	6	7	8	9	10	11	12	13	14	15	16	17	18	19	20
3.0	.050	.199	.423	.647	.815	.916	.966	.988	.996	.999	1.000										
3.2	.041	.171	.380	.603	.781	.895	.955	.983	.994	.998	1.000										
3.4	.033	.147	.340	.558	.744	.871	.942	.977	.992	.997	.999	1.000									
3.6	.027	.126	.303	.515	.706	.844	.927	.969	.988	.996	.999	1.000									
3.8	.022	.107	.269	.474	.668	.816	.909	.960	.984	.994	.998	.999	1.000								
4.0	.018	.092	.238	.433	.629	.785	.889	.949	.979	.992	.997	.999	1.000								
4.2	.015	.078	.210	.395	.590	.753	.867	.936	.972	.989	.996	.999	1.000								
4.4	.012	.066	.185	.359	.551	.720	.844	.921	.964	.985	.994	.998	.999	1.000							
4.6	.010	.056	.163	.326	.513	.686	.818	.905	.955	.980	.992	.997	.999	1.000							
4.8	.008	.048	.143	.294	.476	.651	.791	.887	.944	.975	.990	.996	.999	1.000							
5.0	.007	.040	.125	.265	.441	.616	.762	.867	.932	.968	.986	.995	.998	.999	1.000						
5.2	.006	.034	.109	.238	.406	.581	.732	.845	.918	.960	.982	.993	.997	.999	1.000						
5.4	.005	.029	.095	.213	.373	.546	.702	.822	.903	.951	.978	.990	.996	.999	1.000						
5.6	.004	.024	.082	.191	.342	.512	.670	.797	.886	.941	.972	.988	.995	.998	.999	1.000					
5.8	.003	.021	.072	.170	.313	.478	.638	.771	.867	.929	.965	.984	.993	.997	.999	1.000					
6.0	.002	.017	.062	.151	.285	.446	.606	.744	.847	.916	.957	.980	.991	.996	.999	.999	1.000				
6.2	.002	.015	.054	.134	.259	.414	.574	.716	.826	.902	.949	.975	.989	.995	.998	.999	1.000				
6.4	.002	.012	.046	.119	.235	.384	.542	.687	.803	.886	.939	.969	.986	.994	.997	.999	1.000				
6.6	.001	.010	.040	.105	.213	.355	.511	.658	.780	.869	.927	.963	.982	.992	.997	.999	.999	1.000			
6.8	.001	.009	.034	.093	.192	.327	.480	.629	.755	.850	.915	.955	.978	.990	.996	.998	.999	1.000			
7.0	.001	.007	.030	.082	.173	.301	.450	.599	.729	.830	.901	.947	.973	.987	.994	.998	.999	1.000			
7.2	.001	.006	.025	.072	.156	.276	.420	.569	.703	.810	.887	.937	.967	.984	.993	.997	.999	.999	1.000		
7.4	.001	.005	.022	.063	.140	.253	.392	.539	.676	.788	.871	.926	.961	.980	.991	.996	.998	.999	1.000		
7.6	.001	.004	.019	.055	.125	.231	.365	.510	.648	.765	.854	.915	.954	.976	.989	.995	.998	.999	1.000		
7.8	.000	.004	.016	.048	.112	.210	.338	.481	.620	.741	.835	.902	.945	.971	.986	.993	.997	.999	1.000		
8.0	.000	.003	.014	.042	.100	.191	.313	.453	.593	.717	.816	.888	.936	.966	.983	.992	.996	.998	.999	1.000	
8.2	.000	.003	.012	.037	.089	.174	.290	.425	.565	.692	.796	.873	.926	.960	.979	.990	.995	.998	.999	1.000	
8.4	.000	.002	.010	.032	.079	.157	.267	.400	.537	.666	.774	.857	.915	.952	.975	.987	.994	.997	.999	1.000	
8.6	.000	.002	.009	.028	.070	.142	.246	.373	.509	.640	.752	.840	.903	.945	.970	.985	.993	.997	.999	.999	
8.8	.000	.001	.007	.024	.062	.128	.226	.348	.482	.614	.729	.822	.890	.936	.965	.982	.991	.996	.998	.999	
9.0	.000	.001	.006	.021	.055	.116	.207	.324	.456	.587	.706	.803	.876	.926	.959	.978	.989	.995	.998	.999	1.000
9.5	.000	.001	.004	.015	.040	.089	.165	.269	.392	.522	.645	.752	.836	.898	.940	.967	.982	.991	.996	.998	.999

TABLE D

Control Chart Factors

Sample Size n	$\overline{X}$ Chart A_2	R Chart d_2	D_1	D_2	D_3	D_4
2	1.880	1.128	0.0	3.686	0.0	3.267
3	1.023	1.693	0.0	4.358	0.0	2.575
4	0.729	2.059	0.0	4.698	0.0	2.282
5	0.577	2.326	0.0	4.918	0.0	2.115
6	0.483	2.534	0.0	5.078	0.0	2.004
7	0.419	2.704	0.205	5.203	0.076	1.924
8	0.373	2.847	0.387	5.307	0.136	1.864
9	0.337	2.970	0.546	5.394	0.184	1.816
10	0.308	3.078	0.687	5.469	0.223	1.777
11	0.285	3.173	0.812	5.534	0.256	1.744
12	0.266	3.258	0.924	5.592	0.284	1.716
13	0.249	3.336	1.026	5.646	0.308	1.692
14	0.235	3.407	1.121	5.693	0.329	1.671
15	0.223	3.472	1.207	5.737	0.348	1.652
16	0.212	3.532	1.285	5.779	0.364	1.636
17	0.203	3.588	1.359	5.817	0.379	1.621
18	0.194	3.640	1.426	5.854	0.392	1.608
19	0.187	3.689	1.490	5.888	0.404	1.596
20	0.180	3.735	1.548	5.922	0.414	1.586
21	0.173	3.778	1.606	5.950	0.425	1.575
22	0.167	3.819	1.659	5.979	0.434	1.566
23	0.162	3.858	1.710	6.006	0.443	1.557
24	0.157	3.895	1.759	6.031	0.452	1.548
25	0.153	3.931	1.804	6.058	0.459	1.541

Formulas for using Control Chart Factors

$\overline{X}$ *Chart*

σ Known (z often equals 3)

UPPER CONTROL LIMIT = $\overline{\overline{X}} + Z^*\sigma_{\overline{x}}$

LOWER CONTROL LIMIT = $\overline{\overline{X}} - Z^*\sigma_{\overline{x}}$

σ Unknown

UPPER CONTROL LIMIT = $\overline{\overline{X}} + A_2^*\overline{R}$

LOWER CONTROL LIMIT = $\overline{\overline{X}} - A_2^*\overline{R}$

R Chart

σ Known

UPPER CONTROL LIMIT = $d_2^*\sigma + D_2^*\sigma$

LOWER CONTROL LIMIT = $d_2^*\sigma - D_1^*\sigma$

σ Unknown

UPPER CONTROL LIMIT = $\overline{R} + D_4^*\overline{R}$

LOWER CONTROL LIMIT = $\overline{R} - D_3^*\overline{R}$